Bergdoll

W9-CAY-107

and Hannah wept

THE JEWISH PUBLICATION SOCIETY

1888–1988

and Hannah wept

⊠ *Infertility, Adoption, and the Jewish Couple*

⊠ *Michael Gold*

The Jewish Publication Society   *Philadelphia · New York · Jerusalem 5748/1988*

Copyright © 1988 by Michael Gold
First edition   All rights reserved
Manufactured in the United States of America
Library of Congress Cataloging in Publication Data
Gold, Michael, 1950–
  And Hannah wept.

  Includes index.
  1. Jewish families.   2. Infertility—Religious
aspects—Judaism.   3. Adoption (Jewish law).   I. Title.
HQ525.J4G59 1988   306.8'5'089924   87–22849
ISBN 0–8276–0306–1

Designed by Adrianne Onderdonk Dudden

Contents

᠀ *Preface*

This book grew out of my own experience with infertility and adoption. My wife and I have known the pain of infertility, the discomfort and expense of ongoing medical treatment, the hurt caused by insensitive comments, and the overwhelming joy of successfully adopting a baby.

Evelyn and I were married in the fall of 1979, shortly after I assumed my first pulpit. We dreamed of a large family and spoke about having four children. We soon discovered that it would not be so easy. After several months went by, we saw our doctor, who told us, "Give it more time." We began to share our concerns with close friends. Some tried to shrug off our anguish, saying, "Relax and it [pregnancy] will happen." Others, however, were deeply sensitive, and we soon discovered that we were not alone. Many Jewish couples are suffering or have suffered from fertility problems. Through friends, we were referred to one of the best infertility clinics in the country.

At the clinic, we began a long series of fertility tests and treatments, which culminated in surgery for both my wife and me. Medical treatment has still not been successful in our case, yet we have learned a great deal. We have become experts on the workings of our own reproductive systems and on the latest technologies of conception. We have also discovered that in spite of the Jewish emphasis on children, our religious observance sometimes raised questions regarding infertility.

Does Judaism permit aggressive medical treatment, including experimental surgery, to solve a fertility problem? Does Judaism permit semen testing of males? For couples who observe the laws of *mikvah*, what if their observance is the cause of their infertility? Does Judaism allow artificial insemination using a donor's sperm? In vitro fertilization? What about a Sabbath-observant woman who must have her hormones monitored daily, even if it means traveling on the Sabbath? I quickly discovered that there are few sources that tackle these questions in English and none that do it with a sensitivity to infertile couples.

My wife and I were in the middle of a course of medical treatment when we received a call that changed our lives. A friend, who knew of our desire for children, asked if we were interested in adoption. A baby would soon be born to a pregnant teenager in the South, and the girl was not in a position to keep the baby. Were we interested? They needed an answer immediately.

Up to that point, adoption had been a last resort in our minds. We would have considered it only if medical treatment failed. Now there was no time to wait; a decision had to be made. We knew that adoption is difficult and the opportunity might not arise again. Before we even had a chance to talk with our families, we said yes. And so our son Natan Yosef entered our lives.

Natan's adoption was not totally smooth. We took him into our home at risk, while his biological mother vacillated on signing the final papers. Yet it had a happy ending, and we celebrated his arrival with a large reception in our synagogue. When Natan was four months old, we took him to the *mikvah* (ritual bath) and formally converted him to Judaism.

With Natan's adoption, I learned an important lesson. Adoption is not a "last resort," nor is it settling for "second best." Despite a negative social bias, it is a viable alternative way to build a Jewish family. In fact, adoption has a long history in the Jewish community and has been viewed by Jewish sources in a very positive light.

Shortly after Natan's adoption, two local newspapers wrote stories about us. The newspapers found a human interest story in a rabbi and his wife who adopted a baby and converted him to Judaism. Almost immediately, the phone began to ring. Jewish couples wanted to know how to adopt. Sometimes they wanted my help in arranging the conversion of an adopted child. They wanted my opinion on adopting babies from other countries or of other races. In one case, a young Jewish woman called seeking to place her baby for adoption. Some couples called me simply to talk, to relate difficulties they had faced in adopting a child because they were Jewish.

Because of these many conversations, I knew that there was a scarcity of information on infertility and adoption from a Jewish perspective. I placed an announcement in the *RESOLVE Newsletter*, which goes out to infertile couples throughout the country, stating that I was interested in hearing from Jewish couples about their difficulties with infertility and adoption. The response was overwhelming; letters and phone calls came from all over the country. I heard stories of great sadness: couples who had miscarried or lost babies, couples whose marriages had broken up because they could not accept their infertility, couples who had faced hostility from agencies and from their own relatives when they tried to adopt. I also heard great success stories: Jewish children conceived through artificial insemination or in vitro fertilization; Jewish children adopted from South America, Korea, and throughout the United States. I heard stories of great loneliness, but I learned that persistence pays off when seeking a child, whether by medical techniques or through adoption.

Recently Evelyn and I adopted a second child, our daughter Aliza Chasha. We would have preferred to adopt through a Jewish agency but discovered that the organized Jewish community in many cities has no adoption program.

Evelyn and I adopted our daughter privately, working with three other couples in an adoption support group. All four couples have adopted within a year, proving that successful adoption is possible in the United States and that it doesn't have to cost a fortune.

This book has been written as a guide for Jewish couples who are struggling with infertility and adoption. It can also serve as a resource for rabbis, social workers, and other Jewish professionals who should serve the needs of these couples. It raises an issue that has been ignored by the leadership of the Jewish community—an issue that should be of concern to all committed Jews. Although this book is committed to a liberal interpretation of halakhah (Jewish law), it has been written to guide Jews of all religious persuasions. Some sections may have greater appeal to Reform Jews, whereas other sections deal with problems faced by the Orthodox. Infertility is a community problem that cuts across all ideological levels.

In preparing this book, I spoke with many individuals who shared their expertise with me. In particular, I would like to thank Elizabeth Cessna for her insights into counseling infertile couples, Neil Siegel for his help with the legal material in the book, Dr. Steele Filipek for his advice on medical solutions to infertility, Cyral Sheldon for her expertise on adoption counseling, and Arnold Ryave z"l for sharing his work with families bereaved of an infant.

I would like to thank Dr. Stephen Winters for reading the medical sections and offering many excellent criticisms and comments. My thanks also to Rabbi David Feldman and Dr. Rela Geffen Monson for reading the entire manuscript and offering many valuable suggestions. Deborah Levenstein typed the entire manuscript and added her own suggestions.

I would like to thank The Jewish Publication Society, particularly the editor-in-chief, Sheila Segal, and the managing editor, Barbara Spector, for their faith in my book and their help in perfecting it. A special thanks goes to my wife, Evelyn, for her love and encouragement. This book tells our story, and I pray it will help other couples in our situation. Finally, I wish to thank more than one hundred infertile couples who shared their lives with me. There is strength in knowing that you are not alone.

Michael Gold
Pittsburgh, August 1987

and Hannah wept

There was a man ... whose name was Elkanah. ... He had two wives, one named Hannah and the other Peninnah; Peninnah had children, but Hannah was childless. ... One ... day, Elkanah offered a sacrifice. He used to give portions to his wife Peninnah and to all her sons and daughters; but to Hannah he would give one portion only—though Hannah was his favorite—for the Lord had closed her womb. Moreover, her rival [Peninnah], to make her miserable, would taunt her that the Lord had closed her womb. ... So that she wept and would not eat.

1 Sam. 1:1–7

1

Introduction

On the first day of Rosh Hashanah, in synagogues through-out the world, we chant the Haftarah that tells the story of Hannah. It is a story tied to one of the basic themes of Rosh Hashanah: God remembers. Not only was Hannah childless, but she also was taunted by her more fertile co-wife, Peninnah. Hannah wept and refused to eat. Her husband tried to comfort her. ". . . Hannah, why are you crying and why aren't you eating? Why are you so sad? Am I not more devoted to you than ten sons?" (1 Sam. 1:8). But Hannah would find no solace.

Finally, during a visit to the sanctuary at Shiloh, Han-nah poured her heart out to God. She prayed with such fervor that the high priest Eli thought she was drunk. She answered Eli that she was not drunk but deeply unhappy, for the Lord had closed up her womb.

And she made this vow: "O Lord of Hosts, if You will look upon the suffering of Your maidservant and will remember me and not forget your maidservant, and if You will grant your maidservant a male child, I will dedicate him to the Lord for all the days of his life; and no razor shall ever touch his head."

(1 Sam. 1:11)

Shortly afterward, in keeping with the theme of Rosh Hashanah, God remembered Hannah. She and Elkanah conceived a child, a baby boy whom they called Samuel. When the boy was weaned, Hannah fulfilled her vow and brought Samuel to the sanctuary in Shiloh so that he could dedicate his life to the service of God. Samuel, of course, went on to become the political and religious leader of the people Israel. It was he who anointed King Saul and eventually King David. He was the last and greatest of the judges, the transitory figure before the establishment of the monarchy in ancient Israel.

Our concern, however, is not with Samuel the son but with Hannah the mother. For the infertile couple, longing for a child and unable to conceive, the story of Hannah is particularly poignant. Thousands of Jewish couples can share her sadness and comprehend her prayer. They know the pain of being childless. In my own synagogue, I know a young woman who is deeply religious yet never came to services on the first day of Rosh Hashanah. When I asked her about it, she told me that the Haftarah was too painful and ruined the holiday for her. Only after she and her husband adopted a child did she start coming to synagogue again on Rosh Hashanah.

The story of Hannah in the Bible is rather sketchy. The rabbis of the Talmud, using the interpretative technique called Midrash, fleshed out the text. They put words in Hannah's mouth, words that reflect the anger and sense of injustice she felt at being infertile. They noticed that she was the first to use the term *Adonai Tsevaot*, "Lord of Hosts":

> Said Hannah before the Holy One, blessed be He: "Sovereign of the Universe, of all the hosts and hosts that Thou hast created in Thy world, is it so hard in Thy eyes to give me one son? A parable: To what is this matter like? To a king who made a feast for his servants, and a poor man came and stood by the door and said to him, give me a bite, and no one took any notice of him, so he forced his way into the presence of the king and said to him, Your Majesty, out of all the feast which thou hast made, is it so hard in thine eyes to give me one bite?"[1]

The Midrash continues:

> Sovereign of the Universe, among all the things that Thou hast created in a woman, Thou hast not created one without a purpose, eyes to see, ears to hear, a nose to smell, a mouth to speak, hands to do work, legs to walk with, breasts to give suck. These breasts that Thou hast put on my heart, are they not to give suck? Give me a son, so that I may suckle with them.[2]

I am amazed by how well the rabbis of the Talmud captured the sense of injustice aroused by infertility. I have felt it personally. Shortly before my wife and I adopted our son, during one of our most difficult periods, a young woman in my synagogue became pregnant. She and her husband were close friends of ours and knew of our fertility problems. They had questions to ask me, as their rabbi, questions about names and about a *brit milah,* about raising Jewish children. Yet, as friends, they could not bring themselves to tell me of the pregnancy. They kept it a secret until they could hide it no longer; only then did they almost apologetically break the good news. I was happy for them and thrilled when they gave birth to a little girl some months later. Yet deep down there is always a pain, an anger at God and a sense of injustice.

Like so many biblical tales, the story of Hannah remains timeless. It reflects not only the great pain and sadness felt by a woman unable to conceive but also the feeling of envy toward more fertile friends and neighbors and the gnawing sense of injustice. I have heard so many couples tell me, "Rabbi, it's unfair. We would make such good parents. We know people who abuse their kids, ignore their kids, and have all the children they want. And we have a big, empty house. Where's the justice?"

I can only sigh and empathize with them. I recently spoke to a young couple, one of whom had lost a parent. They told me, "We could have handled the grief. Parents grow old and die. But we could not bear coming home from sitting *shiva* to an empty house. We felt that, with the death of a parent, we were the end of a chain. There was no child to whom we could pass on the tradition. The pain of that empty house was unbearable."

Much has changed since the days of Hannah and Elkanah. By talmudic times polygamy had fallen out of practice, and in the Middle Ages it was outlawed. In the days of the Bible, if a man could not have children by one wife, he could take a second. Our father Abraham, the founder of the Jewish people, did just that. When Sarah could not provide him with children, he took her handmaiden Hagar. But this is no longer an option. Rabbi Gershom ruled in the eleventh century that a man could have only one wife. Suddenly, childlessness became not a woman's problem but a couple's problem.

Doctors have also begun to understand that infertility is a couple's problem. Fertility specialists realize that both men and women can have physical problems that result in infertility. About 40 percent of the time, the problem can be traced to the woman, and 40 percent of the time, it can be traced to the man. That leaves another 20 percent when both the husband and wife contribute to the problem. Fertility specialists realize today that they must treat couples.[3]

Our theology has also changed since the days of Hannah. The Bible saw God as the cause of everything. Barrenness was a curse given by God, often as a punishment for some transgression. Prayer was the cure. Today we may still believe in prayer, but not as the only recourse. We recognize that infertility has physiological causes that will respond to medical treatment. Hormones or surgery can often cure a fertility problem. When these fail, there are often more radical techniques, which raise legal and moral questions. Doctors have been accused of playing God for using such techniques as artificial insemination, in vitro fertilization, surrogate mothering, and embryo transplants. And yet Jewish couples are turning to doctors and asking for these treatments.

The sadness of infertility is felt by couples of all faiths; yet, in certain ways, it is particularly acute in the Jewish community. The clinical definition of infertility is the inability to conceive a child after one year of trying. Between 15 and 20 percent of the couples of childbearing age in the United States are infertile.[4]

There are no data on Jewish couples, yet from my own observation, the percentage of infertile Jewish couples seems higher. The reason is simple. Jews tend to marry later and postpone having children longer than the general population. They tend to go to college, to be attracted to the professions, and to spend several years in the graduate programs that lead into those professions. More Jewish women are remaining in the work force and delaying the decision to have children as long as possible. When educational and professional commitments come first, women usually wait until their thirties to begin childbearing.

Studies have shown clearly that there is a marked decrease in fertility with age. Among normally fertile women in their early twenties, 20 to 25 percent will conceive within the first month. Among women in their early thirties, only 10 percent will conceive in the first month. In the late thirties, the numbers fall to around 8 percent.[5]

I recently spoke with a professional couple in their mid-thirties who were expecting their first child. They told me what a difficult time they had conceiving. They had been through numerous fertility tests, and the woman had taken Clomid, a potent fertility drug, for almost a year. "I guess God was getting even with us," the man said. "We were so fertile for so many years, but we kept Him waiting. We both had to complete professional degrees and establish ourselves in our careers. Then finally we started trying to have a baby. And God said, 'You kept me waiting. Now

I am going to make you wait, so you can see what it is like.' "

While one may not be comfortable with the mystical aspect of their explanation, this couple also touched on a scientific truth, that pregnancy becomes more difficult with age. Nobody knows why, although there are theories. One logical hypothesis says that the problem lies in a physiological difference between men and women. Men are continually manufacturing sperm; women have a fixed supply of eggs from birth. Perhaps the healthiest, most easily fertilized eggs are emitted by the ovaries early in life. To quote one authority, "Generally, the most fertilizable eggs are released early in life. Thus, with advancing years, though the woman may be fertile, her relative fertility diminishes."[6]

Whatever the reason, Jews have delayed their childbearing and thereby increased their fertility problems. Perhaps traditional Judaism recognized this fact when it encouraged Jews to marry and begin a family at a young age. To quote one colorful description in the Talmud, "Until a man is twenty, God waits around to see who he will marry. After twenty, God says, 'blast his bones.' "[7] In traditional Judaism, and even among Hasidic groups today, a man is expected to be married at the age of eighteen. Women were married even earlier. A girl reached the age of majority, when she could effect a marriage, at twelve and a half years and one day.[8] However, although child marriage was permitted in the Talmud and is practiced in some Jewish communities even today, the rabbis discouraged it. In modern Israel, the minimum age for a girl to be married is seventeen. In recent years, the Orthodox community has attempted to lower it to sixteen.

With Jews marrying so young and with no sanction for birth control in religious law—unless there was a clear danger to the mother's health—it is no wonder that Jews had large families and were quite fertile. This is why some Orthodox authorities have called for a return to younger marriages. Yet, ultimately, we cannot turn back the clock. Most Jews today, even many Orthodox women, want to delay childbearing at least until after they establish themselves in professional or business careers. As a result, more and more Jewish couples are having fertility problems.

Infertility is particularly painful to Jews because of the focus on children in much of our religious and communal life. Judaism is a religion of commandments, and the first commandment mentioned in the Torah is "Be fruitful and multiply" (Gen. 1:28).* The Jewish ideal has always been a house full of children. Other religions do not necessarily emphasize this. In the Catholic Church, the religious leadership is expected to take a vow of chastity, neither marrying nor having children. In Judaism, a rabbi is expected to marry and have a large family. The Talmud ruled that a rabbi without children could not sit on the Sanhedrin, the central lawmaking body during the second Temple period.[9] A rabbi who had not fulfilled his own responsibility of procreation could not be appointed to the highest position of community leadership.

So much of Jewish life is built around children. Children are blessed on Friday night; they place coins in a *tzedakah* box before the candles are lit. They add their decorations to the *sukkah* and carry the *lulav* and *etrog* around the synagogue. We give children coins and gifts on Hanukkah as they participate in the candle-lighting ceremony. Our most widely practiced Jewish ritual, the Passover seder, was developed with one purpose in mind: to tell the story of the Exodus to the children and encourage them to ask questions. By answering their questions, we pass the story to the next generation. It is no wonder that Passover and Sukkot and even Shabbat seem to lack something without children present.

Even our communal institutions reflect an emphasis on children. Most synagogues have a family membership category, not couple membership. Childless couples often shy away from synagogues, thinking that they do not have

*This phrase appears as "Be fertile and increase" in *Tanakh*, The Jewish Publication Society's new translation of the Hebrew Bible, which is the source for all biblical quotations in this book. However, the phrase "Be fruitful and multiply" is retained because of its familiar usage.

a place in the institution. The fact is that synagogues are open to all Jews, with or without children. Nevertheless, many congregations do convey an impression of being for families only. I have heard of childless couples inquiring about membership at a synagogue and being told, "Why would you want to join before you have to? Wait until you have children."

The pain of childlessness is greatest when we contemplate our own death. In Judaism, children are our immortality. A child carries on our name, and traditionally, a son says *Kaddish* each morning and evening for a parent. That is why Jewish parents used to call a son "my *Kaddish*." Today many synagogues permit daughters to say *Kaddish* as well. For a Jew, dying childless means that there is no one to say *Kaddish*. Children represent the future, the part of us that lives on after we are gone. It is no wonder that so many childless couples see themselves as the end of a chain.

It is for these reasons that most Jewish couples happily contemplate having children. There is a wonderul moment in the traditional wedding ceremony that guests often miss. It is called the *bedeken*. Immediately before the processional, the groom carefully lowers the veil over the face of his bride. This recalls the wedding of Jacob, who loved Rachel but found himself with Leah, the bride's sister. Ever since, the groom makes sure he does not have the wrong bride by personally supervising the veiling of his bride. The words that are said at that point emphasize one of the primary purposes of Jewish marriage. *At hiyee k'alfei revava.* ". . . 'May you grow into thousands of myriads . . .' " (Gen. 24:60). These words were used in the Bible to bless Jacob's mother Rebecca before she married Jacob's father Isaac. The prayer expressed the hope that Rebecca would have children who would have children and so forth, becoming the mother of myriads. The irony is that Rebecca turned out to be infertile. Only after Isaac's prayer and God's intercession was she blessed with twins.

Most Jewish couples who walk under the marriage canopy (huppah) contemplate having children someday. It used to be my custom, as a rabbi, to encourage this in my wedding charge to the couple under the *huppah*. I would speak of the desperate need for Jewish children and express my prayers that the couple would fulfill the *mitzvah* of "be fruitful and multiply." My counseling of infertile couples has forced me to rethink my wedding talks. I now usually include words like, "I pray that you will be blessed with children because, God knows, we need Jewish children. If you are blessed with children, I pray that you will raise them as educated and caring Jews."

Another aspect of infertility, which puts a particular strain on those couples who care most about their Judaism, is the rising concern about low fertility rates in the Jewish community. Rabbis and communal leaders have expressed alarm at the low Jewish birthrate. Jews are practicing a zero population growth, or worse, a negative growth. We are not replacing ourselves. The rate of intermarriage and assimilation, combined with a low birthrate, is causing the Jewish community to shrink. That is something we cannot afford, particularly after losing one third of our population in the Holocaust.

Rabbis have cried out from pulpits and in written articles on the desperate need for Jewish children. Hearing a sermon on the low Jewish fertility rate only intensifies the pain for the infertile couple, particularly the couple who care about their Jewish identity and want nothing more than to have children. Mixed in with their sadness is often a feeling of guilt. They may feel that the rabbi's words are being directed at them. And a rabbi who is unaware of their fertility problem may indeed have them in mind.

I recall one incident that particularly reminded me of Hillel's dictum, "Do not judge your fellow until you stand in his place."[10] I decided one year on Rosh Hashanah to speak about the importance of having children because they are part of God's plan for the world. I spoke about the danger that zero population growth presented to the Jewish community. I was disturbed by the number of young Jewish professional couples who were abandoning the idea of parenthood altogether. I mentioned in my sermon that a colleague had recently refused to perform a marriage between two Jews because they told him that they had decided never to have children; it would interfere with their careers.

As I prepared my sermon for that Rosh Hashanah, I had in mind one couple in particular, both successful professionals in their mid-thirties. They had two lucrative careers, had recently bought a new home, and were living the suburban good life. Children seemed the farthest thing from their minds. I spoke passionately that Rosh Hashanah about the purpose of Jewish marriage and the need for Jewish families. It was one of my more successful holiday sermons, and several people requested copies. I was particularly pleased when this couple made an appointment to see me shortly after the holidays. "We need your help," they told me. "We have been trying unsuccessfully to have a baby for over five years. We have tried every medical test in the book. We want to adopt a baby, but where can we turn?"

A couple faced with a fertility problem usually have nowhere to turn within the Jewish community. Jewish leaders who do not know their situation might blame them for not carrying their share of the community responsibility to have children. When the problem is known, they will get sympathy but little practical advice. Parents may tell them, "Relax, don't try so hard, and it will happen." Some rabbis will speak of the importance of prayer or tell them to accept God's will. Few rabbis have the expertise to counsel them on medical or adoption alternatives and how Judaism views these alternatives. The organized Jewish community not only has few resources to help them but often appears unsupportive. To quote one rabbi who is also an adoptive parent, "We Jews are often our own worst enemies."

Adoption is particularly difficult for Jewish couples. The Jewish community, with a few notable exceptions, has removed itself from the adoption business. Babies are available through Catholic, Lutheran, and various nonsectarian agencies but rarely through Jewish agencies. Even the most tolerant and ecumenical religious agencies are reluctant to give a baby born of a Christian woman to a Jewish couple. Couples who attempt to adopt independently or internationally often face anti-Semitism.

My wife and I have encountered this community apathy. When we called a Jewish social service agency about adopting a second child, the social worker told us that she could not help us. They no longer placed babies, and if they did, they would not consider us. We already had an adopted child, and the rare baby they placed would go only to a childless couple. I understood this, so I told the social worker that we were seeking a child through independent sources. Visibly upset, she told us, "It is people like you who are preventing us from placing babies. Girls are giving their babies to the highest bidder, and the black market is destroying adoption in this country." It did not matter that my wife and I would never consider a black market baby, only an independent adoption, which is perfectly legal in our state. Rather than feeling guided by a social worker, my wife and I were made to feel guilty. We were not the only couple who have run into difficulty in seeking help from a Jewish social service agency.

This book was written to help infertile Jewish couples deal with the numerous issues they face. When does one seek help? How does one deal with insensitive comments? What are the emotional issues? What medical alternatives are permitted by Jewish law? Is childlessness a Jewish alternative? How does Judaism view adoption?

Not all couples who are childless are unable to conceive. Some conceive but lose their babies by miscarriage or stillbirth. And many couples have coped with the sad experience of carrying a baby to term, only to have that baby die in infancy. How does Judaism deal with these sad situations? Similarly, genetic screening and amniocentesis have opened a Pandora's box of ethical problems for Jewish couples. What guidance can we give to a couple who are frightened to conceive because they are both carriers of a Jewish genetic disease such as Tay-Sachs? What of the couple who discover through amniocentesis that their unborn child has Down's syndrome? How can Judaism serve as a source of guidance and strength for that couple?

I have already mentioned the particular difficulties that Jewish couples face in finding babies to adopt. But even after an adoption goes through, new questions arise. Is a baby considered Jewish because a Jewish family adopted him or her? If the adoptive father is a Kohen, is the adopted son? Whose Hebrew name is used? What are the child's obligations toward biological parents and adoptive parents? How does Judaism view open adoption?

Finally, what can the Jewish community do to help infertile couples? Is halakhah really sensitive to the problems they face? Or do couples find that traditional rabbis have forbidden many of the more unconventional medical procedures that have helped infertile couples conceive? Can Jewish social service agencies reenter the adoption business and find babies for Jewish couples? If 20 percent of young Jewish couples are having difficulty conceiving, that becomes a community problem, and the community must allocate some of its resources to finding solutions.

The bias of this book should be clear: The Jewish community must help Jewish couples become parents. Occasionally this may mean using aggressive means, as long as they are legal by Jewish law and by the law of the state. In the area of medical ethics, this book will consider the Jewish legal issues involved in such procedures as artificial insemination, surrogate mothering, embryo transplants, and in vitro fertilization. It will also examine such particularly Jewish issues as *mikvah* and Sabbath observance as they relate to infertility. The tendency will be to search for a *heter* (a permissive ruling) for the sake of conception, whenever such a *heter* can be countenanced by Jewish law.

Similarly, in the area of adoption, this book advocates aggressive action to help Jewish couples find babies, stopping short only when illegal activity is contemplated. Jewish legal experts must also find ways to minimize the differences between biological and adopted children in terms of their status in Jewish law.

Any discussion of Jewish law and tradition is presented

against the background of the first commandment given in the Torah: "Be fruitful and multiply." That is the over-riding concern. We must keep in mind the beautiful Midrash that the rabbis wrote regarding the giving of the Torah:

> When the people of Israel stood at Mount Sinai ready to receive the Torah, God said to them, "Bring me good securities to guarantee that you will keep it, and then I will give the Torah to you."
>
> They said, "Our ancestors will be our securities."
>
> Said God to them, "I have faults to find with your ancestors . . . but bring me good securities and I will give it to you."
>
> They said, "King of the Universe, our prophets will be our securities."
>
> He replied, "I have faults to find with your prophets. Still, bring me good securities and I will give the Torah to you."
>
> They said to Him, "Our children will be our securities."
>
> And God replied, "Indeed, these are good securities. For their sake I will give you the Torah."[11]

Children are our security for a Jewish future. We need children if we are to survive as Jews. We must muster the resources of our community to help Jewish couples become Jewish parents. We must help make the words of the psalmist come true: "He sets the childless woman among her household as a happy mother of children. Hallelujah" (Pss. 113:9).

Abraham then prayed to God, and God healed Abimelech and his wife and his slave girls, so that they bore children; for the Lord had closed fast every womb of the household of Abimelech because of Sarah, the wife of Abraham.

(Gen. 20:17–18)

✡ 2

The Jewish View of Infertility

Jewish infertility is not a new phenomenon. The Bible is filled with cases of women unable to conceive and men who die childless. The Talmud discusses at great length the legal ramifications of infertility. The barren woman is seen as a metaphor for Jerusalem, a city devoid of children through much of Jewish history. Jewish couples have been struggling with the pain of infertility since the days when Abraham and Sarah, our father and mother, struggled to conceive a child.

A Jewish view of infertility must be viewed within the context of the law "be fruitful and multiply." As we shall see, this law is central to the Jewish outlook. This chapter begins with a careful study of the *mitzvah* of procreation. Only then can we understand how the Bible, the Talmud, and the later codes and responsa view those couples who are unable to fulfill this *mitzvah.*

The Mitzvah *of Procreation*

A Jewish view of infertility must begin with a Jewish view of fertility. How does Judaism understand the responsibility of having children? Is it an option or an obligation? Is it a blessing or a commandment? Is having and raising children one of many life-style options or the only option? Is zero population growth a Jewish consideration, or is it foreign to Jewish tradition? Does the responsibility of propagation fall equally on men and women? Does Judaism permit birth control? By answering these questions, we can begin to understand how Judaism sees the many couples who want children but are unable to conceive.

First, propagation of the species is a blessing given to all life. According to the Bible, God created the fish and the birds on the fifth day of Creation. God looked at the creatures he made and saw that they were good. The Torah continues, "God blessed them, saying, 'Be fruitful and multiply, fill the waters in the seas, and let the birds increase on the earth'" (Gen. 1:22). God continued on the sixth day with the creation of animals. Although no blessing was given explicitly to them, they were included in the overall blessing "Be fruitful and multiply."

It was also on the sixth day that humankind was created. Humans are qualitatively different from animals. The Torah says, "And God created man in His image, in the image of God He created him; male and female He created them" (Gen. 1:27). Humans, unlike animals, were created in the image of God. They have intelligence and the ability to make moral choices.

One difference between humans and animals is in the area of reproduction. Only a man and a woman can choose the circumstances under which they will reproduce; only humans are free to have sexual relations or avoid them.

Unlike animals, humans can have sexual relations even during the infertile times of the month.

Animals reproduce by instinct. They have sexual activity only during their fertile period. In this essential way, humans are different. To quote Dr. Sherman Silber, a leading infertility expert: "But in all animals except for humans there is no interest in sex until the time of heat, just prior to ovulation."[1]

Humans were thus created with free will. Following the creation of man, the Torah continues: "God blessed them and God said to them, 'Be fruitful and multiply, fill the earth and master it; and rule the fish of the sea, the birds of the sky, and all the living things that creep on earth' " (Gen. 1:28). God's words are more than a blessing, they are a commandment. The rabbis looked carefully at the language of the Torah. The word *God* is used twice in this verse, once to indicate God's blessing to humans, once to indicate His commandment "Be fruitful and multiply." In Judaism, having children is a commandment from God.

In fact, Judaism is essentially a religion of commandments. The Talmud speaks of 613 commandments, 365 negative commandments corresponding to the days of the year, and 248 positive commandments corresponding to the rabbinic count of limbs in the body.[2] Rabbinic scholars have sharply disagreed in their attempts to enumerate and classify these 613 commandments. Yet most have agreed that "Be fruitful and multiply" is the first.

Other religions have seen the monastic or the celibate life-style as a religious ideal. A person could find a closeness to God through prayer, meditation, or community service while remaining unmarried. Not so in Judaism, in which it is a commandment to marry and to have children. In classical Christianity, marriage is a compromise. Paul said to the Corinthians, "If they cannot contain, let them marry; for it is better to marry than to burn" (1 Cor. 7:9). To quote Rabbi David Feldman, "One fact is objectively true of the developing Christian tradition; celibacy became the ideal, and marriage was treated as an unworthy concession to the weakness of human will."[3]

Like all commandments in Judaism, the *mitzvah* of procreation is developed in great detail by the Talmud and codes. The exact requirements of the *mitzvah* are spelled out in the Mishnah:

A man should not neglect the commandment of "be fruitful and multiply" unless he already has children. The school of Shammai teaches, two sons. The school of Hillel teaches, a son and a daughter since it says, "male and female he created them." If a man marries a woman and lives with her ten years, and they have no children, he cannot neglect it any longer. When he divorces her, she is permitted to marry another. The second husband can wait for her ten more years. If she miscarries, we begin the count from the time of the miscarriage. A man is commanded to be fruitful and multiply, but not a woman. Rabbi Yohanan ben Berukah said, both are commanded as it says, "And God blessed them and said, be fruitful and multiply."[4]

This Mishnah is discussed at great length by the Talmud and by the later codes of Jewish law. Its most striking feature is the ending. There is a disagreement between an anonymous teacher (known as *tanna kama*, "the first teacher") and Rabbi Yohanan ben Berukah. The former says that women are not obligated to be fruitful and multiply. That is the accepted halakhah. In traditional Judaism, procreation is a man's *mitzvah*. A man must marry and have children, whereas a woman is free to have children or remain single. This basic fact of Jewish law will frequently prove relevant in our study of infertility.

Let us look more closely at this fact. Why does Judaism exempt women from the important *mitzvah* of procreation? The Talmud gives a reason that makes sense within the context of a talmudic society. Yet, admittedly, it sounds rather sexist today. To quote the Talmud:

Where does this [law] come from? Rabbi Illa said in the name of Rabbi Elazar in the name of Rabbi Shimon, the verse teaches '[be fruitful and multiply] fill the earth and subdue it.' It is the way of a man to subdue the earth, but it is not the way of a woman to subdue it.[5]

The Talmud sees man as taking an activist role on the earth and woman as being more passive. It is up to a man to seek out a wife, not up to a woman to seek a husband. We can see this picture clearly from another talmudic passage:

> The Torah says, "when a man takes a wife" and not "when a woman is taken by a man," because it is the way of a man to search for a wife, and not the way of a woman to search for a husband. It is comparable to a man who loses a possession, who searches for whom? The owner of the possession searches for what he lost. (So a man searches for the rib which he lost.)[6]

This entire explanation may be counter to modern sensitivities, yet it contains a grain of truth, even in contemporary society. We live in a world where men still are expected to be the more aggressive, taking the active role in making a date and forming a relationship. Women are expected to be more passive, or at least more subtle in their pursuit of relationships. Society may be changing, but such changes are slow. In a society where a woman cannot actively hunt for a husband, she cannot be obligated by a commandment to propagate.

Modern thinkers have attempted to give more contemporary explanations for the woman's exemption from this commandment. Rabbi Immanuel Jakobovitz, the chief rabbi of England, has suggested that women do not need this commandment since they are already driven by a maternal instinct to have and raise children. It is men who need this external commandment.[7] Unfortunately, modern society has not proved this true, since so many fertile Jewish women are choosing not to have babies today.

What seems to be a more sensible explanation is found in the biblical commentary of Rabbi Meir Simha Ha-Kohen of Dvinsk, a scholar of this century:

> It is not amiss to assume that the reason why women are exempt from the obligation of procreation is grounded in the reasonableness of the judgments of the Lord and His ways. The Torah did not impose upon Israel burdens too difficult for a person to

bear. . . . Women, whose lives are jeopardized by conception and birth, were not enjoined.[8]

It would be unfair for the Torah to impose a commandment on somebody who must endure pain and physical danger to fulfill that commandment.

The Talmud tells a fascinating story that reflects this point of view. "Judith the wife of Rabbi Hiya had great pains when she gave birth. She changed her clothes and came [in disguise] before Rabbi Hiya and asked, is a woman obligated to be fruitful and multiply? He told her no. She drank a cup of roots and became sterile."[9] This is one of the earliest sources permitting the use of an oral contraceptive by a woman.

Most Jewish legal authorities have few problems with the use of birth control pills by women, since women are not obligated by the commandment of procreation. Even Orthodox authorities have permitted it after the husband has fulfilled Hillel's minimum of "a son and a daughter." In general, Judaism is relatively liberal regarding birth control—that is, when it comes to birth control usage by the woman.

For Jewish men, the commandment is not optional. The Torah is clear that a man is expected to find a wife and have children. Usually a man becomes responsible for the commandments of Judaism when he becomes bar mitzvah, at the age of thirteen. Only one commandment is delayed until the age of eighteen, the commandment of procreation. *Pirkei Avot*, "The Ethics of Our Fathers," gives the ages at which a man must make various Jewish commitments. "At five years the study of Torah, ten years the study of Mishnah, thirteen years the commandments, fifteen years the study of Gemarah, eighteen years the marriage canopy."[10] At eighteen, at least in traditional Jewish law, a man was expected to find a wife and begin to build a family.

The Talmud makes twenty the maximum age. "Rava said, and also the school of Rabbi Ishmael taught, until twenty years God sits and waits for a man to find a wife.

When he reaches twenty and hasn't married, God says 'blast his bones.' "[11]

Jewish tradition does recognize that eighteen may be a relatively young age to fulfill the commandment "Be fruitful and multiply." Certainly today, few rabbis outside the Hasidic community will advocate marriage to their eighteen-year-old young men. Tradition says that a man should first build a house, then plant a vineyard, and only then marry.[12] Translated into modern terms, this means that a man should first establish himself economically and find a way to earn a living, and only then marry. Marriage today can be delayed until after college and professional training, but it cannot be delayed forever.

> Rabbi Tanhum ben Hanilai said, whoever is not married abides without joy, without blessing, without good. Without joy—as it is written [Deut. 14:26], "And thou shalt rejoice, thou and thy household." Without blessing—as it is written [Ezek. 44:30] "To cause blessing to rest in thy house." Without good—as it is written [Gen. 2:18], "It is not good that man be alone."[13]

Eventually a man must find a wife and begin to have children.

We see that a man is commanded to procreate but a woman is exempt from that *mitzvah*. That division made more sense in a world where polygamy was permitted, such as in biblical times. If a man had more than one wife, he could fulfill his obligation with only one of them. Today, when monogamy is the rule in the Jewish community, the question becomes more complicated. Fertility becomes a couple's obligation.

How many children should a couple have? Returning to our Mishnah, the school of Shammai teaches two sons. They pattern this after Moses, who had two sons and then separated from his wife. Shammai believed that the economic and military contributions of sons were of ultimate importance to the Jewish community. For Hillel, a son and a daughter are required. This is patterned after the works of creation, when God created Adam and Eve. For Hillel, to give birth to a son and a daughter is to ensure that propagation of the species will be carried on for a new generation. On this issue, Jewish law follows the opinion of Hillel.

The Talmud says further that this son and daughter should themselves be capable of having children, ensuring that procreation is carried to the next generation.[14] However, a man's responsibility does not stop there. The rabbis quote two verses from the prophets to prove that a man has a continual responsibility to produce children. The first is Isaiah 45:18: ". . . He did not create it [the earth] a waste, but formed it for habitation. . . ." Man has a duty to continue to produce offspring to inhabit the world. The rabbis also taught that if a man has brought forth children at a young age, he still has an obligation in his old age. They based this on Ecclesiastes 11:6. "Sow your seed in the morning, and don't hold back your hand in the evening, since you don't know which is going to succeed, the one or the other, or if both are equally good." On the basis of this verse, Rabbi Joshua taught, "If a man married a woman in his youth, let him marry in his old age, if he had children in his youth, let him have children in his old age."[15]

According to Jewish tradition, the *mitzvah* of procreation never stops for a man. One can understand this rabbinic concern with large families. The infant mortality rate was high, and many children did not live to adulthood. Even for those who did reach adulthood, not all would be capable of marrying or bearing children. To ensure the continuity of Jewish tradition through a new generation, many children were required. This is one of the reasons why vasectomies have long been outlawed by Jewish tradition.

Similarly, although Judaism has been liberal regarding birth control usage by women, it is quite strict regarding birth control by men. A man was expected to continue to have children throughout his life. The outlawing of such male birth control devices as the condom was also related to the Jewish prohibition of the wasteful spilling of seed.

Today, outside the very Orthodox community, few Jews are having the large number of children envisioned in the Talmud. It is no longer necessary to have nine or ten children with the hope that three or four will survive to adulthood, marry, and have children of their own. Because of advances in medicine, most children survive to adulthood. Few Jewish women are prepared to sacrifice a career totally and spend a lifetime raising children.

We also speak today about the quality of life of those children brought into the world. Most Jewish families are prepared to have fewer children and to ensure that each of those children can be provided for properly. The cost of raising a child is overwhelming today. College education alone, which is almost a necessity for most Jewish families, demands huge sacrifices for even a two-child family. The large Jewish families of the past are unthinkable for most Jewish couples today.

And yet the importance of procreation as a commandment is still heard among rabbis of all movements. Let us look at a sampling of the writings of some rabbis.

Maurice Lamm, representing the Orthodox community, writes:

> Every Jewish birth today is a commitment to the Jewish future. It is a resounding response to the Hitlers of history that the Jews will survive. Today, bearing children is more than just fulfilling the religious duty to "be fruitful and multiply"—it is an act of faith in the God of Israel and the destiny of the Jewish people.[16]

Robert Gordis, a leading Conservative thinker, writes:

> Jewish families in the future are not likely to run to eight or ten children each, but neither should they be limited to one or two ... three or four children should be adopted as the minimum for Jewish families. Parents should be encouraged to bring a large number of children into the world within the capacity and the scope of their desires. Though the cost of raising a child in modern society is high, modern couples should increase their family size as a matter of Jewish loyalty and social policy, if they

are able to afford it economically, physically, and culturally. They will be richly rewarded as they forge a lifeline to immortality for themselves and their people.[17]

Eugene B. Borowitz, representing the Reform outlook, writes:

The world population problem is quite real—but, though many supporters of Zero Population Growth seem to be Jewish, it has little directly to do with the Jewish people. The cold facts are that every Jewish community that modernized has had little or no natural population increase. That has been true of American Jewry for some decades. . . . A case can easily be made for having larger Jewish families. They would not only make up for the decline in marriage, but bring the Jewish population back to the level it was before the Holocaust.[18]

"Be fruitful and multiply" remains a commandment at the center of the Jewish agenda in all three major movements. Nevertheless, it is important to note that there is more to Jewish marriage than procreation. When the Bible speaks of the institution of marriage, it does not mention procreation. It mentions companionship. The Torah teaches, "The Lord God said, 'It is not good for man to be alone; I will make a fitting helper for him' " (Gen. 2:18). "Hence a man leaves his father and mother and clings to his wife, so that they become one flesh" (Gen. 2:24). To Jews, human fulfillment is found in marriage, irrespective of children. The Talmud and Midrash are full of aphorisms on the joy of married life and the incompleteness of bachelorhood. One of the most beautiful teaches, "No man without a wife, neither a woman without a husband, nor both of them without God."[19]

Companionship takes an equal place with procreation as the purpose of Jewish marriage. To quote one popular Orthodox manual:

Marriage has its own legitimacy, significance, and meaning apart from children. It has its own sanctity. Before God commanded "Be fertile and increase," he set about creating a wife for Adam because "it is not good that man should be alone . . . and I will make him a help-mate." . . . Companionship, and the love and goodwill necessary for that relationship, is presented as the first and primary purpose of marriage. While the importance of having children is stressed, the marriage itself, the coming together as man and wife, has also been a prime target of rabbinic concern.[20]

Because companionship is one basic purpose of Jewish marriage, Judaism has always recommended marriage as the ideal, even for Jews who cannot have children. Even if one aspect of marriage (procreation) could not be fulfilled, the other aspect (companionship) still could be. Rabbi David Abudarham, a fourteenth-century liturgical scholar, was asked why a blessing was not said over procreation when a couple stand under the wedding *huppah*. He answered that the blessing under the *huppah* must be appropriate for all couples, both fertile and infertile. "Thus, the subject of companionship was an appropriate blessing, but procreation was not."[21] True, the Mishnah does speak of divorce as a requirement for a couple married ten years without producing children. However, as we shall see later, this law eventually fell out of practice.

Before turning to the Jewish view of infertility, it will be useful to summarize how Judaism views procreation:

1 In Judaism, procreation is more than a blessing. It is a *mitzvah*, one of the commandments given to the Jewish people.

2 Women are not obligated to be fruitful and multiply. Although Jewish society has pressured women to marry, by Jewish law a woman is free to remain single. Of course, once she is married, she joins her husband in fulfilling the *mitzvah* of procreation.

3 Men are obligated to be fruitful and multiply. The minimum obligation is one son and one daughter. However, the rabbis saw it as a *mitzvah* to continue having as many children as possible.

4 Even today, there is an overwhelming need for Jewish couples to have children. Rabbis of all three move-

ments have spoken out forcefully on the need for more Jewish children.

5 Birth control is permissible for a woman, as long as the basic commandment of procreation has been or will be fulfilled. Most birth control techniques used by men raise serious problems in Jewish law.

6 Procreation is only one of the two primary purposes of marriage. Companionship is the other one. Therefore, marriage is the ideal state even for those Jews who know that they are infertile.

Infertility in the Bible

Although the Bible is the source of the commandment "Be fruitful and multiply," from the beginning, couples were frustrated in their attempts to conceive a child. All of the three patriarchal and matriarchal couples—Abraham and Sarah, Isaac and Rebecca, Jacob and Rachel—were infertile. Of the matriarchs, only Leah had no trouble conceiving. Yet even she went through a period when she was unable to have more children, despite her desire.

The Bible indicates some fundamental theological suppositions that had great influence on later Judaism. Childlessness was not simply a cause for sadness; it was perceived to be a sign of God's displeasure. Infertility in the Bible is a form of punishment.

This is indicated clearly by the quote at the beginning of this chapter. Abraham feared for his life from Abimelech, the king of Gerar. He therefore lied, saying that Sarah, his wife, was his sister. With this false information, Abimelech took Sarah into his household with the hope that she would become his wife. God appeared to Abimelech in a dream, rebuking him for living with a married woman. As a punishment, all the women of his household became sterile.

Only Abraham's intercession was able to cure the women in Abimelech's household. Abraham prayed, and the wombs of the women were opened up. In the next verse, we learn that God remembered Sarah, and she became pregnant with a son of her old age, Isaac. The rabbis learned a beautiful thought from the juxtaposition of these two passages. "Anybody who prays for mercy for his fellow when he himself needs mercy, he will be answered first."[22] Abraham, in spite of his own fertility problem, was willing to pray for Abimelech. In praying for his fellow, his own prayer was answered. Perhaps there is a lesson in this story for modern infertile couples. By helping each other and rejoicing in each other's triumphs, we can ultimately help ourselves.

Another example of infertility as a sign of divine disfavor is the story of Michal, the wife of King David and the daughter of King Saul. When the ark of the Lord was brought up to Jerusalem, after being held by the Philistines, David rejoiced and celebrated. The Bible says, "As the Ark of the Lord entered the City of David, Michal daughter of Saul looked out of the window and saw King David leaping and whirling before the Lord; and she despised him for it" (2 Sam. 6:16). Michal chastised David for behavior unbecoming of a king, and David defended the propriety of his action. The tale ends with the words, "So to her dying day Michal daughter of Saul had no children" (2 Sam. 6:23). Michal was punished for her angry words at her husband; she was to remain childless.

There is an interesting development in this story that should be of great interest to infertile couples. Michal had an older sister named Merab, who was married to Adriel, the son of Barzillai; later the Bible speaks of the five sons of Michal, who were born to Adriel (2 Sam. 21:8). The Talmud questions this biblical passage. Did Michal give birth to five sons? Michal's sister Merab was the mother. The Talmud continues in the name of Rabbi Joshua, "Merab gave birth to them, and Michal raised them, therefore they are called by her name. This teaches that anyone who raises an orphan in his home, scripture considers him as if he gave birth to him."[23] This is the classical justification for adoption in Jewish law.

In the biblical worldview, God is the key to everything that happens in the world. To be childless was taken as a sign of divine displeasure. The Torah even mentions infertility as a punishment for certain sexual crimes (Lev. 20:20–21). If one is afflicted with any disease, one should search his or her behavior for wrongdoing. This is the classical religious view, and for many it still holds great sway today.

Yet most of the women in the Bible who were infertile are not portrayed as being sinful. On the contrary, they are held up to be examples of piety and generosity. Sarah, Rebecca, Rachel, Hannah, and the Shunammite women all exemplify spiritual qualities imitated by future generations of women. Each was barren, yet each eventually conceived.

Sarah is considered the mother of the people Israel. She was Abraham's wife, and her Hebrew name comes from a word meaning princess. The rabbis lavished praise on Sarah for her beauty and good deeds. Yet when we first meet her, the Torah points out only one fact—her barrenness. "Now Sarai was barren, she had no child" (Gen. 11:30). God appeared before Abraham and promised to be his shield and protector. Abraham answered back with words that should be familiar to any childless couple. ". . . 'O Lord God, what can you give me, seeing that I shall die childless, and the one in charge of my household is Dammesek Eliezer! . . . Since you have granted me no offspring, my steward will be my heir' " (Gen. 15:2–3). God answered back, ". . . 'That one shall not be your heir, none but your very own issue shall be your heir' " (Gen. 15:4).

We see a major concern of Abraham. To be childless is to have no heir. It seems that it was the custom of the day for a childless man to "adopt" a servant to be his heir. Abraham adopted his servant Dammesek Eliezer as an heir. Yet one senses the emptiness in the lives of Abraham and Sarah; once again, the sadness behind the words is obvious.

The years passed, and there was still no sign that God's promise would come true. The story continues:

Sarai, Abram's wife, had borne him no children. She had an Egyptian maid servant named Hagar. And Sarai said to Abram, "Look, the Lord has kept me from bearing. Consort with my maid; perhaps I shall have a son through her." And Abram heeded Sarai's request. So Sarai, Abram's wife, took her maid, Hagar the Egyptian—after Abram had dwelt in the land of Canaan ten years—and gave her to her husband Abram as concubine. He cohabited with Hagar and she conceived; and when she saw that she had conceived, her mistress was lowered in her esteem. (Gen. 16:1–4)

The story continues with the birth of Ishmael, son of Hagar and Abraham. Sarah's plan to bring Hagar in as a surrogate mother backfired and thus began a series of domestic troubles within Abraham's household. Trouble developed between Sarah and Hagar, between Sarah and Ishmael, and ultimately between Isaac and Ishmael.

This story can give us a number of insights. First, the rabbis pointed out the fact that Abraham and Sarah had lived ten years in the land of Canaan. This is the basis of the law that if a couple is married ten years without children, the husband should try to fulfill his obligation through another wife.[24] In biblical society, where polygamy was acceptable, this did not present a problem. By talmudic times, when polygamy fell out of favor, having a second wife meant that the couple must divorce. (This issue will be discussed in detail later in this chapter.)

The rabbis learn another insight from this story. They count only the ten years that Sarah and Abraham lived in Canaan, not the many years they lived together previously. According to the rabbinic interpretation, before Abraham lived in Canaan, he was living in a partial state of sin and therefore was unworthy of having children. "[The Torah mentions] the ten years that Abram lived in the land of Canaan to teach us that years lived outside the land do not count toward the ten. Therefore, if he is ill or she is ill or either is in prison, they do not count toward the ten years."[25] There must be ten healthy years of living together.

What is intriguing about the story are the words that

Sarah used. She did not say, "Marry my handmaiden, so you can fulfill the obligation of 'be fruitful and multiply.' " Such language would have been an anachronism. She said, "Consort with my maid; perhaps I shall have a son through her" (Gen. 16:2). The children would become Sarah's children, at least in a fashion. In fact, a similar story takes place when Rachel is unable to conceive a child. She said to Jacob, "Here is my maid Bilhah. Consort with her, that she may bear on my knees and that through her I too may have children" (Gen. 30:3). When Bilhah gave birth, the Torah continues, "And Rachel said, 'God has vindicated me; indeed he has heeded my plea and given me a son.' Therefore she named him Dan" (Gen. 30:6). Rachel called the son born to her handmaiden "my son."

The stories of Sarah and Rachel provide biblical sources for allowing an infertile couple to build a family. It is a form of surrogate mothering. We will find many other examples in the Bible of one person giving birth to a child, who is then called by someone else's name. Of course, the child of the handmaiden never acquires the status of a biological child. Isaac's status as Sarah's biological child is greater than that of Ishmael. Similarly, Joseph and Benjamin, Rachel's biological children, have greater status than Dan and Naphtali, the two sons of Bilhah.

Despite a lesser status, this was an acceptable method for a barren woman to have a child from her husband. In biblical times, concubinage was an acceptable social institution. Several ancient documents from Nuzi, a city in northeast Iraq, speak about the custom of a childless woman giving her husband a handmaiden as a concubine so that he will have an heir. The child born of the handmaiden becomes the wife's child.[26] In passing, we should also note that these Nuzi documents speak about a type of adoption. A man with no heir can adopt an outsider to be his heir. This seems to explain Abraham's words to God, that Dammesek Eliezer, his servant, will inherit from him.

Modern scholars have written that there was a popular belief that adopting the handmaiden's child would be a cure for infertility. In fact, this worked for both Rachel and

Leah. This will ring a responsive chord for every modern couple who have been told after adopting, "Now you will become pregnant." In fact, the whole procedure did not work out well for Sarah. Because she was barren, her esteem was lowered in the eyes of Hagar. Ultimately, she treated Hagar harshly and forced both Hagar and Ishmael out of her household and into the wilderness.

In the end, God appeared to Sarah and promised her a son. She laughed and said to God, ". . . 'Now that I am withered, am I to have enjoyment—with my husband so old?' " Sarah put the blame on Abraham. God reported the story to Abraham but changed the wording slightly. ". . . 'Why did Sarah laugh, saying, "Shall I in truth bear a child, old as I am?" ' " (Gen. 18:12–13). The rabbis picked up on this change of wording. They saw the value of *shalom bayit* (peace in the home) if even God was willing to tell a white lie for the sake of peace between Abraham and Sarah. This story is one of the first times the Bible mentions that the man, and not only the woman, may be the cause of infertility. An important modern step is the recognition that infertility is a problem for both the man and the woman; it is a couple's problem. We find a hint here.

In the end, God did remember Sarah and blessed her with a son, Isaac (from the root *tz-h-k*, "to laugh"). Abraham was one hundred years old, and Sarah was ninety. With Isaac, and his wife Rebecca, fertility problems were passed on to a new generation.

The portion *Toledot* begins when Isaac was forty years old and had just taken Rebecca to be his wife. It says, "Isaac pleaded with the Lord on behalf of his wife, because she was barren; and the Lord responded to his plea, and his wife Rebekah conceived" (Gen. 25:21). When Isaac was sixty, Rebecca gave birth to twins, Jacob and Esau. The question is immediately raised, Why did Isaac allow twenty years to go by without fulfilling the *mitzvah* of procreation? Certainly he could have taken a concubine as his father Abraham did.

The answer is given by the Talmud. Isaac, not Rebecca, was the infertile one.[27] Therefore he waited longer, hoping prayer would cure his sterility. The Talmud equivocates about this and then suggests that they both were infertile. Yet there is a hint of Isaac's infertility in the language of the Bible. It says that "Isaac pleaded in the presence of his wife," rather than "Isaac pleaded for his wife."* He understood that he was, at least partially, the cause of the infertility. Later, the Torah says that God answered him, not her or them. There is no proof, but all of these suggest that Isaac was infertile.

Once again, we see that infertility is a couple's problem. As often as not, the man is the physiological cause. It is not a judgment against a man if he is infertile, nor should it be a challenge to his masculinity. Jewish tradition looks at Isaac as an example of great piety; after all, he willingly allowed himself to become a sacrifice. In fact, the same page of Talmud that discusses Isaac's infertility states, "Rabbi Isaac says, why were our ancestors barren? Because the Holy One, blessed be He, longs to hear the prayer of the righteous."[28] It is a fascinating bit of irony that is common in the Bible. In the case of Michal, infertility is a sign of sinfulness. For Isaac, it is a sign of righteousness.

With Rachel and Jacob, infertility becomes a problem for a third generation. Here we encounter a situation that we have already seen with Hannah and Peninnah, the loved wife and the unloved wife. Jacob had two wives, Leah and Rachel. Leah, the unloved wife, had the children. Rachel, the beloved wife, was barren. It is a constant theme in the Bible. Hannah, the beloved wife, was also barren, whereas Peninnah, the unloved co-wife, had the children. In fact, the book of Deuteronomy warns, "If a man has two wives, one loved and the other unloved, and both the loved and the unloved have borne him sons, but the first-born is the son of the unloved one—when he wills his property to his sons, he may not treat as first-born the son of the loved one in disregard of the son of the unloved one who is older." (Deut. 21:15–16).

---

*This literal translation differs from the new Jewish Publication Society (*Tanakh*) translation ("Isaac pleaded . . . on behalf of his wife").

The Bible warns against playing favorites with two wives. A frequent punishment seems to be that the favored wife is infertile. Leah, the unloved wife, kept hoping to find favor in her husband's eyes through her many children. For example, when Reuben the firstborn is named, the Torah says, ". . . [Leah] named him Reuben; for she declared, 'It means: "The Lord has seen my affliction"; it also means: "Now my husband will love me" ' " (Gen. 29:32). When Simeon is born, she says ". . . 'This is because the Lord heard that I was unloved and has given me this one also'; so she named him Simeon." (Gen. 29:33). Even after delivering six sons and a daughter to Jacob, she remained the hated wife. Only Rachel, the infertile wife, was beloved.

From Rachel, we have the cry that any woman who longs for children can understand. "When Rachel saw that she had borne Jacob no children, she became envious of her sister; and Rachel said to Jacob, 'Give me children, or I shall die' " (Gen. 30:1). The cry of anguish can be felt by infertile couples in all generations. On the basis of Rachel's words, the Babylonian teacher Joshua b. Levi said that to be without children is a kind of a death.[29]

Many couples with children do not realize that childlessness is like a death. There is a period of mourning that the infertile couple go through when they realize that they are unlikely to conceive a child. It often includes all five stages of grief that Elisabeth Kübler-Ross identified among dying patients—denial, anger, bargaining, depression, acceptance.[30] A couple unable to conceive must work through their loss just as must a person who has a death in the family. Only after they have mourned for the child they cannot have are they ready to ask the question, "Where do we go from here?"

To Rachel, childlessness was a form of death. She saw no reason to live. Rachel's emotional statement can be understood by anybody who has faced infertility. What is surprising is Jacob's unsympathetic response. Rather than loving his wife and trying to empathize, he answered cruelly. The Torah says, "Jacob was incensed at Rachel, and said, 'Can I take the place of God, who has denied you the fruit of the womb?' " (Gen. 30:2). How different is Jacob's reaction from Hannah's husband, Elkanah. Elkanah at least tried to comfort Hannah and proclaim his love for her.

The rabbis condemned Jacob for his answer. To quote the *Midrash*, " 'And Jacob's anger was kindled.' Said the Holy One blessed be He to him, Is this the way to answer the troubled? By your life, your sons are destined to stand before hers [i.e., Joseph]."[31] Nehama Lebowitz, the great Bible teacher, points up a parallel between Jacob's use of the phrase "Can I take the place of God . . .?" and Joseph's use of a similar phrase (see Gen. 50:19).[32] Jacob used it in an insensitive and angry way, whereas Joseph used a similar phrase in a comforting way toward his brothers after their father's death. Joseph, Rachel's son, learned a sensitivity from his mother that his father lacked.

Rachel's statement is also questioned by the rabbis. She must have said something to provoke such an angry response. Some rabbis said that Rachel expected Jacob to have some kind of magical powers. If only he prayed harder, or said the right words, she would be cured. There is no magic, and no automatic formula, for curing infertility. Some things are in the hands of God.

A relevant explanation for modern Jews of Jacob's anger is found in the commentary by Isaac Amara, *Akedat Yitzhak*. Amara speaks of the various names given to woman when she was created, and the various roles given to her. This explanation is sufficiently important that it is worth quoting at length:

The two names "woman" [*ishah*] and "Eve" indicate two purposes. The first teaches that woman was taken from man, stressing that like him you may understand and advance in the intellectual and moral field just as did the matriarchs and many righteous women and prophetesses and as the literal meaning of Proverbs 31 about "the woman of worth" (*eshet hayil*) indicates. The second alludes to the power of childbearing and rearing children, as is indicated by the name Eve—the mother of all living. A woman deprived of the power of childbearing will be deprived of the secondary purpose and be left with the ability to do evil or good like the man who is barren. Of both the barren man and woman Isaiah [56:5] states: "I have given them in My house and in My walls a name that is better than sons and daughters," since the off-spring of the righteous is certainly good deeds [see Rashi on Gen. 6:9]. Jacob was therefore angry with Rachel when she said, "Give me children or else I die" in order to reprimand her and make her understand this all-important principle that she was not dead as far as their joint purpose in life because she was childless, just the same as it would be, in his case, if he would have been childless.[33]

Akedat Yitzhak is teaching a basic Jewish idea. A woman was not simply created to bear children. She was given the name *ishah* to prove that like a man, *ish*, she can develop her moral and intellectual skills; today we would add her professional skills. This is an early recognition of the feminist agenda of today. A woman's role cannot be limited to bearing and raising children; there are too many other reasons to live. When Rachel said, "Give me children, or I shall die," she was denying other important parts of herself. A modern feminist would be upset by Rachel's statement, as Jacob was. Judaism would answer Rachel by saying, "There are many areas of life where you can find fulfillment besides motherhood." As Rashi put it, "This comes to teach us that the descendants of a righteous person are his good deeds."[34]

This explanation for Jacob's anger is fine on a philosophical level, but Rachel's cry was a cry of anguish. She was not discussing philosophy but was opening her heart to her husband. As a counselor, I have spoken to many women with great professional and intellectual accomplishments who have poured their souls out to me saying, "What good is it all, since I can't have children?" It is difficult to respond, "There's more to life than having children. Look what you have accomplished with your life." Such an answer would be insensitive in the extreme. Professional accomplishments do not lessen the pain of infertility.

Rachel, like Sarah, used her handmaiden to have children in her place. Leah, who had stopped conceiving, also gave her handmaiden to Jacob. The jealousy and competition continued between the two sisters. When Leah's eldest, Reuben, picked some mandrakes, Rachel wanted them because they were thought to have the power to reverse infertility. Ultimately, Rachel gave birth to two sons, Joseph and Benjamin. She died giving birth to Benjamin.

There are still other examples of the barren woman in the Bible. Samson's mother was childless when an angel of God appeared to her and told her she would conceive. Her son would be a nazirite, a man whose life would be dedicated to God. He was not to drink wine, or touch unclean things, or shave his hair (see Judg. 13:2ff). Similarly, a Shunammite woman was very kind to Elisha. Yet she was childless, and her husband was old. Elisha promised her a child, a promise that did come true. Later Elisha brought the child back to life after he died (2 Kings 4:8ff).

In all these cases, God is the one who gives or withholds the ability to bear children. The Talmud teaches, "Rabbi Yohanan said, three keys are in the hands of the Holy One, blessed be He, and those are not given to anyone else. The key to rain, the key to giving life, the key to resurrection of the dead."[35] In the Psalms, we praise God, saying, "He sets the childless woman among her household as a happy mother of children. Hallelujah" (Pss. 113:9). In the biblical view, God holds the key, and only prayer and proper behavior can change God's mind and grant an infertile couple children.

In Judaism, the theme of the barren woman has metaphorical power. Jerusalem itself, destroyed by the Babylonians and later by the Romans, is compared to a woman without children. Jews have always had faith that just as the barren woman is remembered by God, so too will Jerusalem be recalled. Thus the prophet Isaiah, from the exile of Babylonia, could deliver his optimistic prophecy to Jerusalem, "Shout, O barren one, You who bore no child! Shout aloud for joy, You who did not travail! For the children of the wife forlorn shall outnumber those of the espoused—said the Lord" (Isa. 54:1).

Throughout the long exile, Jews have always prayed that God would remember Jerusalem and return her children to her. Every Jewish wedding served as a reminder of Jerusalem's childless status. The fifth of the *sheva berakhot* (seven blessings) chanted under the marriage *huppah* reads, "Be extremely joyous and be gladdened, O barren one, as your children are gathered inside her with happiness. Praised art Thou, O Lord, who gladdens Zion (Jerusalem) with her children."

The theme of a barren wife is a frequent one in the Bible. From the women we have studied, we get a sense of the emotional anguish of infertility. Yet, in terms of Jewish law and tradition, female infertility is not as serious as male infertility. Men were expected to be fruitful and multiply, whereas women were exempted. In biblical times, if a man's wife was infertile, he could always take a second wife. It may have caused domestic problems, as it did for Sarah and Abraham, but at least he was fulfilling his obligation.

In the Bible, a childless woman was regarded with pity, but for a man to be childless was particularly tragic. First, there was the concern that a man have an heir—by biblical law, a daughter could inherit property if there are no sons (see Num. 27:1–11). A greater concern in the Bible was that a man who died childless would have no one to carry on his name.

A man who was capable of having children was not permitted to avoid his responsibility. The Bible tells the story of King Hezekiah, one of the truly virtuous kings of Judah, who was afflicted with a serious illness. The prophet Isaiah came to visit him, but his words were hardly comforting. ". . . 'Set your affairs in order, for you are going to die; you will not get well' " (2 Kings 20:1). Hezekiah prayed for healing, and God granted him extra life.

The Talmud comments on this story.

> What is the meaning of Isaiah's words, "you are going to die; you will not get well"? "Thou shalt die in this world and not live in the world to come." Hezekiah said to him: "Why so bad?" He replied: "Because you did not try to have children." He said; "The reason was because I saw by the holy spirit that the children issuing from me would not be virtuous." He said to him: "What have you to do with the secrets of the Almighty? You should have done what you were commanded, and let the Holy One, blessed be He, do what pleases Him."[36]

The implications of the story are clear: Nobody knows what the future will bring. Yet even if a man fears for the future, that is no excuse for avoiding the responsibility of procreation. Hezekiah had a responsibility to bring children into the world; how those children would turn out was in God's hands. To avoid having children was considered a grievous sin in the Bible.

What of the man who dies childless? We can learn a great deal from the story of Er and Onan. Er was the oldest son of Judah and the grandson of Jacob. He married a woman named Tamar. The Bible tells the story of Er and Onan:

But Er, Judah's first-born, was displeasing to the Lord, and the Lord took his life. Then Judah said to Onan, 'Join with your brother's wife and do your duty by her as a brother-in-law, and provide offspring for your brother.' But Onan, knowing that the seed would not count as his, let it go to waste whenever he joined with his brother's wife, so as not to provide offspring for his brother. What he did was displeasing to the Lord, and He took his life also. (Gen. 38:7–10)

The rabbis asked, What was Er's evil deed that God should slay him at a young age and without children? The Bible does not say, but rabbinic Midrash fills in the story. Er also spilled his seed upon the ground. He did not want to ruin Tamar's beauty by making her pregnant. Once again, we see the seriousness of a man not fulfilling his obligation to have children.

This is the first time the Bible mentions the institution of levirate marriage, in which the brother of the deceased man has an obligation to marry the widow and have children. The children are called by the name of the first husband. Even after his death, it was unthinkable that a man should be without seed. Here is another biblical example of one person having a child and that child being raised in the name of someone else. Onan should have fulfilled his responsibility to raise children in his brother's name. By spilling his seed upon the ground, he was committing a grievous sin.

The laws of levirate marriage are found in the book of Deuteronomy (25:5–10):

When brothers dwell together and one of them dies and leaves no son, the wife of the deceased shall not be married to a stranger, outside the family. Her husband's brother shall unite with her: take her as his wife and perform the levir's duty. The first son that she bears shall be accounted to the dead brother, that his name may not be blotted out in Israel. But if the man does not want to marry his brother's widow, his brother's widow shall appear before the elders in the gate and declare, "My husband's brother refuses to establish a name in Israel for his brother; he will not perform the duty of the levir." The elders of his town shall then summon him and talk to him. If he insists, saying, "I do not want to marry her," his brother's widow shall go up to him in the presence of the elders, pull the sandal off his foot, spit in his face, and make this declaration: Thus shall be done to the man who will not build up his brother's house! And he shall go in Israel by the name of "the family of the unsandaled one."

It was considered a disgrace to refuse to marry the widowed sister-in-law and to refuse to raise up children in the brother's name. The ceremony of *halitzah*, the removal of the shoe and spitting in the face, were affronts to one's dignity. This brother, by leaving his dead brother childless, deserved those affronts. But Jewish law has changed in this area; today it mandates the ceremony of *halitzah* and has outlawed levirate marriage. As archaic as it may seem, among traditional Jews today, a childless widow must be released by her brother-in-law before she can marry again.

In the Bible, levirate marriage was an important *mitzvah*. To refuse was a disgrace, and to spill one's seed upon the ground, as Onan did, was a sin worthy of death. We still call the wasting of seed "onanism." Judaism frowns on any wasting of seed, whether by masturbation or the use of a condom. The laws against onanism will become quite relevant when we discuss male sperm testing.

What is important about the law of levirate marriage is the seriousness with which the Bible responds to a childless man. A man must have an heir as well as someone to continue his name. Once again, in a world where polygamy was a norm, it was not problematic for a man with a wife to marry his sister-in-law. As the Jewish community became monogamous, levirate marriage would become a serious problem. Eventually, it would be outlawed.

To summarize the biblical view of infertility:

1 The Bible sees infertility as a tragedy. Sometimes it is a sign of disfavor by God, yet many of the most righteous biblical figures were infertile.

2 For a woman to be infertile is sad; for a man to die without an heir is worse still.

3 The Bible suggests ways for infertile couples to build a family. These include adoption (Michal and Abraham), surrogate mothers (Sarah and Rachel), and *levirate* marriage.

4 God ultimately is the key to fertility and infertility. Proper prayers and proper behavior can cure infertility.

All of these ideas are developed further in the Talmud and later Rabbinic literature.

Infertility in Rabbinic Literature

Judaism does not end with the Bible. The Bible is actually the beginning. To understand Judaism, one must first understand the vast corpus of rabbinic literature based on the Bible. This literature includes the Talmud, the Midrash, the various codes of Jewish law, and the responsa of various rabbis to inquiries on Jewish law.

Rabbinic literature can be divided into two categories: *aggadah* and *halakhah*. Aggadah is any material of a non-legal nature. It can range from legends and stories to moral tales to aphorisms to history and folklore. Halakhah, on the other hand, is the meat of rabbinic literature. It consists of the intricate legal discussions that make up the bulk of the Talmud. Halakhah is concerned with only one question: what does God expect of a Jew as a member of a holy people? Aggadah can give us a sense of the world outlook of the rabbis. Halakhah is a practical guide.

We have already dealt with numerous aggadic statements in our study of the Bible. Many of the insights about Sarah, Rachel, Hannah, and Michal were selected from the aggadah.

The Talmud is full of aggadic stories of infertility and successful cures. Although these stories are often fascinating and can give us some Jewish insight, aggadah is not binding on Jews the way halakhah is. An aggadic statement regarding a cure for infertility must be judged within the context of talmudic medicine, not by modern medical standards.

One such aggadic statement says that eating small fish can stimulate propagation.[37] Fish were always seen as a symbol of fertility; that is one reason why in talmudic times brides were married on Wednesday.[38] The first intercourse would then take place on the fifth day, the day the fish were blessed with the words "Be fruitful and multiply." The Talmud speaks of the great fertility of the Israelite women in Egypt before the Exodus.[39] According to the Midrash, when the women went to draw water, their buckets filled with small fish. They cooked these, ate them, and fed them to their husbands, causing great fertility. The population went from 70 to 600,000 in four generations, a feat that can be achieved only through exceptional fertility.

Other medical cures for infertility are also offered in the Talmud. Ezra, the scribe and religious leader of the Jews during the beginning of the Second Commonwealth, made numerous enactments, among them, "A man should eat garlic on Friday because of '*onah*' " (the traditional requirement of regular sexual relations, the ideal evening being Friday). Garlic was thought to increase the sperm.[40] In a similar way, the Talmud mentions eight things that cause a decrease in sperm: "salt, hunger, scalls [scaly eruptions of the skin], weeping, sleeping on the ground, lotus, cucumbers of the season, and bloodletting below the waist."[41]

If this list seems silly, it is worthwhile to remember that infertile couples today are often given a similar list of folk remedies by well-meaning friends.

Other reasons for infertility are given in the Talmud. One reason was the long discourses of Rabbi Huna. "Rabbi Aha bar Yakov said, sixty students were at a lecture, and all became sterile from the discourses of Rabbi Huna except for me."[42] The Talmud suggests a reason for this mass sterility. It was caused by holding one's urine in and not relieving oneself during a long lecture. Once again, the story seems somewhat silly at first, yet it is possible to see a new attitude emerging in the Talmud. In the Bible, infertility is due to God; in these talmudic stories, there is a direct physiological cause. The understanding of physiology is primitive, but the idea is a vital one. Seeking a medical cure is thus a legitimate Jewish path.

A more relevant story for modern couples about infertility involves the son of Rabbi Yehudah Ha-Nasi, the redactor of the Mishnah. It is found in a discussion on the laws of *onah*, the right of a Jewish wife to regular sexual relations with her husband. The issue is a husband who goes away to study for a long time. The son of Rabbi Yehudah Ha-Nasi (Rabi) went away to study thirteen years, leaving his wife behind. By the time he returned, she had become infertile. His father said, "Divorce her." He said, "People will say, 'This poor one waited all these years in vain.' " His father said, "Take a second wife." He answered, "People will say, 'This is his wife and this is his concubine.' " Rather he prayed for her, and she was cured.[43]

The story is primitive, yet it reflects a real truth for many couples who have chosen to delay childbirth until after a period of study. The period of study ends, and they discover that they are no longer able to achieve pregnancy.

Much insight can be gained from this story. With it, we leave the realm of aggadah and enter the realm of halakhah. What should Rabi's son have done when he discovered that his wife could not become pregnant? The basic law is clear: "If a man marries a woman and lives with her ten years and they have no children, he cannot neglect it [the *mitzvah* of procreation] any longer."[44] The law says that he must either divorce her and remarry or take a second wife. He is obligated to have children. Rabi's son chose neither of these options. Both would have been unfair to his loving wife who waited for him all those years. He chose prayer instead as a cure for their infertility.

Here we have a classical problem in Jewish law. What if a happily married couple is unable to conceive after ten years of marriage? As Rabbi David Feldman said, "What if a conflict occurs among the stated purposes of marriage—if the duty of procreation clashes with the privilege of marital bliss?"[45] There are two choices in the Mishnah. A childless man after ten years of marriage must either marry a second wife in addition to the first or divorce and then remarry. We will explore each of these options.

The first option, marriage to a second wife, was not favored by the rabbis. Although the Torah permits polygamy, monogamy is the ideal. The Torah says, "Hence a man leaves his father and mother and clings to his wife, so that they become one flesh" (Gen. 2:24). The Bible presents monogamous marriage as the proper life-style for a man and woman. The Talmud, although permitting polygamy, truly frowned upon it. Not one of the more than 2,000 sages quoted in the Talmud had a second wife. It is no wonder that the second wife is called a *tzarah*, from a root meaning "trouble."

By the Middle Ages, polygamy was outlawed altogether. Rabbi Gershom of Mayence (d. 1028), known as Meor Ha-Golah, "the light of the exile," is credited with the ban on polygamy. He decreed a ban of excommunication on any man who took a second wife. (Incidentally, he also placed a ban on any man who divorced his wife against her will.) Some authorities did permit bigamy as a solution to childlessness, but most authorities forbade it.

This ban on bigamy for purposes of "be fruitful and multiply" was presented most strongly in a responsum by Eliezer ben Joel Halevi. He wrote:

There was a man who would interrupt the prayers and make manifest in public on a number of occasions his inability to carry out the commandment of "be fruitful and multiply"—all in order to be exempted from the ban of the great Gershom Meor Ha-Golah. But the Council did not agree to grant him the exemption, and held it preferable that one soul should be lost, than that a corruption [*kilkul*] be carried out as precedent for generations to come. He came to Bonn also, but to no avail, since the Rabbis did not agree to grant him exemption. Hence we also are fearful of agreeing lest we commit a corruption, Heaven forbid. And even though it was whispered that he was living with another woman in secrecy, they still did not grant him exemption.[46]

> The language is clear; to take a second wife would be a great corruption. It is better that they should remain childless.
>
> Bigamy is not an option. In biblical times, when Sarah was unable to conceive, Abraham took a second wife. By talmudic times, the ideal of monogamy was well established in the Jewish community. For a man who wished to fulfill the obligation of procreation, one solution was left. Let the man divorce his wife and remarry. Yet as can be seen from the story of Rabi's son, divorce was not looked upon favorably. Infertility is grounds for divorce in Judaism, but there is an overriding sense that such a divorce is improper and unfair. Rabi's son would not divorce his wife, saying, "This poor woman waited all these years in vain."
>
> The feeling of the rabbis toward such a divorce is revealed in a beautiful way by a story in the Midrash:

A couple who lived in Sidon had been married for ten years without having children. The husband demanded a divorce, and the couple went to see Rabbi Simeon bar Yohai. The rabbi, who strongly opposed divorces, tried to convince them to stay together. But the husband was adamant.

"Since you are resolved to divorce," the rabbi told them, "you should give a party to celebrate your separation just as you gave one to celebrate your wedding."

The couple agreed. During the course of the party, the husband, who had drunk much wine, said to his wife, "My dear, before we separate, choose whatever you consider most precious in this house, and take it with you when you return to your father's house to live."

After her husband had fallen into a drunken sleep, the woman ordered her servants to carry him to her father's house and put him to bed there. In the middle of the night, the husband awoke.

"Where am I?" he called out.

"At my father's house," his wife replied. "You told me to take whatever I considered most precious to me. There is nothing in the world more precious to me than you."

Moved by his wife's love, the husband decided to remain married, and they lived together happily after that.[47]

Infertility may be a legitimate ground for divorce by Jewish law, but it was not deemed proper by the rabbis. They sensed that it was more important for a couple to stay together, even without children. As the Talmud says, "over him who divorces the wife of his youth, even the altar of God sheds tears."[48]

Still, after ten years of marriage with no children, both the husband and the wife can present a claim before the court and ask the court to compel the other to grant a divorce. In terms of Jewish law, it is easy to see why a man can ask for a divorce if he is obligated to be fruitful and multiply and cannot fulfill this *mitzvah*. It is more difficult to justify why a woman has a right to ask for a divorce since she has no obligation. In fact, such a case did come before the courts in the time of the Talmud. A woman asked for a divorce, claiming childlessness after ten years. When the rabbis told her that she was not obligated to have children, she answered, "I know, but I want children to be a staff for my old age." Rav Nahman ruled that in such a case we compel him to give a divorce and pay her *ketubbah* (her marriage settlement).[49]

Another issue is raised by the rabbis: if the husband makes a claim that his wife is barren and therefore he wants to divorce her, does he have to pay the *ketubbah*? The answer is interesting.

He says, she's the cause (of infertility). She says, he's the cause. Rabbi Ami said, in private matrimonial affairs, the wife is believed. And what is the reason? She is in a position to know whether the emission is forceful (literally, "shoots like an arrow"); he is not in a position to know.[50]

> The *Tosafot* asks a pertinent question on this: "What is the relevance of a forceful emission? Even if the emission is forceful, he pays her *ketubbah*. Perhaps he is not worthy to be built through her."[51] The *ketubbah* must be paid in all circumstances, whether the husband or the wife has the fertility problem.
>
> Thus we see a certain trend taking place in Jewish law. According to the Mishnah, after ten years of childless marriage, a man cannot put off his obligation. Yet as Jewish law developed, bigamy was outlawed and divorce was discouraged. If divorce does take place, even if the wife is infertile, the husband must pay her the *ketubbah*, although some authorities disagree. Ultimately, staying married without children was still the best solution since the purpose of marriage was not simply to have children but to provide companionship. Infertility as grounds for divorce fell out of favor in Jewish law.
>
> This is shown clearly in the *Shulkhan Arukh*, the basic code of Jewish law followed by observant Jews today. The *Shulkhan Arukh* mentions the law of a couple married ten years with no children. The Rama, the leading sixteenth-century Ashkenazic authority, writes:

Today it is not the custom to force somebody on this issue. Similarly, anybody who has not fulfilled the commandment "be fruitful and multiply" and goes to marry a woman who is not capable of having children because of sterility, age, or youth, because he loves her or for her wealth, even though by law we should prevent such a marriage, it has not been the practice for many generations for the court to interfere in the affairs of couples. Similarly, if a man marries a woman and waits ten years (without children), we do not force him to divorce her, although he has not fulfilled the commandment "be fruitful and multiply." Similarly for other matters regarding couples.[52]

The Rama's view that we do allow a marriage to take place, even though the woman is infertile, marks a definite change in Jewish law. The original law in the Talmud says that a man without children must marry a woman capable of having children; only if he has children can he marry an infertile woman.[53] By the sixteenth century, this law was not enforced. The rabbis did not want to involve themselves in issues of coupling.

One further question may be pertinent. The Talmud states that a childless man must marry a woman capable of having children. Is it permissible for a woman to marry a man who is infertile? The Torah says, "No one whose testes are crushed or whose member is cut off shall be admitted into the congregation of the Lord" (Deut. 23:2). This is a reaction to the ancient fertility cults, which often used eunuchs for religious leadership. The Mishnah's interpretation of this is clear. A man who becomes a eunuch cannot marry an Israelite woman. He could marry a slave who was freed or a convert to Judaism, but not a woman born a Jew.[54]

The rabbis of the Talmud had difficulty with this law. They limited its application only to those who inflict an injury upon themselves. One who deliberately castrates himself may not marry, but one who is born with such an injury may. "Rab Judah said in the name of Samuel: A man whose testes have been injured by a supernatural agency is regarded as a fit person."[55] The Rambam rules that although a man who deliberately castrates himself may not marry, if he does marry the marriage is valid. (Numerous authorities disagree.)

If applied literally, this law may have surprising consequences for today. Technically, it would mean that a man with a vasectomy is not permitted to be married since this procedure is a violation of Jewish law. In fact, Jewish law forbids the sterilization of any males, whether animal or human.[56] (Sterilization of females is not explicitly forbidden but is deemed improper.) However, if a man with a vasectomy contracts a marriage, it is valid, according to Rambam. And as the Rama said, today rabbis do not concern themselves with such questions when couples meet with them prior to marriage.

With all its emphasis on procreation, rabbinic literature does see a legitimacy to a person remaining childless, as long as he or she is involved in other works of goodness. Ben Azzai, a well-known rabbi from the time of the Mishnah, is the best example. The scholar was known for his strong words against people who failed to have children, yet he never married.

His students said to Ben Azzai, "There are those that speak well and behave well, those that behave well and do not speak well, you speak well but do not behave well." Ben Azzai said to them, "What can I do? My soul craves for the study of Torah. The world will have to be populated by others."[57]

In the Talmud, the intensive study of Torah is a legitimate option. A man like Ben Azzai, whose life is dedicated to Torah, can be relieved from the obligation of procreation. In a similar way, a couple unable to have children may be able to fulfill their Jewish obligations in other ways. We have already learned that good deeds are the true descendants of a person. The Jewish community needs active, involved Jews. Having children is only the first of 613 *mitzvot*. There are still 612 others.

Conclusions for Modern Jews

Jewish tradition is a continuum. The situation of the Jewish people may change from generation to generation, but the Judaism of future generations is built upon the Judaism of the past.

For the infertile Jewish couple today, much has changed

since the days of Sarah and Abraham, the days of Hannah and Elkanah, the days of the son of Rabi and his wife, or even the days of the man in the Middle Ages who wanted a second wife because his first could not have children. Modern medicine has opened new vistas in our understanding of infertility. Whereas the barren Shunammite woman turned to Elisha to pray for a cure, the modern Jewish couple will turn to obstetricians and gynecologists who specialize in infertility. Whereas the women of the talmudic period ate small fish to open their wombs, today women will take powerful drugs such as Clomid and Pergonal. With this change in technology has come a change in theology. We no longer believe that all the answers are in God's hands.

And yet, there is much we can learn from Jewish tradition. The Torah is still an eternal document that offers insights into most human problems. In particular, there are three insights about infertility that will provide a foundation for the rest of the book.

1. Judaism is not a fatalistic religion. Not everything that happens in this world has to be accepted as God's will. On the contrary, it is the role of the Jewish people "to perfect the world as a Kingdom of God."[58] If something is imperfect in this world, our job is to change it and make it as perfect as we can.

Similarly, Jews do not bemoan their fate, accept it as God's will, and wait for their reward in the world to come. We are a this-worldly religion. As the Talmud tells us:

> Rabbi Hiyya ben Abba fell ill and Rabbi Yohanan went to see him. Rabbi Yohanan asked him, "Are your afflictions welcome to you?" To this, Rabbi Hiyya replied, "Neither they nor their reward." Rabbi Yohanan then said to him, "Give me your hand." Rabbi Hiyya extended his hand, and he [Rabbi Yohanan] raised him [i.e., cured him].[59]

This example suggests that it is better to be cured in this world than to have a reward in the next. To passively accept the problems that life deals us is not the Jewish way; Judaism teaches that we struggle to correct them. Neither Sarah nor Rebecca nor Rachel nor Hannah nor Michal nor the Shunammite woman passively accepted her infertility. They prayed, they asked their spiritual representatives to intervene, they brought their handmaidens to their husbands, they adopted, they did what was necessary to ensure themselves a child.

2. There are legitimate nonbiological ways to build a family. Traditionally, a family is built when the husband contributes the genetic material in the sperm and the wife contributes the genetic material in the egg. Yet it does not have to be that way. The Bible provides examples of another woman contributing the egg, another man contributing the sperm, or strangers contributing both the egg and the sperm.

In the cases of the handmaidens Hagar and Bilhah, another woman contributed the egg. Yet both Sarah and Rachel considered the offspring their children. Thus we have a clear biblical precedent for surrogate mothers. In a later chapter we will learn about a talmudic precedent for an embryo transplant.

In the case of Er and Onan, and in other cases of levirate marriage, another man supplies seed for his brother. True, the brother was dead, but this could not have been done when the brother was alive without the commission of adultery, since the impersonal techniques of artificial insemination were not yet invented. Yet we will see a talmudic precedent for artificial insemination in a later chapter.

We have mentioned only two examples of adoption in the Bible: Abraham adopted his servant Eliezer, and Michal adopted her sister's children. There are numerous others. Pharaoh's daughter raised Moses as her own child. Mordecai adopted his niece Esther. Later we will explore at great length the Jewish legal ramifications of adoption.

It is true that most of us would prefer to be the source of our children's genetic makeup, but this is not always possible. Judaism teaches that someone else can provide the biological material for the children we raise and love.

3. Having children is not the only purpose of marriage. Not every infertile Jewish couple is prepared to go through medical procedures that can be costly and unpleasant. Not every infertile Jewish couple chooses to go through the emotional trauma of adoption. Judaism does consider it improper for a fertile couple to be childless. Yet Jewish couples who are infertile should not feel that they have nothing to live for.

Judaism sees the essential purpose of marriage as companionship. It teaches that even people who are unable to have children should be married and establish a household. When Rachel cried out, "Give me children, or I shall die," Jacob became angry with her. Rachel was limiting her entire life to one purpose—being a mother; Jacob was saying, "There's more to live for."

There is much that a childless Jewish couple can live for. As Rashi taught, their good deeds become their descendants. There are vital child-oriented tasks to be done in the Jewish community and in society in general. There are foster children needing homes. There are children in our religious schools who need to be taught. There are youth groups that need leadership. There is a need for Jewish Big Brothers and Sisters. There are children's hospitals that need volunteers.

The rabbis of the Talmud argued about a verse in Psalms (55:20). "God . . ., who will have no successor, hears and humbles those who have no fear of God." Rabbi Yohanan and Rabbi Joshua ben Levi differed on the meaning of this. According to one, a child is meant; according to the other, a student.[60] The intent of the Talmud is clear. One does not have to leave a child in the world in order to have a successor. It is sufficient to leave a student, somebody who learns from us. "Rabbi Samuel the son of Nahmani said in the name of Rabbi Yohanan, whoever teaches the child of his friend Torah, scripture considers it as if he gave birth to the child."[61]

A song of ascents.
Happy are all who fear the Lord/who follow His ways./You shall enjoy the
fruit of your labors;/you shall be happy and you shall prosper./Your wife
shall be like a fruitful vine within your house;/ your sons, like olive saplings
around your table./So shall the man who fears the Lord be blessed./May the
Lord bless you from Zion;/may you share the prosperity of Jerusalem/all the
days of your life,/and live to see your children's children./ May all be well
with Israel!

(Pss. 128:1–6)

3

Dealing with Infertility

Psalm 128 gives the traditional Jewish dream, at least from
a male point of view. It speaks of a wife who is a fruitful
vine and children who grow like olive saplings. It speaks
of God's blessing, of living to see children and grandchildren. This, says the psalmist, will be the reward for the
man who fears the Lord.

Most Jewish couples who marry share this dream. They
may choose to delay having children until they finish school,
are established in their careers, or have had a chance to
concentrate on their own relationships. But children are
part of the ultimate picture—children who will look like
their parents and carry on their biological heritage.

For most couples it happens this way, automatically

and naturally. They pick a date, give up using birth control, and within a few months the wife is pregnant. All the parts of the dream fit together. Yet for 20 percent of married couples, life does not turn out like the dream.[1] Month after month passes without a pregnancy. A year goes by. The couple become alarmed as the loss is felt more acutely with each menstrual period. At some point they begin to seek medical help.

Confronted with infertility, a couple must deal with numerous issues. There are feelings of anger and guilt. There are insensitive comments and well-meaning but ineffective pieces of advice. There are threats to one's own sexuality and to a couple's marriage. Jews, for whom bloodlines and genealogy are so important, have a particularly strong sense of loss. Yet for every religious person there is the ultimate question: How can we reconcile the unfairness of infertility with a belief in God's justice?

Decisions must also be made. When does one seek medical help, and when does one stop seeking it? Is it appropriate to tell friends or relatives? When does adoption become an option? There are real emotional issues for infertile couples of all faiths, and certain problems for Jewish couples in particular. This chapter attempts to give a Jewish perspective for dealing with infertility.

The Emotional Issues

It is important to recognize that infertility involves a loss that is similar to the loss of a loved one. There are grief and mourning, anger and guilt, all the emotions that we associate with a death. For as the Talmud put it, infertility is a kind of a death.[2] It is the death of a dream, a dream we hold from childhood. When a loved one dies, we have a rich tradition to help us cope and mourn. There are *shiva, Kaddish, yahrzeit*; the community supports us and shares our suffering. But for the loss felt by the infertile couple, there is no tradition or community. Couples facing infertility usually feel isolated and alone. Jewish tradition has no ritual to mark the loss of a dream. On the contrary, the Jewish community often adds to the guilt felt by the infertile couple by its pressure to produce children.

How does a couple deal with infertility? The first step is to recognize that it is a loss, similar to the loss of a loved one. Judaism has great wisdom when it comes to helping Jews cope with the death of a family member. Perhaps some of that wisdom can be applied to infertility. There are different periods of mourning of varying length and intensity. As time goes on, the intensity lessens and the mourner slowly leaves his or her grief and reenters the real world. First, there is *shiva,* when a mourner stays home, sitting on low benches, wearing nonleather shoes, and being comforted by friends and family. Then there is *sheloshim,* the thirty-day period when the mourner wears a torn piece of clothing or ribbon, the rip symbolizing the grief and anger. Then there is a year with *Kaddish* each morning and evening. The mourner still avoids weddings and other festive occasions. Finally, the period of mourning ends and life returns to normal. From then on, once a year on the *yahrzeit,* the family lights a candle, gathers in synagogue for *Kaddish,* and cherishes the memory of a loved one.

There is no similar scheme for infertility. (There is also no similar scheme for a miscarriage, stillbirth, or death of a premature baby. I will discuss this in a later chapter.) Yet there is a need to mourn the dream that has died. There is a need to feel the loss and work out one's feelings. Let us look at some of the emotions felt by a couple confronting infertility.

Grief. Just as with the loss of a loved one, an infertile couple needs an opportunity to grieve. In her studies on death and dying, Elisabeth Kübler-Ross has described five stages of mourning: denial, anger, bargaining, depression, and, finally, acceptance.[3] The infertile couple may feel all or some of these emotions, and the order and intensity may vary. The emotions are real.

A couple, learning of their infertility, are often told

by well-meaning friends, "You can always adopt." Yet until the grieving period ends, it is difficult to consider other options, such as unconventional medical treatment, adoption, or childlessness. Relatives and friends must respect this need to mourn. It is no more appropriate or helpful to say, "You can always adopt," to a couple who have learned of their infertility than to say, "You can always have another," to a couple who have lost a child.

Infertility is a loss felt by both the husband and the wife. Traditionally, the male is the one who passes on his name to a new generation; he also passes on his status as a Kohen, Levi, or Yisrael. Yet most important, the mother gives the child his or her identity as a Jew. For this reason, infertility is particularly painful for Jewish women.

Judaism teaches that when a person mourns, he or she should avoid joyous events such as weddings and other *simhah*s where music is played. A parallel can be drawn to the mourning of infertility. It is not inappropriate, and in fact is understandable, for an infertile couple to avoid occasions where many children will be present, such as a Hanukkah party or Passover *seder*. Many infertile couples will avoid going to a *brit milah* or baby naming. Judaism places great emphasis on these family occasions. Yet for the infertile couple, they simply make the pain more acute.

RESOLVE, a national infertility support group, publishes a monthly newsletter. In the November and December issues, articles on one theme seem prevalent: how to avoid family get-togethers during the holiday season. For family members with children, this seems selfish. Yet for infertile couples, Thanksgiving, Hanukkah, and Christmas are the most difficult times of the year. The newsletter often recommends that a couple spend the holiday with other childless couples.

For the Jewish couple, it is permissible to miss a *brit milah* or baby naming, a *seder*, or a holiday dinner if such an experience is too painful. It is permissible to mourn, and no one expects a person in mourning to attend joyous events. There may be moments when friends and family members will have to be sensitive and understanding. They must realize that before a couple can fully reenter society, they must work through their own grief.

Threat to sexuality. For many people, sexual identity is linked to the ability to conceive a child. I see this regularly in my counseling of infertile couples. A man unable to impregnate his wife may feel that his masculinity is threatened. A wife unable to experience pregnancy may feel incomplete as a woman. Sadly, our culture tends to confuse both masculinity and femininity with fertility. In her book *New Conceptions,* Lori Andrews tells the story of a man who told his co-workers of his fertility problem. They responded by hiding copies of *Playboy* in his locker and offering to teach him the facts of life. Their ignorance only added to his pain. Yet such ignorance is prevalent in our culture.

In the case of one couple whom I counseled, the husband was sterile and the wife was willing to consider artificial insemination by donor or adoption. The husband, however, would not consider a child unless he was the biological parent. He was adamant on this point, and it was putting a serious strain on their marriage. Part of my job as a counselor was to convince him that masculinity is unrelated to the ability to produce children. This basic Jewish teaching is contrary to the macho image of sexuality that is part of our contemporary culture. Traditional Judaism defines male identity through certain community activities such as Torah study, participation in synagogue ritual, and community leadership, not the ability to sire children.

In Judaism, masculinity is established not by being a biological parent but by being a spiritual parent. Judaism puts more emphasis on the ability to teach a child than on the ability to sire a child. This is seen most clearly in a somewhat strange but relevant Mishnah:

> If [a person finds] his father's lost property and his teacher's lost property, that of his teacher comes first. For his father brings him into this world, but his teacher teaches him wisdom to bring him into the world to come. . . . If his father and his teacher are carrying a burden, he must relieve his teacher first, then he

relieves his father. If his father and his teacher were taken captive, his teacher is redeemed first, then his father.[4]

The basic statement of this Mishnah is clear. That is why Judaism says "whoever teaches a child, scripture considers him as if he gave birth to that child." Of course, these sources refer to teaching Torah, but the idea can be applied to any kind of teaching. A man does not have to produce children to prove his masculinity in Jewish culture.

For a woman, a similar difficulty arises. Her femininity and her sense of self-worth as a woman are often reflected in her ability to produce children. We recall the prayer of Hannah:

"Sovereign of the Universe, among all the things that Thou hast created in a woman, Thou hast not created one without a purpose, eyes to see, ears to hear, a nose to smell, a mouth to speak, hands to do work, legs to walk with, breasts to give suck. These breasts that Thou hast put on my heart, are they not to give suck? Give me a son, so that I may suckle with them."[5]

Her body was created to produce children, and it was not fulfilling its God-given function.

A woman's feeling that her femininity is being threatened by her infertility cannot be dismissed lightly. Yet Judaism does teach that a woman's role is not limited to childbearing. In fact, traditional Judaism says that a woman is not obligated to have children. There are numerous other ways that she can find fulfillment in this world.

Judaism places greater emphasis on nurturing and raising a child than on giving birth to that child. In Judaism it is the woman who has the greater responsibility to pass on the heritage to children. That is one reason why the religion of the child follows that of the mother. Obviously, pregnancy is an ideal; yet a woman unable to achieve pregnancy should not consider herself any less of a woman. There are other ways to nurture a child as a Jew: adoption, foster care, religious school teaching, volunteer work. All of these are legitimate Jewish options.

The important point is that infertility has nothing to do with masculinity or femininity. Judaism has always recognized that marriage has a purpose above and beyond producing children. Being a biological parent is only one of many ways that a man or woman can find fulfilment with each other and in the larger world.

Threat to Marriage. Along with the threat to one's sexuality, infertility brings a greater threat that the marriage itself may unravel. A husband and wife, each trying to cope with the loss that infertility entails, may blame one another. The Talmud and codes speak of marriages that were dissolved because of infertility. Traditionally, a couple who lived together ten years without children divorced and tried to find new partners with whom to fulfill the *mitzvah* of procreation. Yet in the evolution of Jewish tradition we see that companionship, not reproduction, is considered to be the primary purpose of marriage.

Companionship is the key to saving a marriage whenever adversity strikes. In the *sheva berakhot* (seven blessings) recited under the *huppah*, husband and wife are called *reim ahuvim* (loving friends). They must be more than lovers; they must be best friends to one another. A husband and wife must be able to talk with one another and communicate openly about infertility or any other problem. They must support one another. The key is communication.

In infertility, there is no room for blame; it is nobody's "fault." The word *fault* implies a moral culpability. Infertility has a physical cause, not a moral cause. The physical cause may lie with either the husband or the wife, but often it lies with both partners. It is a couple's problem, not a woman's problem. Infertility is a time for communication and mutual support, not for castigation and blame.

Ultimately, infertility, like any other loss, can threaten a marriage. Counseling can help a couple work through their fertility problems and teach them to communicate better with one another. For this reason, most fertility specialists have professional counselors on their staffs. A local rabbi, or a local agency such as a Jewish family service, should be able to provide counseling with sensitivity to Jewish issues.

In Judaism, the marriage is of ultimate importance. By being *reim ahuvim,* loving friends, by supporting rather than blaming one another, by communicating openly, by knowing when to seek help through counseling, a couple can strengthen their marriage. In fact, this is an unexpected plus of infertility. Couples who have worked through the loss together discover that their marriages are stronger than ever. As true life partners, they can move forward to the next decision, be it medical treatment, adoption, or childlessness.

Loneliness. Another emotion felt by virtually every infertile couple is loneliness. Everybody else is having children; there is nobody with whom to talk and no way to share one's feelings. One woman, unable to become pregnant, told me about one of her worst moments. She was coping very well with her infertility. Then she went to a synagogue sisterhood luncheon, and the women at her table began sharing stories about their pregnancies. She told me later that she never felt so alone.

My wife and I made a discovery when it became known that we had a fertility problem and were going to adopt a child: we discovered that we were not alone. Numerous couples in my synagogue shared similar problems with me. Some had eventually achieved pregnancy, some had adopted, some had decided to remain childless. All had felt alone at one point.

In the Jewish community, there is no support system for infertile couples. Unfortunately, most couples delay joining a synagogue until they have children. For an infertile couple, the synagogue may not give them the support they need. Even if they belong to a synagogue, most couples choose not to share such personal matters with other congregants or even with their rabbis.

To help couples deal with infertility, RESOLVE is an excellent support group with chapters throughout the United States. A RESOLVE meeting provides not only emotional support but also the latest information on infertility treatments and leads for adoption. Most of all, it lets an infertile couple know that they are not alone. The national office is:

RESOLVE, Inc.
5 Water Street
Arlington, MA 02174
(617) 643-2424

Anger and Guilt. Anger and guilt are opposite sides of the same emotion. A couple facing infertility will become angry at themselves, at each other, at fertile friends, at God. Then they will feel guilty about the anger. In fact, guilt is simply a self-directed anger.

Couples with a fertility problem often feel guilty. A woman may feel that she caused the problem by delaying childbirth or by wearing an intrauterine device (IUD). A man may feel responsible because he worked in an environment that lowered his sperm count. Often the partner will feel guilty for a physical cause beyond his or her control, such as a blockage in the fallopian tubes. Guilt that results from being unable to provide children for a spouse may manifest itself as anger toward that spouse, or the more fertile spouse may grow angry at a partner who is unable to produce children, then feel guilty about that anger. These are normal emotions associated with the sense of loss. The cure is time and communication.

For the religious Jew, there is another aspect of anger and guilt. We grow up believing in God's justice, yet infertility is unjust. It strikes couples without regard for their desire to be parents or their ability to care for children. I know personally that whenever I read in the newspapers of a neglected or abused child, I am overcome with waves of anger. "How could they be parents, and we can't?!" The anger is directed at God. Sometimes such anger may be suppressed and become self-directed guilt.

Unfortunately, there is not perfect justice in this world. From the days of the Bible when the book of Job was written, Jews have struggled with the problem of theodicy, or evil in the world. Rabbi Harold Kushner, who suffered the loss of a child, has written a beautiful, sensitive book, *When Bad Things Happen to Good People,* in which he concludes that ultimately God cannot guarantee us perfect justice. What God can do is give us the strength to cope with the injustice we face. I will deal more with God's role in the section Prayer as a Solution.

Loss of Control. In my counseling of infertile couples, the one emotion I have encountered in almost every case was a sense of not being in control. Couples feel swept along by events, by emotions, by doctor's orders and find themselves deeply depressed at having no control over a vital part of their lives.

I personally felt this loss of control most strongly when my wife and I sought a private-placement adoption. I found that there was little correlation between how hard we worked at locating a potential birth mother and how successful we were. Some weeks we would cover our state with adoption ads and fliers, without a nibble. Other weeks we did virtually nothing, and a phone call with a potential situation would come in.

Many couples express a similar emotion when seeking medical treatment to become pregnant. Infertility causes a couple to seek treatment with a desperation akin to that of cancer patients seeking a cure. With the hope that the physician will have all the answers, a couple often passively accept the doctor's course of treatment. As a general rule, patients are reluctant to question their physicians, let alone disagree with a course of treatment. Sometimes the more desperate a patient, the more reticent to question the doctor. Infertility patients will often go through a course of treatment they do not understand or do not agree with for fear of upsetting the doctor.

Finally, couples often feel a lack of control over their emotions. An infertile woman will see a pregnant woman in the supermarket and burst into tears. A man will find himself moody, angry, or depressed at the wrong time. Infertile couples feel that their emotions have the better of them. Regaining control of one's emotions and situation is often the first step in coping with infertility.

In her excellent book *Infertility: How Couples Can Cope*, Linda Salzar provides some good advice on gaining control of one's emotions:

> Whenever people experience crises in their lives, a sense of being out of control may prevail. Emotions take over and it is easy to feel as if you are on a runaway train, powerless to put on the brakes. . . . It may seem impossible to you at first, but you can develop the skills to take control of these powerful feelings rather than allowing them to control you.[6]

Salzar lists several practical suggestions, including recognizing and expressing feelings, putting one's thoughts into writing, developing the skill of inner encouragement, allowing oneself to cry, and learning relaxation techniques.

A vital step in gaining control is getting the necessary professional help. This means actively seeking out the right physician, counselor, spiritual leader, or attorney for advice. The importance of a sympathetic counselor cannot be overemphasized. Similarly, a good physician should possess not only the medical knowledge but also the willingness to let you be a partner in your own treatment.

In seeking medical treatment, one should never passively accept a doctor's orders without seeking a full understanding of why they are being given. To quote one study on infertility:

> The greater the patient's understanding of his or her body, of the reasons for certain tests and therapies, the more responsibility he or she may assume in sharing the information with the physician, and the more capable he or she may become in understanding and coping. Explanations of tests and treatments help allay fears engendered by misinformation and ignorance. The patient may assume a more active, less helpless role. He or she can begin to feel involved in the treatment rather than its victim.[7]

Limit to Mourning. Judaism teaches that when we suffer a loss, it is proper to mourn. But it is also proper to move beyond mourning: "A season is set for everything, a time for every experience under heaven: . . . A time for weeping and a time for laughing, A time for wailing and a time for dancing" (Eccles. 3:1,4).

An infertile couple need time to mourn, to talk, to work out their feelings. Then, at some point, they must get on with their lives. They must decide whether to seek more unconventional medical treatment or perhaps stop treatment altogether. They must decide whether to remain childless or begin to explore adoption. The hurt may always be present, but at some point they must seek resolution and move on.

Dealing with Insensitive Comments

Although most couples learn to accept the reality of their infertility, few issues are as difficult as unthinking and insensitive comments from relatives and friends. I remember with anger one evening when a couple came over to visit us with their small child. The child was being cranky and difficult, and the parents kept commenting on how lucky we were to be childless. "Look at all the difficulties children bring." Finally I lost my temper and told them, "It is not our choice to be childless, and I don't think it would be your choice either." They were dumbfounded and meekly apologized.

It is important for people to realize that a childless couple may not be childless by choice. They may have a fertility problem, which they may choose to discuss or keep to themselves. Recently I spoke with a middle-aged woman from my synagogue whose daughter and son-in-law were childless after many years of marriage. This woman was lamenting the fact that her daughter was not pregnant. "How long am I going to live without being a grandmother? When is she going to stop pursuing her career and become pregnant already?" After hearing this refrain many times, I finally spoke with her. "You know, it is not so easy for everybody." People, particularly parents, must realize that pregnancy does not always happen easily or automatically.

For a couple trying to conceive there are few things more frustrating than parents who constantly harp on their wish to become grandparents. A couple must decide whether to share their infertility with their parents and with other family members. There are no right or wrong answers. I happen to believe that it is useful to be open and honest with one's parents whenever possible. Honesty can make parents less critical and more supportive.

It is important to be honest for another reason. An infertile couple will often turn to adoption to build a family. As a couple, they need time to get used to the idea of adoption as an alternative. In the same way, grandparents need time to get used to the idea of adoption as a way to have grandchildren. One older couple in my synagogue shared with me a painful moment. "For years we were waiting for our daughter-in-law to be pregnant. They never said that anything was wrong. Now all of a sudden, they adopt a baby. We were the last to know. Can we love this baby like a grandchild?" The truth is, they will love that baby like any other grandchild, but they needed a chance to get used to the idea. It is important to share infertility with parents and not let an adoption, or childlessness, be a surprise.

Needless to say, infertility is a private matter, and a couple should weigh carefully how open they wish to be, especially since openness can bring other insensitive or ignorant comments. Every infertile couple has heard too often: "Relax, and it will happen." "Go away on a vacation, and it will happen." "Adopt, then you will get pregnant." All of these statements are false. Infertility usually is not the result of stress; most often, stress is the result of infertility.[8] It is rare that a couple cannot conceive because of tension or stress, and the link between adoption and subsequent pregnancy has been scientifically proved to be a myth. If there is a physical cause for infertility, adoption will not make that physical cause go away. However, it will certainly relieve some of the pressure of being childless.

I find that when people make ignorant comments, it is best to try to educate them. I have a set answer to the words, "You two should relax, then your wife will get pregnant." I say, "I wish it were that simple. Relaxation has nothing to do with pregnancy, but we are getting the best medical treatment." Sometimes people like to pry. "Tell me what the problem is." Then I can only answer, "That is a personal matter between my wife and myself."

Unfortunately, sensitivity is a difficult thing to teach people. Even the most sensitive people will occasionally make a comment that is extremely painful because it hits a sore spot. I recently went to a *brit milah* for a young professional couple, who had their first baby while in their late thirties. While making small talk with a young couple among the guests, I innocently remarked, "We need more *simhah*s like this." The woman turned red and retorted, "Rabbi, we are getting the best medical treatment we can."

Ultimately, an infertile couple must realize that friends and relatives will become pregnant and that pregnancy and childbirth are joyous times. It is not fair to detract from that joy. A couple having a baby must share their good news with infertile friends in as sensitive a way as possible. I will always remember a beautiful phone call from a woman in my synagogue who had just given birth to a healthy baby boy. She told me that although she and her husband were overjoyed, they kept thinking of us. They knew that calls like theirs had to be hard for us, but they were praying that we would be blessed with a child soon. Her words brought tears to my eyes.

Prayer as a Solution

Judaism has a classic solution for any problem: prayer. Many couples have told me that they have discussed their infertility with their rabbi and have been told, "Why don't you pray to God to give you a child?" For many rabbis, this is the limit of their advice. One Orthodox manual on raising a Jewish child contains a short section on infertility that specifies, "Before any medical treatment can be used, a competent rabbinic authority must be consulted. Meanwhile, try prayer. It worked for Rebecca, Rachel, and Hannah."

My wife and I have often received similar advice. When we adopted our son, we had to spend some time in a small community in the South. We called a local Orthodox rabbi to find out about kosher food, the *mikvah*, and other Jewish facilities. The rabbi expressed surprise that we were there. I remember his words well. "Why don't you send a letter to the Lubavitcher Rebbe and ask him to say a prayer for you?" There was an attitude that the right prayer could effect what fertility specialists could not.

There is a Hasidic story of a couple unable to conceive. They spoke to their rabbi, who told them, "Check the *mezuzzah* on your house." They took out the mezuzzah scroll and found that the word *children* in the *Shema* text had worn away. They had a scribe repair the scroll and shortly afterward the wife became pregnant.

Most Jews would look at these anecdotes as magic and superstition. Yet one often hears the words in Jewish circles: "Pray and it will work." It is worthwhile to take a moment and look at prayer as a solution to infertility.

I believe that this well-intentioned advice misconstrues the idea of Jewish prayer. I call it the "vending machine" approach to prayer. With a vending machine, if a customer puts in the correct coins and pushes a button, the desired candy or soda comes out. Similarly, many Jews believe that if they only say the right words to God, the solution will come forth. That is why people often ask me to pray for them; they feel that I will know the right things to say to get the correct response.

In truth, "vending machine" prayer is not a genuine Jewish concept. Only a tiny percentage of our liturgy asks God for favors, and even that is done on a community, and not an individual, level. Most of the prayers that make up the *siddur* are either praises of God or hymns of thanksgiving. They set a mood of reverence and add a spiritual dimension to our lives. They do not present God with a list of favors or automatically expect God to grant our every wish.

The Hebrew word for prayer is *tefillah,* coming from the Hebrew root *l'hitpallel.* This means literally "to judge oneself." Prayer is not something we do to change God; it is something we do to transform ourselves. Our prayers are meant to give us a strength to cope, even if our circumstances remain unchanged. If we pray to God to grant us children, our prayers may not automatically open our wombs. Ideally, they will give us the strength to persist and pursue all the options open to us and to accept our situation, whatever it may be.

Jewish prayer does not depend on miracles from God. We learn in the Talmud, *Ein somkhin al ha-nes.* "Do not depend on miracles."[9] There is an excellent talmudic insight in the story of the parting of the Red Sea, the miracle par excellence in Judaism. The Israelites were trapped between the sea and the approaching Egyptian army. Moses was standing in prayer. Finally God said to Moses, " '. . . Why do you cry out to Me? Tell the Israelites to go forward' " (Exod. 14:15). According to the Midrash, the Israelites went forward into the sea. Only when the leader, Nahshon ben Aminadav, was up to his neck in the water did the sea finally part. Only when the Israelites took action did the miracle come true.[10]

Action, not prayer, is the keystone of Judaism. An infertile Jewish couple who want a family must act in the medical sphere, or they must act to adopt. Often they must do both at the same time. Prayer may give them the strength to take action, but it cannot be a substitute.

Does that mean there is no room for prayer as a solution? Not at all. Medicine is still an imperfect science, and there are still events in this world that are beyond human control. One Jewish couple I know went to numerous fertility specialists and tried a number of painful and expensive procedures. Nothing would work. They were told by doctors that it was hopeless—there was no way that the wife would become pregnant. They went home and began making arrangements to adopt. As they were about to adopt a baby, she found herself pregnant. She gave birth to a child and within a year had a second child. Nothing could convince this couple that prayers are not answered.

Jewish theology has changed since the days of Hannah. Prayer alone is not a solution to infertility because God requires our active participation. Prayer combined with action can succeed. Prayer keeps our faith alive and gives us the strength to pursue our dream of having a family. When we have taken action and done everything we can, the rest is in God's hands.

Remaining Childless and Other Options

A couple coping with infertility must make several critical choices. They must decide when to seek medical treatment, how to find the right doctor, and how far to pursue a medical solution to their infertility. Fortunately, modern medicine is helping more and more couples become parents, often by using powerful drugs or microsurgery.

Physicians have many new, unconventional techniques to help the infertile couple. Artificial insemination, in vitro fertilization, surrogate mothering, and embryo transplants all raise legal, emotional, and religious issues. In the next two chapters, we will put a Jewish perspective on these medical solutions to infertility, including some of the less conventional solutions.

Another critical choice couples may face is when to stop medical treatment, when to say enough is enough. Every couple reach a limit to both their emotional and financial resources. It is wise to say, "We shall go so far and no farther. We will try one last surgical procedure or one last drug, then no more." Such a couple may choose to pursue adoption or perhaps to remain childless.

Adoption presents its own choices. There are agency and independent adoption, the adoption of an infant or an older child. There are questions about how open to be, how much contact to have with a birth mother, and how much to tell a child. Jewish law raises numerous questions on adoption and the importance of biology to a child's identity. We will deal with these questions in later chapters.

Childlessness is a legitimate Jewish choice for an infertile couple. Medicine is still an imprecise science and cannot help every couple. Not all couples feel prepared for the financial and emotional commitment of adoption. Some couples may feel that they would resent an adopted child, never loving him or her as their own. Needless to say, such couples should not adopt. For any number of reasons, sometimes by active choice and sometimes by not taking any action, some couples choose childlessness.

No couple should ever feel ashamed of having no children. We have already spoken of Ben Azzai, the second-century rabbi who chose never to marry and never to have children. He felt that he was too attached to the study of Torah to give proper attention to a wife and children. There is a Jewish legal principle, *Ha-osek b'mitzvah patur me-mitzvah*. "Somebody who is occupied with one *mitzvah* is freed from another *mitzvah*."[11] If somebody is busy studying Torah, he is relieved from the obligation of procreation.

A couple unable to have children should occupy themselves with other concerns in the Jewish community. Childlessness can give a couple more time for other Jewish pursuits, whether it be Torah study, synagogue involvement, or activity in philanthropic organizations. Childless couples should be urged to join synagogues, perhaps by lower membership rates. A synagogue is a place of worship not just for families but for all Jews. No couple should have to feel that, without children, they do not belong. A childless couple often have more time and more money to contribute to a synagogue. Ben Azzai put it well: Other Jews can complete the task of populating the world; for a childless couple, there are numerous important tasks to be done as Jews.[12]

Blessed art Thou, Lord our God, King of the universe, Who has formed man in wisdom and created in him many ducts and organs. It is revealed and known before the throne of your glory, that if but one of these be opened [that should be closed] or if one be closed [that should be open], it would be impossible to survive and to stand before Thee. Blessed art Thou, Lord, Who heals all flesh and works wondrous things.

(Morning prayer)

4

Medical Solutions to Infertility

An observant Jew says the above blessing each morning shortly after rising. The blessing recognizes the intricacy and beauty of the human body. It expresses the fact that our bodies are a marvelous work of creation; they are truly God's handiwork. Therefore, we praise God for the miracle that our bodies function properly.

Few systems in our body are as intricate and complex as our reproductive organs. Most people take for granted that sexual intercourse at the right time of the month will lead to pregnancy. Yet the system is so complex, and so many things can go awry, that we ought to praise God when the system succeeds. Numerous components must function smoothly for the sperm to reach and fertilize the ovum. There are hazards every step of the way. If one hormone is off balance in either the man or the woman, if one organ is malformed, if one event is ill timed, the process will fail.

The Reproductive System

Our assessment of medical solutions to infertility should be preceded by a quick overview of the reproductive process.[1] This overview is by necessity sketchy; for a more thorough description, the reader should refer to the many excellent books on infertility.

For the woman, the monthly cycle is controlled by a delicate balance of various hormones. In the early days of the cycle, LH (luteinizing hormone) and FSH (follicle-stimulating hormone) produced by the pituitary gland stimulate the ovary to produce estrogen, permitting the development of an egg. At mid-cycle, the large amounts of estrogen secreted induce a surge of LH, which causes the egg to break forth from the follicle. This process is known as ovulation. Estrogens also stimulate the growth of the lining of the uterus (endometrium), preparing it to receive the fertilized egg.

With ovulation, the cells of the ruptured follicle change form, becoming the corpus luteum and producing a hormone called progesterone. The progesterone allows further growth of the endometrium to nourish the implanted fertilized ovum. If pregnancy occurs, the placental hormone HCG, (human chorionic gonadotropin) sustains progesterone secretion to support the conceptus. The detection of HCG in the urine is the basis for current tests for pregnancy. Without pregnancy, the corpus luteum ceases to produce progesterone, the lining of the uterus is shed, and menstruation begins. The whole cycle then starts again.

Obviously, normal ovulation requires a delicate balance of these various hormones. In fact, birth control pills containing estrogen and progesterone work by throwing the entire process off balance. On the other hand, a basic part of infertility evaluation and treatment is the careful monitoring of these hormones. Sometimes infertility can be treated by administering these hormones artificially. In some cases the hormone level must be monitored daily. (This can be problematic for Sabbath-observant couples, an issue addressed later in this chapter.)

Even if the hormone levels are normal and ovulation occurs as expected, the process is still complicated. The newly released egg must be scooped up by the fallopian tube and slowly moved to the center of the tube by tiny hairlike tentacles called fibriae. The tube is extremely narrow, in some spots as tiny as a pinpoint. Sometimes it is blocked by adhesions or scars as a consequence of abdominal infection, injury, or a disease called endometriosis. Sometimes the fallopian tubes have been deliberately blocked when the woman has been sterilized by a tubal ligation. In these cases, surgery can sometimes cure a fertility problem.

Even if the tube is unblocked and the egg can enter it normally, pregnancy is not assured. There is only a six- to eight-hour period each month when the egg is ripe and capable of being fertilized. A sperm must be present at exactly the right time. To increase these chances, the female body was designed to allow a steady flow of sperm into the fallopian tubes. The sperm must cross numerous barriers to arrive at the egg. The biggest barrier is the cervical mucus, a jellylike substance covering the cervix at the entrance to the womb. For most of the month, this mucus is too thick for sperm to penetrate. Only around ovulation does the texture of the mucus change, allowing sperm to pass. Still, of the 50 million to 200 million sperm deposited in one ejaculation, only 100,000 make it past the mucus. Of these, only about 400 sperm find their way into the fallopian tube. Both the egg and sperm are tiny, and it is only by chance that they meet at the correct time.

Numerous problems can occur with the passage of the sperm through the vagina into the uterus and the fallopian tube. The cervical mucus may be too thick. Although controversial in the medical literature, vaginal infections and antibodies to sperm may play a role as well. A fertility specialist will want to test the mucus for thickness and viscosity and for any allergic reaction to the husband's sperm.

Another common cause of infertility is endometriosis, a scarring of the tubes and other nearby organs by endometrial tissue, which normally lines the uterus. The symptoms of endometriosis are painful menstrual periods, painful intercourse, and infertility. An accurate diagnosis can be made only by a laparoscopy. With this minor procedure, done under a general anesthetic, a tube attached to a viewfinder and a camera is passed through a woman's navel to explore her reproductive organs. If endometriosis is identified, it can sometimes be treated by drugs or surgery. A strange irony is that pregnancy is an excellent cure for endometriosis.

Sometimes fertilization does occur, but the fertilized egg fails to move from the fallopian tube to the uterus. This is called an ectopic pregnancy, a dangerous condition requiring surgery. At other times pregnancy begins normally, only to result in a miscarriage. This can be caused by a genetic or chromosomal problem, a hormonal imbalance, or a problem with the uterus.

From this brief review, it is obvious that the entire female reproductive system is exceedingly complex and delicate. It is easy to understand how an accurate fertility work-up on a woman takes many months.

The male also has a delicate system, so that 40 percent of the time the cause of infertility lies with him. The testicles are really sperm-producing factories. A woman is born with all the eggs she will ever use in a lifetime; a man must continually manufacture sperm. The temperature of the testicles must be maintained at the right level—in this case 94°F. That is the reason the testicles hang outside the body; the body temperature of 98.6°F is too warm to manufacture normal sperm.

It is likely that an increase in the temperature of the testicles can cause a fertility problem. It has been suggested that something as simple as tight underwear or too many hot baths can affect a man's sperm count. A varicocele (varicose vein in the scrotum) also appears to raise the temperature of the testicles. As many as 25 to 33 percent of infertile men have varicoceles; however, it should be noted that varicoceles are also found in some fertile men. The varicocele is treated by minor surgery and by new radiologic methods. These procedures can lead to a dramatic improvement in sperm count.

A man also must have the proper balance of hormones. As in the female, the pituitary gland produces FSH and LH, which must be balanced to cause the production of sperm. There are successful hormonal treatments for infertility in men who have proven hormonal deficiencies; however, these cases are uncommon. For otherwise normal men, hormone treatments are not generally successful. The contribution of infectious diseases, sperm antibodies, and genetic and environmental factors to poor sperm output remains controversial.

Assuming that the sperm are manufactured correctly, it is still a long process before the sperm reach the ejaculate. The sperm mature while being carried down a twenty-foot-long microscopic tube called the epididymis. They then go into the vas deferens, the male sperm duct. Occasionally there are congenital problems with the epididymis or vas deferens. The latter is sometimes deliberately blocked through a vasectomy, a procedure prohibited by traditional Jewish law.

The entire manufacturing process of sperm takes seventy-two days. Thus, even if a problem is corrected, it takes nearly three months to know if the correction was successful. Once the sperm reach the ejaculate, they must have sufficient quality and concentration to fertilize an egg. A high percentage of the sperm must have the correct morphology (shape) and motility (ability to swim). These are simple to test by a sperm count. However, sperm counts require masturbation, which raises questions of Jewish law. I will consider these questions later in this chapter.

Even if both the male and female reproductive systems are functioning properly, success is still not guaranteed. Sexual relations must take place with sufficient frequency and during the correct time of the month. A couple leading active professional lives and reserving the weekends for intercourse will not achieve pregnancy if the woman ovulates in the middle of the week. By taking her temperature daily with a basal body thermometer, a woman can predict fairly accurately when she will ovulate. The trick is to have sexual relations right before ovulation (i.e., before the temperature goes up on the thermometer).

Sometimes a sexual problem such as impotence prevents intercourse from occurring normally. This can have an organic or psychological cause. A couple must support each other in seeking treatment. Today there are excellent treatments for both organic and psychological impotence. One valuable book on the problem is *The Male* by Dr. Sherman Silber (Charles Scribner's Sons, 1981).

For observant Jewish couples, there is another possible cause of infertility. Jewish law prohibits sexual relations during certain parts of the month, namely from the onset of menstruation and for seven clean days following the completion of the woman's menstrual period. For most couples, these laws increase the chances of fertility by concentrating sexual relations during the woman's most fertile period. However, for some observant couples, such laws have the opposite effect. If the woman has a short menstrual cycle, these laws may cause them to avoid relations during her fertile period. This is a serious problem in Jewish law, and it will be dealt with later in this chapter.

As this overview has shown, the process of achieving pregnancy is complex. Our knowledge of medicine is far from complete, yet with improvements in medical knowledge and technique, more childless couples are achieving pregnancy each year.

Jewish Attitudes Toward Medical Treatment

It is fascinating to contrast the scientific description of reproduction outlined previously with the Talmudic description of conception:

> Our rabbis taught, there are three partners in [the creation of] man. The Holy One, blessed be He, his father and his mother. His father brings forth white seed that produces bones, nerves, nails, the brain in his head and the white in his eye. The woman brings forth red seed which produces skin, flesh, hair, and the dark of the eye. The Holy One, blessed be He, gives the spirit, the soul, the personality of the face, the sight of the eye, the hearing of the ear, the speech of the mouth, the locomotion of the legs, understanding and wisdom. When the time comes to part from this world, the Holy One, blessed be He, takes His portion, and the part of the mother and the father are laid before them.[2]

The physiology of this description may be primitive, for the Talmud is not a scientific textbook. Yet it contains an essential religious truth. To the religious Jew, the creation of a human life is not a matter of random chance. God is a partner in creation. It is the classical argument by design; the complexity and intricacy of the human reproductive system reflect the hand of God. For this reason, we bless God whenever a new life is created.

Where does this leave the infertile couple? If God is a partner in creation, perhaps God is ignoring the couple unable to conceive. Perhaps He is withholding life, for reasons only He knows. The Bible saw infertility as a punishment from God. Perhaps a couple facing infertility ought to accept it as God's will. There is a basic religious question: Is it proper for a couple facing infertility to seek medical help? Or should they stoically accept their fate, trusting in God's wisdom?

I recall counseling one couple who were considering in vitro fertilization, an expensive and still experimental procedure. Some religious and well-meaning friends had told the couple, "It is God's will that you not have a baby yet. Perhaps eventually God will answer your prayers. But aren't you subverting His will by going through this procedure?" Religious individuals, both Jewish and non-Jewish, have made this kind of comment frequently when discussing infertility. Many people believe that reproduction ought to be in the hands of God and off limits to humans and their technology.

Before we study the particular problems raised by medical treatment for infertility, we must look at a more general problem. How does Judaism view medical treatment in an area that is not life threatening, such as infertility, particularly when such treatment is both experimental and expensive?

Among the religions of the world, there are two approaches to medical treatment: passive and active. The passive approach questions the need for medical treatment. Illness is, after all, God's will and should be treated through prayer and repentance. To turn to a doctor is to subvert God's will. This religious philosophy finds its fullest development in Christian Science. The Christian Scientist denies the very reality of disease and calls for spiritual exercises to move a person beyond the affliction.

Jewish tradition does contain a strand supporting this passive view toward medical treatment. In the Torah, God, not man, is considered the healer:

He said, "If you will heed the Lord your God diligently, doing what is upright in His sight, giving ear to His commandments and keeping all His laws, then I will not bring upon you any of the diseases that I brought upon the Egyptians, for I the Lord am your healer" (Exod. 15:26).

The strongest advocate of this passive approach toward medical problems was the medieval commentator and philosopher Nahmanides. He wrote:

This is the general rule: when Israel is perfectly [in accord with God] and many in number, their affairs will not be conducted according to nature, not in their bodies nor in their land, not as a group and not individually. For God will bless their bread and their water and remove all sickness from them to the point that they will need no doctor nor need to care for themselves according to the rules of medicine. As it is written, "I am the Lord your healer." Thus the righteous did in the time of prophecy, when they sinned and became ill, they did not seek out a doctor but a prophet.[3]

To Nahmanides, illness was the result of an imperfect relationship with God. Therefore, in a perfect society we won't need doctors. Later in his commentary, Nahmanides did give reluctant permission to seek healing because people are accustomed to turning to a doctor when they are ill. But, ultimately, a religious person should turn to God for healing.

Nahmanides' point of view shows that Judaism has produced rabbis who prefer a passive approach toward healing. However, this has not been the normative Jewish opinion. On the contrary, Jewish tradition has reacted strongly to the passive acceptance of disease as God's will. Judaism teaches that a physician has a responsibility to heal. The Torah speaks of a man injured by another man. "If he [the injured man] then gets up and walks outdoors upon his staff, the assailant shall go unpunished, except that he must pay for his idleness and his cure" (Exod. 21:19). The rabbis interpreted this verse as an activist approach toward medicine; a physician must seek a cure.[4]

The activist approach toward healing is best illustrated in a Midrash:

> Once Rabbi Ishmael and Rabbi Akiva were strolling in the streets of Jerusalem along with another man. They met a sick person who said to them, "Masters, tell me how I can be healed." They quickly advised him to take a certain medicine until he felt better.
>
> The man with them turned to them and said, "Who made this man sick?"
>
> "The Holy One, blessed be He," they replied.
>
> "And do you presume to interfere in an area that is not yours?" the man explained. "He is afflicted and you heal?"
>
> "What is your occupation?" they asked the man.
>
> "I'm a tiller of the soil," he answered, "as you can see from the sickle I carry."
>
> "Who created the field and the vineyard?"

"The Holy One, blessed be He."

"And you dare to move in an area that is not yours? He created these and you eat their fruit."

"Don't you see the sickle in my hand?" the man said. "If I did not go out and plow the field, cover it, fertilize it, weed it, nothing would grow!"

"Fool," the rabbis said, "just as a tree does not grow if it is not fertilized, plowed and weeded—and even if it already grew but then is not watered it dies—so the body is like a tree, the medicine is the fertilizer and the doctor is the farmer."[5]

This activist approach toward medicine has become the normative Jewish position. Many of our greatest rabbis, including Judah Ha-Levi and Maimonides, earned their livings as physicians. Jews have always been attracted to the medical profession and have been quick to seek medical help when confronted with a health problem. The passive acceptance of illness as God's will is not the Jewish approach.

This activist approach can also be applied to seeking a cure for infertility. I once knew a childless couple who were deeply religious Christians. They had chosen not to seek medical help but to stoically accept their infertility as God's will. "I suppose God has other plans for us," they said, not with sadness but with a strength built on faith. I have a deep respect for them, but I found their particular approach to be extreme. Stoic acceptance would not be a normative Jewish reaction.

Jewish tradition would teach the infertile couple to seek the best medical help to solve an infertility problem. Judaism is not a fatalistic religion, and not everything that happens in this world has to be accepted as God's will. Not one biblical matriarch passively accepted her infertility. Hannah and Rebecca prayed, Sarah and Rachel brought in surrogate mothers, Michal adopted her sister's children, Tamar married her brother-in-law. In the Talmud, infertility is shown to have physical cause. Sitting too long in a lecture without emptying one's bladder, too many years of separation between husband and wife, improper nutrition—all of these were known to cause infertility. If a problem has a physical cause, it is proper to seek a physical cure.

Judaism advocates an activist approach. And the Jewish people, faced with zero population growth, desperately need Jewish babies to be born. If the miracles of modern medicine can help create more Jewish children, the Jewish community can only benefit.

Professor Seymour Siegel, an expert on bioethics from the Jewish Theological Seminary, has written most persuasively on the human right to seek medical treatment and tamper with nature to help conceive a child. The following quote is from his response on the case of Louise Brown, the first test-tube baby:

> The theological question, is it *permissible* to tamper with nature, raises an important concept in biblical thought. In contrast to pagan religion, the Bible asserts that both nature and man are creatures of God. Nature is not divine. God's glory is *reflected* in nature, the heavens do *declare* the *kavod* [glory] of God. God is above Nature as its Lord and Creator. Of all creatures, man is the highest, being a *shutaf* [partner] with the Almighty in the formation of the world. It should also be stressed that mind is part of nature. Therefore, we are called upon to care for nature and to preserve it—but not to worship it. We are also called upon to use our ingenuity, our imagination and intelligence to improve nature when human happiness and well-being [are] thwarted. This is the basis for the whole medical enterprise.[6]

Siegel is saying that to seek medical treatment to cure infertility is not only permissible, it is an obligation. If a couple are unable to fulfill the God-given commandment, "Be fruitful and multiply," and if there is a physical cause, they have a responsibility to find a cure for that cause.

Many health specialists have raised another ethical issue regarding medical treatment for infertility. Some thinkers have called it a luxury that we cannot afford. After all, infertility may be painful, but it is not life threatening. Research funds can be better used to cure cancer or heart

disease, not to create more babies in an already overpop-
ulated world. Some have called infertility research and
treatment a luxury of the rich.

An editorial in the *Journal of the American Medical Association* makes this point most forcefully. Dealing with the
difficult issue of in vitro fertilization, which we shall discuss
in the next chapter, the editorial calls for a moratorium on
further experiments in that area. Supporting this position,
it quotes a point made by one bioethics expert, L. R. Kass:
"Infertility in marriage is not a 'disease' and therefore intrauterine implantation of a laboratory conceptus is not
treatment of a disease but of a woman's 'desire.' "[7] Other
ethicists have made a similar claim that infertility is not a
disease.

Judaism would differ on this issue. The Torah almost
explicitly calls infertility a disease. According to the Book
of Exodus, "You shall serve the Lord your God, and He
will bless your bread and your water. And I will remove
sickness from your midst. No woman in your land shall
miscarry or be barren. I will let you enjoy the full count
of your days" (Exod. 23:25–26). Judaism, from the Torah
through modern responsa literature, has advocated aggressive medical treatment to cure infertility. To produce
children is a *mitzvah,* so any treatment that will help a couple fulfill that *mitzvah* can be justified in Jewish tradition.

Besides, calling infertility treatment a luxury fails to
recognize the real emotions of couples who cannot conceive. Their pain is as real as the pain caused by any other
disease. If the medical profession can justify cosmetic surgery for psychological reasons, it can certainly justify infertility treatment for psychological reasons. The couple
facing childlessness are not interested in arguments about
overpopulation. They feel that they should not be forced
to make the sacrifice and remain childless. If reasonable
medical treatment can help them conceive a child, Jewish
tradition advocates that they aggressively pursue that treatment.

This chapter is written for the Jewish couple who choose
to pursue such medical treatment. It will not cover all the

possible diagnoses of infertility and their treatment; these can be found in any basic text on infertility. Rather, it will look at some particular Jewish issues raised by treatment. The next chapter will explore a Jewish approach to some of the more unconventional medical treatments such as artificial insemination, in vitro fertilization, surrogate mothers, and embryo transplants.

Beginning Medical Treatment

Most couples who suspect a fertility problem first turn to modern medicine for treatment. It is only after the medical option has been exhausted that they consider the other options—adoption or childlessness. In thinking about medical treatment, couples first ask: When should we begin?

There are no absolute rules. The usual rule of thumb is, if a couple have tried to conceive for one year without success, they should seek help. If a couple are older, or if there is any history of medical problems such as uneven or painful menstrual periods or perhaps no menstrual periods in the woman, undescended testicles or adult mumps in the man, they should seek help earlier. They should also recognize that a good fertility work-up takes many months. As a couple approach their mid-thirties, each month counts. It makes sense that they should seek medical help as soon as they feel that there is a problem. However, they also should remember that even a normal fertile couple have only a 25 percent chance of achieving pregnancy in any particular month. If several months go by without pregnancy, it may be simply a question of odds, not a medical problem.

There are two sobering considerations for any couple contemplating medical treatment for infertility. First, medical treatment is expensive. Since the average obstetrician-gynecologist is not trained to deal with most fertility problems, a trained specialist should be consulted, preferably a member of the American Fertility Society. Such specialists are costly. Also, many types of infertility treatment are not covered by insurance because infertility is not a "disease" as defined by the insurance companies. If a couple should try an experimental procedure such as in vitro fertilization, costs may run as high as $6,000 a month. This will come out of the couple's pocket.

Infertility treatment is also intrusive. Traditionally, Judaism sees sexual relations between husband and wife as very beautiful and very private. The Jewish conception of modesty dictates that what happens in the bedroom should not be discussed with anybody. Infertility treatment brings a third party into the bedroom, the doctor. A good fertility specialist will want to know all aspects of a couple's sexual life, including their frequency and position of intercourse, any lubrication they use, and any sexual problems they may have. The wife will have to keep a daily temperature chart to check ovulation, and certain times of the month will be marked as ideal for intercourse. Many couples resent the loss of spontaneity in their sex lives, as they seek to time their intercourse to doctor's orders. Most couples find the whole course of medical treatment to be emotionally difficult, particularly if it becomes extensive.

A couple should learn as much as possible about their reproductive processes and about infertility before beginning treatment. One of the strengths of Jewish tradition is its emphasis on knowledge. A couple who understand their own reproductive systems can assist their physician in making a diagnosis. It also is important to ask about the side effects of any test or treatment. I know of many women who have driven themselves to the physician for a fertility test and found themselves unable to drive home afterward.

Many excellent books have been written on infertility. Among the best are Dr. Sherman Silber, *How to Get Pregnant* (Charles Scribner's Sons, 1980) and Barbara Eck Menning, *Infertility: A Guide for the Childless Couple* (Prentice-Hall, 1977, soon to be reissued and updated). The *RESOLVE Newsletter* also contains articles on the newest medical procedures. Armed with such information, a couple can talk intelligently with their doctor to find out what is wrong.

It is vital that a couple seek out the best medical treatment. Not only should a doctor be sensitive and discreet, but he or she should be an expert in the field. Many obstetrician-gynecologists and urologists do not have the expertise for successful infertility treatment. The doctor should be an expert in infertility. A list of such doctors can be found by writing:

American Fertility Society
1608 13th Ave. S., Suite 101
Birmingham, AL 35256-6199

While couples are pursuing medical treatment, it is important to try to keep a sense of humor. It can be quite difficult to have sexual relations according to doctor's orders or to take temperatures every morning. The joy and spontaneity, which are the ideal in marital relations, often disappear. A good sense of humor can help see a couple through the stress. RESOLVE recommends that a couple occasionally take a vacation from infertility treatment. They should put away the thermometer and live spontaneously for a while—perhaps take a trip. Treatment can be resumed later.

Finally, it is important to recall that since infertility is a couple's problem, a husband and wife should always seek treatment together. When my wife and I first suspected that we had a fertility problem, we shared our concerns with a physician and his wife who are personal friends. The physician pulled me aside and said, "Don't worry. Your wife will go to a doctor, and he'll take care of her. She'll be pregnant in no time." This physician did not realize what I already knew, that I would shortly be going into the hospital for surgery. Even this doctor reflected one of the oldest prejudices: blaming infertility on the wife.

The evaluation of an infertile couple raises a strange anomaly in Jewish law. Certain tests for women tend to be fairly complicated, uncomfortable, and even painful. These include an examination of the cervical mucus, various blood hormone tests, an endometrial biopsy, a hysterosalpingogram (an x-ray of the fallopian tubes), and finally a laparoscopy under a general anesthetic. The basic test for a man is simple and takes minutes. A sperm count or a series of sperm counts and other semen tests can reveal fairly quickly whether a man is likely to be fertile.

Because of this difference, it seems logical to test the male first and, only if he provides a normal ejaculate, to then test the female. Yet many rabbis disagree with this order. The tests on a female, for all their complexity, raise no questions of Jewish law; semen analysis does. Jewish law is very strict about *hotzaat zera l'vatalah* (emitting semen in vain). Therefore, many rabbis will permit a semen test only after the wife has had a full fertility work-up. In fact, some authorities outlaw such fertility tests for males altogether or insist on waiting until the couple remain childless for ten years. In any case, they see semen testing as a last resort.

There is something unfair about an interpretation that requires a woman to go through a series of complicated, expensive, and painful tests first and only then permits the simple procedure for testing the man. If infertility is a couple's problem, they should be treated as a couple from the beginning. Both the man and woman should go in for medical histories, physical examinations, and some basic tests, including a semen analysis. We must look more closely at the question of whether such tests on the male are permissible by Jewish law.

Semen Testing for Men

Judaism has always frowned on the wasteful emission of seed. Rabbinic literature has waxed eloquent on the evils of *hotzaat zera l'vatalah* (emitting seed in vain) or, to use the more popular term, *hash-hatat zera* (wasting of seed). The word *hashat* means "to waste," but more than that, it means "to corrupt." There is a degree of corruption involved in spilling seed. According to tradition, the wasteful spilling of seed was one of the sins of the generation of the Flood.

With this attitude, rabbinic tradition has outlawed both masturbation and the use of male contraceptive devices such as a condom. The Talmud quotes Rabbi Elazar as saying, "What is meant by the verse, 'Your hands are full of blood' [Isa. 1:15]? This refers to those who pollute themselves with their hands."[8] With those strong words, not only is *hash-hatat zera* immoral but also is compared with murder. The Talmud merely outlaws the spilling of seed, but the *Zohar* and other mystical literature condemn it in the harshest terms. According to the *Zohar*, this is a sin whereby "one pollutes himself more so than through any other sin in this world or the next."[9]

What is noticeable about this law is that, although *hash-hatat zera* is considered a major sin in Judaism, it is difficult to pinpoint its biblical source. The story of Onan's refusal to impregnate Tamar, spilling his seed upon the ground instead, is frequently quoted as the basis of this law (see Gen. 38:9–10). In English, *onanism* has come to mean the wasteful spilling of seed. Yet that story is complicated by other factors, in particular Onan's avoidance of his levirate obligations. In fact, Jewish tradition is unclear as to Onan's sin. Rashi, quoting the Midrash, says Onan "threshed inside her and winnowed outside," that is, practiced coitus interruptus. The Talmud claims that Onan practiced anal intercourse (*lo k'darkah*),[10] which technically is permitted by Jewish law. By the talmudic explanation, Onan sinned by avoiding his levirate responsibilities. In his analysis of the law of *hash-hatat zera*, Rabbi David Feldman cites many other possible sources for the prohibition. The large number of sources quoted by Feldman is proof of the difficulty in pinpointing the origin of this law.

Whatever the biblical source, Judaism has always outlawed the wasteful spilling of seed. However, this law was never construed to mean that every act of intercourse must have the potential to result in pregnancy. Judaism permits intercourse between husband and wife even if the wife is sterile, already pregnant, or postmenopausal. Judaism also permits birth control to be practiced by the wife under certain circumstances. As long as the sexual relations were natural, such intercourse was not considered the wasting of seed. The term *hash-hatat zera* is used only to refer to such acts as coitus interruptus, masturbation, and the use of condoms.

From this point of view, it is clear that semen testing raises serious questions of Jewish law. The same applies to the removal of seed by the husband to be concentrated or treated by a physician and then planted in the wife's uterus, the procedure known as artificial insemination by the husband (AIH). (The question of artificial insemination by donor [AID] is more complex and will be discussed in the next chapter.) As a result of the difficulties raised by semen testing, many Orthodox authorities have said that the husband should be tested only as a last resort. To quote one prominent Orthodox authority, Rabbi Eliezer Waldenberg, "For an infertile couple, one should administer first every test that can be made on the fertility of the wife, and only if these are found to be negative, is it permissible to test the husband by checking his sperm."[11] As mentioned, there is an unfairness about this position, particularly considering the pain and expense involved in most fertility tests for women.

Actually, there is precedent for semen tests in the Talmud. That precedent is not concerned with infertility, but rather with the case of a man who has had part of his penis cut off. According to the Torah, "No one whose testes are crushed or whose member is cut off shall be admitted into the congregation of the Lord" (Deut. 23:2). This was interpreted to refer to anybody who deliberately mutilated himself, as opposed to an accident. It was a protection against people deliberately becoming eunuchs, a common practice in ancient times.

The Talmud states that if the penis was cut and had healed, the man may once again enter the congregation and marry a Jew. Yet if it was cut and the wound opens up when sexual intercourse takes place, he cannot enter the congregation. The question was asked of Rabbi Yosef: How do you test for such a condition? His answer, although extremely strange for modern Jews, does give us some insights:

> Our rabbis taught, how do we act [in such a case]? It was answered, bring warm barley bread and put it on his anus, so that he ejaculates and we can see [if the wound is healed]. Abbaye said, do we need all this? Are we dealing with Jacob our father . . . who never had a sexual emission all his days [until his first-born was conceived]? Rather Abbaye said, wave colored [female] clothing in front of him [until he ejaculates]. Rava said, do we need all this? Are we dealing with Barzillai the Gileadite [who was sexually promiscuous]? Rather, do what was taught in the first place.[12]

Two things are clear from this unusual passage. First, under certain circumstances, ejaculation for purposes of a medical examination is permissible. Second, indirect stimulation, as opposed to masturbation, is preferable. On the basis of these considerations, Rabbi Waldenberg built a hierarchy of methods to obtain the sperm for testing.

> The removal of sperm for purposes of medical examination—after the woman has been thoroughly examined—is not considered the wasteful spilling of seed. But one should strive to do the examination in a manner that causes the fewest halakhic difficulties.
> The ideal method, according to halakha, is when the doctor removes the seed from the woman's vagina immediately after natural intercourse.
> If this is not possible (for medical, technical or emotional reasons), use the method of threshing within, and winnowing without into a jar (coitus interruptus).
> If this is not possible, it is permissible to retrieve the seed through use of a condom and natural intercourse.
> If this is not possible, it is permissible to put a receptacle within the vagina of the wife and ejaculate there.
> If all these are not possible, it is permissible to ejaculate

manually, yet it is preferable that the doctor use an instrument for this. If this is impossible, it is permissible for the husband to ejaculate by hand.

If there is a need, a testicular biopsy is permissible, but it is preferable that the left testicle be used.[13]

It is clear that, according to Waldenberg, masturbation is to be discouraged and can be used only as a last resort. The more natural the ejaculation to remove semen, the less objectionable in terms of Jewish law. The basis of Waldenberg's preference for the left testicle is unclear; today testicular biopsies are taken from either or both testicles.

A similar concern with the method of obtaining sperm is raised by another prominent Orthodox authority, Dr. Moses Tendler, who writes:

During the medical work-up of a sterility problem, it is occasionally necessary to test the semen of the husband for quantity and quality of sperm. Jewish law generally prohibits obtaining the semen by an act of manual masturbation. Post-coital examination, using a rubber or plastic covered tampon as a vaginal plug which is inserted immediately after intercourse, may suffice. If deemed necessary, a specially prepared condom which does not have any toxicity to the sperm can be used during the act of intercourse, or the semen sample might be obtained by interrupted coitus. The condom or interrupted coitus are not ordinarily permitted by Jewish law. However, when the intent of the act is to enable the couple to fulfill their desire and obligation to have children, competent rabbinic authorities should be consulted as to the permissibility of condom or interrupted coitus or other methods.[14]

The "other methods" probably refer to masturbation.

As we have seen, Orthodox authorities are fairly strict, permitting a man to provide a sperm sample only after the woman has been tested. The view that masturbation should be used only as last resort is problematic because most physicians believe masturbation to be the best method of obtaining a sperm specimen. Other methods are too inaccurate, since the highest concentration of sperm is found in the first half of the emission. Whether the sperm sample is being given for purposes of semen testing or artificial insemination, an accurate, highly concentrated sample must be obtained. It is clear that masturbation, although the most problematic halakhically, is the best method medically.

In truth, there is room for a more liberal opinion. In Judaism, there is a principle that a doctor is to be trusted, even if it is a matter that is usually forbidden.[15] For example, if a doctor requires a patient to eat on Yom Kippur, the patient must follow the doctor's orders. Similarly, if a doctor says that a good semen sample can be obtained only through masturbation, the doctor is to be believed.

There is a stronger reason to permit such semen testing. Ultimately, the prohibition is against the "wasting" of seed. One would be hard pressed to call a sperm test, or AIH, a "wasting" of seed. Rabbi Aaron Walkin, a twentieth-century Lithuanian authority, makes this very clear. When asked by a colleague about the use of the husband's sperm to artificially inseminate the wife, he carefully analyzed the legal precedents. He then wrote:

> To conclude matters, I see no basis for a prohibition of this, in that the prohibition of "emitting seed in vain" does not apply. This is not like wasting seed on trees and rocks, rather it will be brought into the womb of the woman under the supervision of a physician and by this it will be easier for her to conceive; that is not "in vain."[16]

Similarly, Rabbi Moshe Feinstein has written that it is not a forbidden destruction of seed if a proper purpose is served. Rabbi Feinstein speaks of a case of coitus interruptus, which he permits if the mother's health is threatened by normal intercourse.[17] In the same way, seed brought forth to permit the diagnosis and treatment of a fertility problem, or to artificially inseminate the wife, cannot be considered "semen brought forth in vain."

In conclusion, Judaism does outlaw *hotzaat zera l'vatalah* (emitting seed in vain). But the decisive term here is *l'vatalah* "in vain." The emission of semen for fertility testing is not a vain purpose; on the contrary, it contributes to the performance of a *mitzvah*. Precedent does state that the method of procuring the semen should be as indirect as possible. Yet we follow a doctor's orders even on matters that are usually forbidden, and most doctors have stated that masturbation is the best technique for procuring sperm.

Therefore, it would seem clear that Jewish men should have no qualms about using masturbation to produce a semen sample for examination. Since this test is so simple and economical compared with most fertility tests performed on women, the semen analysis should be done fairly early in the couple's fertility work-up. If a doctor recommends artificial insemination using the husband's sperm, Jewish law would permit this procedure. Ultimately, the overriding factor is the *mitzvah* of procreation, permitting a doctor to use the best medical knowledge if the result will be another Jewish baby.

Mikvah *as a Fertility Problem*

I know a couple, struggling with infertility, who put out the word in the Jewish community that they were hoping to adopt. One day they received a package in the mail from a stranger. It contained a book on the laws of *mikvah* and a note: "If you observe these laws, God will give you a baby." Needless to say, they were quite upset and quickly threw the book into the trash. It is unfortunate that the laws of *mikvah* are associated with superstitions, for these laws can convey a powerful symbolism for the infertile couple, as I will show at the end of this section. At the same time, the laws of *mikvah* may be the cause of infertility.

A number of difficult problems can arise for Jewish couples who observe the laws of *mikvah*—often euphemistically called *taharat ha-mishpahah,* or "family purity." These laws regulate the sexual life of a married couple, defining when sexual relations are permitted and when they are forbidden. The regulations are complicated and difficult for nonobservant Jews to understand, yet they are appealing to more and more young Jews who are attracted to tradition. Many are not strictly Orthodox; some are affiliated with Conservative or even Reform synagogues. Yet the laws hold an attraction, for they bring a holiness into marital relations.

The Torah states: "Do not come near a woman during her period of uncleanliness to uncover her nakedness" (Lev. 18:19). The use of the word *unclean* for the Hebrew *tamei* is difficult for modern Jews; some prefer to say "ritual impurity," although there is no exact English equivalent. Whichever translation is chosen, the Torah clearly forbids sexual relations between husband and wife for seven days beginning with the onset of the woman's menses.

Rabbinic law applied a stricter standard. There are times when a woman may have a discharge of blood that is not menstrual. In such a case, the Torah says: "When she becomes clean of her discharge, she shall count off seven days, and after that she shall be clean" (Lev. 15:28).

The problem for the rabbis of the Talmud was the discrepancy between these two laws. A menstruating woman (called a *niddah*) must separate from her husband seven days altogether. A woman with another discharge (called a *zavah*) must wait for the bleeding to stop, then wait an additional seven clean days. Only then can she resume marital relations. The problem was that a woman who sees bleeding may not know if she is a *niddah* or a *zavah*. Therefore, the rabbis ruled that the strictest law must be applied in every case; all women must wait seven clean days. "Rabbi Zira said, the daughters of Israel are strict upon themselves, so that even if they see a drop of blood the size of a mustard seed, they wait seven clean days."[18] Waiting seven clean days has become the accepted ruling among all observant Jews.

The laws of "family purity," as practiced by a modern Jewish couple, would be as follows[19]:

1 When the woman feels or sees that her menses has begun (or on the day that it was scheduled to begin

if it is regular), she separates from her husband. The strictest adherents sleep in separate beds and even avoid all physical contact.

2 The woman waits until her period ends, but she can wait no fewer than five days. Late in the afternoon on the fifth day she checks herself to be sure all bleeding has stopped (called *hefsek taharah*).

3 She then counts seven clean days, checking herself daily.

4 On the evening of the eighth day she bathes, cuts her nails, removes all jewelry, and then immerses herself in a ritual bath called a *mikvah*. A *mikvah* attendant is there to ensure that she immerses completely and the water touches every part of her body. She says a *berakhah* (a blessing) and immerses twice more. She is then free to resume sexual relations with her husband.

Rabbis have presented numerous arguments as to the advantages of these laws. The strongest is that they force a couple to have marital relations during the woman's most fertile period since most women ovulate halfway through their cycle. A woman with a twenty-eight-day cycle will ovulate around the fourteenth day. To achieve fertility, the couple must have relations on that day or the day before. If they practice the laws of family purity, they separate for twelve days. On the thirteenth day they resume relations, right at the ideal moment for pregnancy. These laws are the exact reverse of the rhythm method of birth control; they are a means of achieving high fertility in the observant Jewish community.

Yet for many couples these laws have the opposite effect. Rather than ensuring fertility, they act as a form of birth control. A woman with a short cycle, who ovulates on or before the twelfth day, will find herself avoiding relations during her fertile period. This is an immense problem for observant Jewish couples who are infertile. Marsha Sheinfeld, an Orthodox Jew, writes in the *RESOLVE Newsletter* of the frustration Orthodox couples sometimes have in explaining these laws to their doctor:

The Orthodox patient must make further demands on this relationship by asking the physician to adhere to a strict set of
religious regulations and rabbinic opinions.

The doctor who becomes impatient with this situation, either
because of a lack of understanding or interest, further increases
the burden on his patient by making cynical and/or discouraging
remarks, such as advising the patient to "cheat." The patient is
then forced to choose between their doctor, who they believe to
possess the "cure," or their religious conscience.

The Orthodox patient whose physician takes the time to
become knowledgeable and understanding of this problem is
truly to be envied. Most often the well-informed physician will
be sympathetic and cooperative, and will be willing to spend time
with the couple and their rabbi to decide the course of their
fertility treatment.[20]

For some observant couples, the solution to a short
cycle is fairly easy. Sometimes fertility drugs can manipulate the time of ovulation. If this fails, some Orthodox
authorities have permitted the use of artificial insemination
to treat infertility. Thus, Rabbi Tendler writes:

Artificial insemination with the husband's sperm may be considered as part of the total approach to the management of an
infertile couple. Such insemination is especially useful in cases
in which, due to a short menstrual cycle, cohabitation does not
occur during the fertile period. If hormonal manipulation fails
to sufficiently postpone the time of ovulation, rabbinic guidance
should be sought with regard to the use of husband sperm during
the niddah [separation] period.[21]

Both the use of hormones and the use of artificial
insemination are possible solutions to infertility problems
caused by the observance of *mikvah*. Yet neither solution
is totally satisfying. Hormones can have side effects, and
they are occasionally dangerous. They are also extremely
expensive. Artificial insemination raises other problems of
Jewish law, which were dealt with earlier in this chapter.
The husband, for religious or psychological reasons, may
not be able to produce a semen sample. Or it may be im-

possible to find a doctor who will participate in such treatments to satisfy a couple's religious scruples.

The basic problem is still that the couple is resuming sexual relations too late in the woman's cycle. The question remains, would it be permissible for a woman to go to the *mikvah* earlier in order to increase the chances of fertility? Can the seven clean days be shortened? The answer from Orthodox authorities seems to be no. Rabbi Moshe Feinstein does give permission to shorten the first five-day period of separation after the menses.[22] In fact, Feinstein gives a fascinating responsum regarding a woman who ovulates on the tenth day of her cycle and bleeds for only two days. The couple can separate three days before her menses begins, plus the two days of the menses, making five days. She can then do the *hefsek taharah*, count seven clean days, and be reunited with her husband before she ovulates. However, if the wife's period lasts the normal four or five days and she ovulates early, there is no recourse. She must count the full seven clean days.

To my knowledge, no Orthodox rabbi has publicly permitted a woman to go to the *mikvah* before seven clean days (although some may have permitted it privately). Because these laws are not widely observed in the Conservative or Reform communities, the rabbis of these movements have not even dealt with the question. I know of two Orthodox couples who were confronted with this problem. One was told by their rabbi, "There is no recourse. You have to accept it as God's will." They ultimately rejected their observance rather than accept a life of childlessness. Another couple, an Orthodox rabbi and rebbetzin, shortened the days of counting and went to the *mikvah* early. She did become pregnant but has been consumed with guilt over breaking Orthodox practice to achieve pregnancy.

It is a shame when Jewish couples are forced to choose between their religious observance and their desire to have children. Actually, there may be a solution that is worthy of consideration by halakhic authorities, for what we have here is a classic case of the clash of two commandments in

Judaism. As mentioned, counting seven clean days was a rabbinic enactment, meant to prevent confusion. The Torah requires only seven days of total separation between husband and wife; the rabbis brought the number to twelve days, including seven clean days. On the other hand, "be fruitful and multiply" is a law from the Torah. If a law from the Torah is not being fulfilled because of a rabbinic enactment, there may be room to set that enactment aside. If we accept the doctor's word as authority, that counting seven clean days is preventing a couple from having relations during the woman's fertile period and fulfilling the *mitzvah* of procreation, there may be room to shorten the abstinence period.

I must end this section with a personal note. Like many observant couples, my wife and I have struggled with the laws of family purity. They are perhaps the most difficult laws in Judaism to observe, but they never made such sense as when we realized we had a fertility problem. Suddenly these laws took on a powerful symbolism.

In her essay on *tumah* and *taharah*, Rachel Adler explains these laws as a metaphor of death and rebirth:

> All that is born dies, and all that begets. Begetting and birth are the nexus points at which life and death are coupled. They are the beginnings which point to an end. Menstruation, too, is a nexus point. It is an end which points to a beginning. At the nexus points, the begetter becomes tameh. The fluids on which new life depends—the semen, the rich uteral lining which sustains embryonic life—the departure of these from the body leaves the giver tameh. The menstrual blood, which inside the womb was a potential nutriment, is a token of dying when it is shed. Menstruation is an autumn within, the dying which makes room for new birth.[23]

For us, the monthly menstrual period was a sign of death. Once again, that potential child would not be born. Once again, we went into mourning as we remained childless another month. It was only natural to separate from one another. After all, Jewish law forbids marital relations during mourning. On the other hand, the monthly trip to the *mikvah* was a time of hope and rebirth. Perhaps this month a child would be created. My wife would tip the *mikvah* attendant, and she would express the hope that they would not see one another for nine months.

The laws of *mikvah* are ancient. Yet for this modern Jewish couple they create a powerful symbol. They represent the monthly brush with death and the monthly renewal of hope that are familiar to any infertile couple.

Sabbath Observance and Medical Treatment

One final area of Jewish observance may cause problems for a couple seeking medical treatment. The Sabbath is a day when one is cut off from the regular weekday world. Traditional Jews do not shop, conduct business, or travel in an automobile from Friday at sundown until Saturday night. Certainly, doctor appointments are not permitted, unless there is a medical emergency. In such a case, in order to save a life, all the laws of the Sabbath are suspended.

Yet for an infertile couple, certain medical procedures must be performed on certain days of the week regardless of the Sabbath. Artificial insemination must be performed on a particular day of the cycle. Here, twenty-four hours may not be critical; I know couples who have gone in for artificial insemination late Friday afternoon, Saturday night, or even Sunday morning. Also, through hormones, doctors can sometimes control the day of the week on which ovulation occurs. There is no substitute for a sensitive physician who will respect a couple's religious scruples and try to accommodate them.

Certain fertility drugs, particularly Pergonal, must be monitored on a daily basis. Either blood tests or sonograms, or possibly both, may be required. Without daily monitoring, this drug can cause hyperstimulation of the ovaries, a dangerous condition. Death has resulted from improper monitoring of this drug. In a similar way, complicated procedures like in vitro fertilization require daily monitoring of hormone levels with the possibility of surgery on very short notice. Ovulation may not wait until the Sabbath ends.

Once again, a candid discussion with the physician is necessary. Is it possible to take hormone levels on Friday afternoon and Sunday? If not, is there a way to arrange these tests near one's home, so that driving on the Sabbath can be avoided? How can Sabbath violations be kept to a minimum? Ultimately we are dealing with a possible danger; if the drug is not monitored, the woman's life would be threatened. But should a woman take a drug that requires daily monitoring, knowing such monitoring will mean breaking the Sabbath? There is no easy answer to any of these questions; once again we have a conflict between two basic Jewish concepts, "be fruitful and multiply" and "observe the Sabbath." The only guidance from our tradition is the statement in the Talmud regarding treating the sick on the Sabbath. "Rabbi Shimon ben Manasya said, 'The children of Israel shall keep the Sabbath.' Desecrate one Sabbath for him so that he can keep many Sabbaths."[24] To paraphrase, desecrate one Sabbath so that a Jewish child may be born to observe many.

And they said, "Come, let us build us a city, and a tower with its top in the sky, to make a name for ourselves; else we shall be scattered all over the world." The Lord came down to look at the city and tower that man had built, and the Lord said, "If, as one people with one language for all, this is how they have begun to act, then nothing that they may propose to do will be out of their reach. Let us, then, go down and confound their speech there, so that they shall not understand one another's speech."

(Gen. 11:4–7)

5

Unconventional Treatments

Today a number of new infertility treatments have become available. As a result, thousands of couples who could not have benefited from the conventional treatments of surgery or drugs have successfully conceived. For many couples, such techniques as artificial insemination by donor (AID), in vitro fertilization, surrogate mothering, and embryo transplants have answered their prayers for a child.

Yet these techniques raise numerous legal and social problems. To quote one expert: "A child may now have as many as five 'parents': the egg donor, the sperm donor, the surrogate who bears the child and the couple who raise it. The potential emotional ramifications are so troubling that many infertility clinics now employ a staff counselor."[1] Civil law is still struggling with such legal ramifications as the "paternity" or "illegitimacy" of a child born from artificial insemination, and ethicists are arguing whether such a complex and expensive procedure as in vitro fertilization can be justified. This is only one of a number of areas in which medical technology and sophistication have bypassed existing legal and social mores.

How does Judaism view these techniques? Would a Jewish couple, faced with no other alternative, be justified in using them? There is no simple answer, for each treatment raises different questions of Jewish law. Some, such as artificial insemination, are medically simple procedures that raise great difficulties halakhically. Others, such as in vitro fertilization, are exceedingly difficult medically but present few halakhic problems.

Many other religious leaders, particularly in the Catholic Church, have objected to these procedures as "unnatural." Catholic theologians have proclaimed any procedure that bypasses natural intercourse between husband and wife to be morally illegitimate. Thus, one Catholic theologian has attacked artificial insemination as immoral "because it is a violation of the natural law which limits the right to generate to married people, and which demands that right to be exercised personally and not by proxy."[2] In vitro fertilization also has been attacked by the Catholic Church as contrary to natural law. To quote a recent Catholic legal document: "Advances in technology have now made it possible to procreate apart from sexual relations through the meeting in vitro of the germ cells previously taken from the man and the woman. But what is technically possible is not for that very reason morally admissible."[3] This statement of Church law goes on to outlaw all the techniques of conception discussed in this chapter as well as artificial insemination with the husband's sperm and experimentation on human embryos. The document does express sympathy for infertile couples but states, "Marriage does not confer upon the spouses the right to have a child, but only the right to perform those natural acts which are per se ordered to procreation."[4]

Judaism takes a very different view. First, Jewish tradition does not accept a doctrine of natural law. From the beginning, Judaism has taught that humankind is a partner in creation. Humans have the right to tamper with nature, as long as the tampering is consistent with Jewish ethics. Therefore, Judaism permits surgery and other medical treatments, even if those treatments are risky, in order to save a life or cure a disease. Certainly, if medical treatment can be justified to postpone death, it can be justified to assist with birth. Natural law does not enter the picture. As Professor Seymour Siegel writes, "We are called upon to use our ingenuity, our imagination and intelligence to improve nature when human happiness and well-being [are] thwarted."

In judging the permissibility of a particular procedure, we must look at two criteria: (1) Is the purpose of the procedure in keeping with the ethical values of Judaism? (2) Are there any particular halakhic objections?

Let us explore the first question. What is the overall purpose of the procedure, and is it in keeping with the ethical values of Judaism? A technological skill is usually morally neutral; it can be used for good or bad purposes. A good example is the Tower of Babel, quoted at the beginning of this chapter. There was nothing intrinsically evil about a tower. The evil was that the tower was to be used to challenge God. Similarly, there is nothing intrinsically evil about the new medical techniques. But we must ask, what is their purpose? A sperm bank established to help couples conceive would be ethically justified by Judaism. A sperm bank established to create a perfect race or to collect sperm of Nobel Prize winners would not be. In vitro fertilization to help a woman with blocked fallopian tubes conceive would be ethically justified by Judaism. In vitro fertilization to obtain embryos for experimentation would not be justified. Genetic manipulation to cure a deadly disease like Tay-Sachs would be ethically justified by Judaism. Genetic manipulation to choose the sex of a baby would not be justified.

Clearly, any of these techniques can be misused. Some ethicists have used the slippery slope argument, which says that even a justified procedure should be avoided if it might lead to experiments that are ethically objectionable. Siegel, arguing passionately against this approach, writes:

[T]he good sense and the ethical sensitivity of scientists operating under the regulatory powers of government acting in the interests of the public, can establish the ground rules that will encourage research and avoid the dehumanization we all fear.[5]

In the context of our discussion, the various new techniques of conception have a purpose that is in keeping with the ethical values of Judaism: to help a Jewish couple, otherwise infertile, conceive and have a baby. The fact that these techniques can be misused is beside the point. If a technique is used to help a couple have a baby, it is justifiable by Jewish ethics to fulfill the first commandment to be fruitful and multiply.

The question of particular halakhic objections is more complex. We therefore must turn to each of the new fertility techniques, explore the halakhic issues raised, and ask whether they can be justified in terms of Jewish law. Since some of the material is somewhat technical, the implications will be summarized at the end of each section.

Artificial Insemination by Donor (AID)

In artificial insemination the sperm is artificially administered to the wife by a physician. When the husband has a low sperm count, his sperm may be concentrated by the doctor and then placed into the woman's cervix at midcycle. This is called artificial insemination by husband (AIH). As mentioned, this technique raises the problem of *hotzaat zera l'vatalah* (wasting of seed) but is now considered permissible by many authorities.[6]

Most artificial insemination uses the sperm of an anonymous donor. This alternative may be used if the husband has *azoospermia* (absence of sperm), has *oligospermia* (very low sperm count), or is impotent (unable to ejaculate). AID can also be used when the husband carries a genetic disease that he wants to avoid passing to his child or when he has had a vasectomy and reversal is unsuccessful. It is estimated that 10,000 to 20,000 children are born each year as a result of AID. The process has a 57 percent national success rate.[7]

Artificial insemination by donor raises a number of serious questions of Jewish law, among them:

1 Is it permissible for a couple to participate in AID?

2 Is it considered adultery? Is the wife then forbidden to her husband as an adulteress?

3 What is the status of a child conceived this way? Is the child a *mamzer* (illegitimate) or legitimate?

4 Who is the legal father—the husband or the donor? What if the donor is a Kohen or Levi? If the husband dies and the children are the result of AID, must the wife go through the ceremony of *halitzah* (discussed in the second chapter)? Is the husband, the father of children conceived through AID, really childless?

5 Do we worry about the possibility that a child conceived by AID will someday marry an unknown half-sibling conceived by AID?

Because of these serious legal issues, most Orthodox authorities have outlawed AID. In fact, some have denounced the procedure in the harshest terms. To quote Rabbi Immanuel Jakobovits:

> If Jewish law nevertheless opposes AID without reservation as utterly evil, it is mainly for moral reasons, not because of the intrinsic illegality of the act itself. The principal motive for the revulsion against the practice is the fear of the abuses to which its legalization would lead, however great the benefits may be in individual cases. By reducing human generation to stud-farming methods, AID severs the link between the procreation of children and marriage, indispensable to the maintenance of the family as the most basic and sacred unit of human society.[8]

Similar questions are raised by Rabbi Moses Tendler:

The sanctity of the family unit serves as a major tenet of the Jewish faith. The parent-child unit is an essential means of perpetuating the great values of our civilization. Any act that weakens this bond cannot be condoned. It is for this reason that artificial insemination with donor sperm cannot receive routine rabbinic approval.[9]

Numerous other Orthodox authorities have denounced AID in equally strong language, yet it is not clear that the early Jewish sources bear out such a strong prohibition. There are three classical Jewish sources that touch on the issue of AID.

The first source is found in the Talmud, which discusses the biblical rule that the high priest must marry a virgin (Lev. 21:13):

It was asked of Ben Zoma, may a virgin who is pregnant marry a high priest? Do we take into account Samuel's statement, for Samuel said, "I can have repeated intercourse without blood," or is Samuel a rare case? He answered, "Samuel is a rare case, but we take into account that she might become impregnated in a bath."[10]

Ben Zoma claims that it is possible for a virgin to be impregnated in a bath; therefore, she can marry a high priest. This indicates that the Talmud was aware of the possibility of insemination without intercourse. It also indicates that such insemination does not make the woman forbidden to the priest, although natural intercourse would have.

A second source is the medieval Midrash regarding the background of Ben Sira. This Midrash is first mentioned by Rabbi Jacob Moellin Segal (1365–1427) in his work *Likutei Maharil*. According to the Midrash, the prophet Jeremiah went to the bathhouse, where he was attacked by a group of wicked men who forced him to emit semen into the water. Later Jeremiah's daughter came to bathe and was impregnated by the seed of her father. The Midrash is based on the fact that by gematria, the names *Sira* and

Jeremiah both have the same numerical value. (Each letter in Hebrew has a numerical value, and both these names add up to 271.)

A basic fact is clear from this source. Ben Sira was the result of a seed by the father and an egg by the daughter. If he had been a child of normal intercourse, he would have been a *mamzer* (the illegitimate child of adultery or incest). The fact that he was not a *mamzer* seems to indicate that there can be no stigma of illegitimacy placed on a child of AID. What's more, since Ben Sira is considered the child of Jeremiah, it shows that the sperm donor is considered the father in terms of Jewish law.

The third source comes from Rabbi Perez ben Elijah of Cabeil in his work *Haggahot Semak*:

> A woman may lie on her husband's sheets but should be careful not to lie on sheets upon which another man slept lest she become impregnated from his sperm. Why are we not afraid that she become pregnant from her husband's sperm and the child will be conceived of a niddah [menstruating female]? [Note: to be the child of a niddah was considered a blemish by traditional sources.] The answer is that since there is no forbidden intercourse, the child is completely legitimate even from the sperm of another, just as Ben Sira was legitimate. However, we are concerned about the sperm of another man because the child may eventually marry his sister.[11]

This source states explicitly a number of facts relevant to AID. First, the child born of AID is *kasher* (legitimate); he or she is not the child of adultery since adultery requires an act of intercourse. Therefore, the child is not a *mamzer* and is free to marry any Jew. (By Jewish law, a *mamzer* may not marry a born Jew.) Similarly, the wife is not forbidden to her husband, as she would be if she committed adultery. These sources prove quite clearly that AID is not to be considered adultery.

But the third source does raise the major halakhic problem with AID: the possibility that the child might accidentally marry a biological sibling, conceived by sperm from the same "donor." The possibility of accidental incest can be decreased by using any one donor for only a limited number of inseminations. A leading medical expert has written:

While doctors like to continue using donors of proven fertility, widespread use of a single donor in a limited geographical area could lead to unwitting incest if children of the same donor grow up and marry each other. The possibility is remote, but in Tel Aviv, a marriage has already occurred between two AID children fathered by the same donor. In the United States a similar marriage was stopped by a doctor who revealed to the couple their genetic link. Thus, it seems wise to put some limit on the number of donor pregnancies a man is allowed to initiate.[12]

Certainly doctors have a responsibility to limit the number of inseminations by any one donor. Yet even the remote possibility of incest should not be a major barrier to AID in Jewish law. Rabbi Moshe Feinstein, a leading Orthodox authority, has written:

If the donor is unknown, he [the child of AID] can marry any woman since we go by the majority of women who are permitted to him. In fact, we do not worry that the donor is Jewish, since the majority of such donors are gentile, for we live in cities where the majority is gentile.[13]

Rabbi Feinstein seems to permit AID when the donor is gentile because such a donor would not raise the issue of incest by Jewish law. Similar rulings have been made by Orthodox authorities in Israel.

All of these facts seem to indicate that there is room for a permissive ruling on AID. In fact, there are authorities in the Orthodox, Conservative, and Reform movements who have permitted it. (There are also authorities in all three movements who have forbidden it.) The truth is that for many couples there is no choice. If they wish to achieve pregnancy and if the husband is sterile, AID is the only alternative. It is not explicitly forbidden by Jewish sources; on the contrary, these sources clearly indicate that it is not adultery and that a child conceived by AID is legitimate. Therefore, AID should be considered a legitimate medical alternative for infertile couples.

One major legal obstacle remains. The child, for purposes of Jewish law, remains the child of the donor. If the donor is a gentile, the child is Jewish, since he or she follows the religion of the mother. Yet if the donor is Jewish, questions are raised. If the donor is Kohen or Levi, the child would be a Kohen or Levi regardless of the status of the husband. Similarly, if the husband is a Kohen or Levi and the donor unknown, the child would be a Yisrael. When the husband dies, technically he is still childless, and his wife must submit to *halitzah* (the symbolic release by the brother-in-law allowing the widow to remarry). These are major halakhic problems, particularly if the parents wish to keep the child's biological background a secret.

One fact remains clear from this; since the donor can claim paternity by Jewish law, he would always remain anonymous. Some couples have requested that a relative of the husband donate sperm, keeping it in the family, if you will. This raises numerous problems. When asked whether the seed of the father and brother can be mixed in with that of the husband, Rabbi Solomon Freehof, the leading halakhic scholar of the Reform movement, wrote:

> In the question asked here, the process is much more unacceptable than that of a booster of the husband's seed with the seed of some unknown donor. Here there is added to his seed the seed of his brother and his father, and to the extent that the added seed is the effective seed, which it is meant to be, to that extent it is an incestuous relationship, for the woman is impregnated by the seed of her living husband's brother and/or her husband's father, a totally forbidden incestuous relationship . . . such a mixture should be forbidden by every state. But it must be stressed again that aside from these especially forbidden mixtures, all mixtures of seed seem to be generally prohibited by all the Halachic authorities who have written on the subject.[14]

Freehof's language seems exceptionally strong, considering that such a mixture does not constitute incest. Yet it seems clear that since a relative might try to claim paternity in the future, the preference should be for an anonymous donor. Some doctors mix the sperm of the husband and the donor, but this is not recommended by recent research. Practitioners prefer that the husband and wife have sexual relations the night of the insemination, perhaps increasing the likelihood that one of the husband's sperm might have fertilized the egg.

Although the problem still remains that a child born of AID is halakhically the child of the donor, even this has a possible halakhic solution whereby the child can be called the child of the husband.

Jewish law, like any legal system, is dependent on particular "presumptions." There is a presumption in Jewish law that a child born of a married woman is the child of her husband. The Book of Exodus teaches: "He who strikes his father or his mother shall be put to death" (Exod. 21:15). The question is, how do we know for sure that he is the father. The Talmud says, "Are we not worried lest he not be the father. Rather, we learn that we go by the majority of cases, and the majority of time, sexual relations are with the husband."[15]

This law is developed further in the codes. Even if the husband and wife were separated for up to twelve months before birth, there is a presumption that the child is the husband's.[16] Even if the word goes out that the wife has committed adultery, the child is considered to be the husband's.[17] Jewish law goes by the majority of cases. The husband can deny paternity, but the onus is on him to prove it.

In a case of AID, we may apply the same presumption: that the baby is the child of the husband. If the husband is a Kohen, the child then becomes a Kohen. It is true that by Jewish law, the husband can deny paternity and bring proof that he is not the father. For this reason, AID should never be used without the husband's concurrence. In fact, most physicians insist that the husband sign a legal consent before AID occurs.

One could ask, how can there be a presumption that the husband is the father when in fact he might be sterile? In legal systems legal presumptions are often made whether or not they match the facts. However, in Jewish law we do have another case in which a man is considered the father of a child even though he is not biologically. That case is levirate marriage. When a man dies childless, his brother marries the widow and raises the children in the deceased brother's name. Here is a case in which one man supplies the sperm, but another man claims paternity. Levirate marriage seems to be a strong precedent for AID. The Torah's concern that no man be left childless, even after death, should convince us to permit AID so that no couple be forced to remain childless.

To summarize the Jewish view of this complicated question:

1 Artificial insemination by husband is not a wasting of seed and therefore is permitted.

2 Artificial insemination by donor raises serious questions of Jewish law, causing some authorities in all three movements to forbid it. Yet classic sources seem to indicate that it is permissible, and some contemporary authorities concur.

3 Artificial insemination is not adultery, and the wife is not forbidden to her husband. The child of AID is considered legitimate in every way.

4 There is a concern that the child might marry a biological sibling. Therefore, some authorities insist that the donor be gentile. Couples who use AID should insist that the donor be limited in the number of pregnancies he can cause. If the donor is unknown, there are no limits on whom the child can marry, since we go by the majority.

5 The use of a relative's seed and the mixing of seed are not recommended.

6 A child conceived by AID is presumed to be the child of the husband for purposes of Jewish law. AID should never be done without the husband's consent.

Two other social questions remain. First, should a child born of AID be told of his or her biological origin? There is no simple answer. Adoptions were once kept secret. Today almost all experts say that a child should be told from the beginning that he or she is adopted. We have removed the stigma from adoption. Unfortunately, the stigma has not been removed from AID. Therefore, there is no reason for it to be public knowledge that a child was born after donor insemination. However, a child does have a right to information about his or her biological background. The facts of a child's AID background should be shared with a child when he or she is old enough to understand.

Second, should an unmarried Jewish woman have a child through AID? Once again there are no easy answers. Judaism sees marriage and family as an ideal; a single-parent family built by AID should never replace a family built through marriage. It is true that single-parent families are becoming more common in the Jewish community, and adoption by singles has become legally and socially acceptable. Generally these involve a *b'deavad* (after the fact) situation in which a child or a pregnancy already exists; this is vastly different from creating a child *l'hathilah* (before the fact).

Yet the use of AID is a very real issue for many single Jewish women in their mid- to late thirties. Often such women feel the biological clock ticking but see no prospects for a spouse, particularly if they choose not to intermarry. It is true that a woman is not obligated by traditional halakhah to have children. Yet halakhah does recognize the legitimacy of a woman's desire for children by making marriage to a sterile husband grounds for divorce with the full payment of the *ketubbah*.[18]

An unmarried woman who contemplates AID must realistically assess her motivation, her financial situation, and the implications of her decision. Unfortunately, single women with children are often at a financial disadvantage in our society. It is one matter to be a single parent as a result of divorce, widowhood, or an accidental pregnancy and quite another to deliberately choose that route. How will child care be arranged? How will family and the community at large react? Most important, what are the emotional consequences of a child being raised with an unknown sperm donor as a father? Such a child would need an exceptionally mature, stable, loving mother.

With all these reservations, the use of AID by an unmarried woman cannot receive routine rabbinic approval. Yet the Jewish community ought to be cognizant of the feelings that would motivate a woman to consider this option. Before pursuing AID, an unmarried woman ought to obtain thoughtful rabbinic counseling.

In Vitro Fertilization

In vitro fertilization, sometimes misnamed "test-tube babies," is becoming more and more common. The procedure is exceedingly complicated, very expensive, and still considered experimental by insurance companies and regulatory agencies. Any couple contemplating in vitro fertilization should investigate thoroughly what is involved, what the costs are, and the chances of success. Some couples may feel that the cost and complexity of the procedure are not worth it; they may prefer adoption. For other couples, in vitro fertilization can be the answer to their prayers for a child.

In vitro fertilization raises far fewer questions of Jewish law than artificial insemination because in most cases it is the wife's egg and the husband's sperm that are used. Fertilization itself is artificially accomplished in a petri dish (in vitro means "in glass"). The fertilized ovum is then replanted in the wife's uterus with the hope that it will successfully implant.

Only certain couples are eligible for in vitro fertilization. Both husband and wife must be in good health, and the husband must have a normal sperm count (although in vitro fertilization is occasionally being used when the sperm count is low). The fertility problem must be caused by blockage or damage of a fallopian tube, the place where fertilization normally occurs. This technique makes it possible to bypass the tubes and fertilize in a petri dish.

For in vitro fertilization to succeed, the woman must take a potent fertility drug such as Pergonal to stimulate and regulate ovulation. The effect of this drug must be monitored daily, particularly as ovulation approaches. At the appropriate time, an injection of HCG is given to trigger ovulation. With daily blood tests and sonograms of the ovaries, ovulation can be pinpointed with some accuracy. This daily monitoring may be problematic for Sabbath-observant couples, as discussed in the previous chapter.

When ovulation is imminent, the woman goes into the hospital for a laparoscopy, performed under a general anesthetic, to retrieve the eggs. Pergonal will usually stimulate the development of more than one egg, enabling the doctor to retrieve as many as possible. Meanwhile, the husband is called to the hospital to provide a fresh sperm sample. Sometimes the husband's sperm has been obtained earlier and frozen, in case he is unable to provide a sample at that time. The sperm is treated with chemicals similar to those in the wife's genital tract.

The sperm and the eggs are then placed together in a petri dish with the hope that fertilization will occur. Sometimes as many as five eggs are fertilized at once. They are allowed to sit in a chemical solution until they begin to divide. When an embryo contains four to eight cells, it is replanted in the woman's uterus. Usually, the three healthiest embryos are replanted at one time, with the hope that one will take. Thus it is not unusual for patients using in vitro fertilization to have twins and even triplets.

Recently, a similar procedure, called GIFT (gamete interfallopian transfer), has been developed that is being done experimentally in some cities. Rather than growing in a petri dish, the fertilized ova are transferred directly back into the fallopian tube. The whole procedure can be done while the woman is asleep. This technique can improve the odds and can also bypass some of the ethical problems of growing a conceptus in a petri dish. Yet with either in vitro fertilization or GIFT there is a major problem: What should be done with any extra embryos that are fertilized? The proper handling and disposal of a fertilized ovum raise halakhic questions.

There are several possible options if there is an extra fertilized embryo. These include freezing the embryo for future use by the couple, transplanting the embryo to another woman with no eggs of her own, using the embryo for research, or disposing of the embryo. I will examine each of these possibilities. The Orthodox halakhic scholar Dr. J. David Bleich recommends that only enough eggs be removed from the ovary so that they all can be implanted at one time.[19] This would limit physicians to removing no more than three eggs. Nevertheless, according to physicians, the more eggs that can be removed, the better the success rate.

The freezing of an embryo for future implantation is not routinely practiced in the United States. It is common in some other countries, particularly Australia. Recently it has been done successfully in Israel. While it does raise questions of fetal experimentation, doctors claim that this is a valid way to help infertile couples, that such freezing does not damage the embryos, and that it allows implantation to take place in the next month without the risk of surgery. If it could be shown that such freezing is clinically successful, it could be justified by halakhah.

The freezing of an embryo led to a complicated legal case in Australia. An extremely wealthy couple, being treated by in vitro fertilization, had several embryos frozen for future use. Sadly, they were killed in a plane crash before implantation could take place. The question arose whether these embryos, if successfully implanted in another woman and allowed to come to term, could someday inherit the wealthy couple's estate. The question remains unanswered. I will try to prove in this section on embryo transplants that, for purposes of Jewish law, the embryo is the child of the mother in whose womb it grew.

Questions about experimentation on embryos or their disposal can arise. Is such research permissible by Jewish law? When asked how research on embryos can be justified, one scientist answered:

In our program, all embryos with a normal appearance and growth rate are transferred to patients or are stored frozen for future use by the couple. If an embryo is abnormal, the IVF [in vitro fertilization] team may study it to try to determine the cause of the abnormality. It is thought that because an abnormal embryo is degenerating and will probably soon die, it no longer has the potential for life.[20]

All of these questions are extremely difficult if an embryo is considered a human life. That is the reason why religious groups who believe that life begins at conception have opposed in vitro fertilization. Antiabortion groups, including the Catholic Church, have been vocally against in vitro fertilization.

Judaism does not view this as a problem. Our tradition has never equated abortion with murder. Judaism teaches that a fetus has a potential for life but is not yet a human life. More important, the Talmud says, "Until the fortieth day, the embryo is merely water."[21] To use a small group of cells for medical research or to dispose of them cannot be equated with experimentation on a developed fetus.

Actually, there is scientific evidence that a group of cells at this early stage of development is not yet life. Modern Jewish law defines death as brain death, when there are no longer brain waves. By the same definition, life begins with the first differentiation of brain cells, usually around the sixth week of gestation (parallel to the Talmud's forty days). A blastocyst, or eight-celled embryo, has not yet achieved the status of life.

Another serious halakhic objection to in vitro fertilization has been raised by several authorities. Scholars as varied as J. David Bleich in the Orthodox movement and Solomon Freehof in the Reform movement have warned of the danger of birth defects.[22] It is unknown whether the human manipulation of a sperm and an egg can cause chromosomal or structural damage. If there is a significant danger of birth defects, halakhah would frown on the entire procedure.

Fortunately, the use of in vitro fertilization has not resulted in an increase in birth defects.[23] About 3 percent of babies from naturally occurring pregnancies have some type of defect. The number seems no higher, and may be lower, for in vitro fertilization. Some anticipated dangers, such as the egg being fertilized by two or more sperm, have not been borne out in practice. The body seems to have a way of naturally aborting such embryos so that they do not develop normally.

In vitro fertilization is still in the early stages of development and has a long way to go until perfected. The very process of fertilization outside the body has given us valuable insights into the human reproductive system. There are halakhic objections, but they are relatively minor. The whole procedure can be a valuable tool to help infertile Jewish couples conceive. Yet, like any procedure, in vitro fertilization is particularly open to abuse. Attempts can be made to use in vitro fertilization to grow a baby totally outside the womb. Or it can be used for trivial pursuits, such as picking the baby's sex or hair color. Experiments such as cloning may also be attempted. Once again we must ask: What is the purpose of the experiment? Are scientists trying to help an infertile couple conceive, or are they trying to reenact Huxley's *Brave New World*?

To summarize the Jewish view of in vitro fertilization:

1 In vitro fertilization and GIFT are two procedures that fertilize the wife's egg with the husband's sperm outside the womb. Since there is no donor involved, there are no serious halakhic objections.

2 The largest halakhic problem is the proper disposal of unused fertilized eggs. This concern is addressed by the recommendation that only enough eggs be fertilized as can be immediately reimplanted in the mother.

3 For the first forty days, a fertilized ovum is "mere water," that is, chemicals without intrinsic life. Therefore, Jewish tradition would not forbid freezing of ova

for future implantation, disposal of ova, or even experimentation on those with abnormalities. However, growing a fertilized ovum outside the womb beyond a very short period would not be permitted.

4 Jewish ethics would be concerned with the possibility of birth defects. However, this fear has not been borne out in practice.

5 Therefore, if a couple feel that in vitro fertilization is the best solution to their fertility problem, Jewish law would permit the procedure.

Surrogate Mothers

One day a young Jewish woman made an appointment to see me. She was a professional woman, happily married and mother of two small children. When we met in my office, she told me that she was interested in becoming a surrogate mother. She had enjoyed her two pregnancies but felt that she was not in a position to raise a third child at this time. She wanted to help a Jewish couple unable to conceive, and her husband supported her decision.

I was impressed with her maturity and sincerity. I told her that being a surrogate mother was a wonderful *mitzvah*. I discussed with her the emotional ramifications: How would she explain the pregnancy to family and friends? What would she tell her children? I also warned her of the legal complications, particularly if she received money from the couple adopting the baby. She answered that she did not need the money; she simply felt that this was the right thing to do. Satisfied with her answers, I put her in touch with an attorney who runs a surrogate program. She recently gave birth to a baby boy who was placed with a Jewish couple.

There have been hundreds of surrogate mother arrangements over the last several years. Most go smoothly, to the satisfaction of all parties. However, the recent court case known as "Baby M" sparked a national debate on surrogate motherhood and demonstrated the potential for heartache when something goes wrong. In that case, a couple contracted with a woman to be inseminated with the husband's sperm, and paid her $10,000 for her services. When a baby girl was born, the birth mother refused to give her up, sparking a custody battle that would have tested the wisdom of Solomon. A family court judge upheld the validity of the surrogate contract, awarding custody to the father and his wife and terminating all rights of the surrogate mother. As of this writing, the case is under appeal.

The Baby M case reinforced many of the stereotypes of surrogate mothering. While the contracting couple were wealthy and well educated, the surrogate mother never finished high school and was in a lower income bracket. Many people, including Jewish and Christian religious leaders, feminists, and adoption advocates, attacked surrogate arrangements for developing a class of poor breeder women selling their wombs to the rich. The "Baby M" case also raised Jewish issues, for it involved a contracting father who was Jewish and a surrogate mother who was Christian. In fact, the father told the media that he had sought a surrogate because he had lost his family in the Holocaust and desired a child with a biological connection.

Following the Baby M case, it is important to clarify the Jewish view on surrogate motherhood. How would Judaism view a contract to "rent a womb"? Is this a legitimate option for Jews? What if the surrogate is not Jewish? Finally, what guidance can Judaism give state legislatures that are struggling to regulate this procedure?

It is important to note that the first surrogate mother is found in the Bible. Sarah, unable to conceive, brought her handmaiden Hagar to Abraham. As a result of their union, Ishmael was born. In a similar manner, both Rachel and Leah brought their handmaidens Bilhah and Zilpah to Jacob. Two sons were born to each. Of course, the social milieu of the Bible was quite different from that of today. Polygamy was common, and it was socially acceptable for a man to have a wife and several concubines. The surrogate mother and child simply became part of the man's household.

Today surrogate mothering is a different matter. Couples in which the husband is fertile and the wife infertile use it in order to have a child with a biological connection to the father. Medically the whole procedure is simple, but it can become an emotional and legal quagmire. Some have called surrogate mothering the exact opposite of AID: In the former there is a male donor of sperm; in the latter, a female donor of an egg and a womb. Yet the analogy stops there. There is a world of difference between taking fifteen minutes to give a sperm sample for twenty-five dollars and renting a womb for nine months for thousands of dollars.

Rabbis opposed to surrogate motherhood have identified several problems in terms of Jewish contract law. First, there is a principle that one cannot contract for something not yet in existence.[24] The rabbis of the Talmud would have considered as null and void a contract to place a baby not yet conceived. Another problem with a surrogate contract is the principle of *asmakhtah*. According to Jewish law, a contract is valid only if we can reasonably presume that the intentions of both parties are serious, deliberate, and final. Without such deliberate intention, the contract is an *asmakhtah* and is void, for "an *asmakhtah* does not give title."[25] It is questionable whether a contract that binds a woman to terminate her parental rights to a child not yet conceived could be done with full intent and no equivocation, as required by Jewish law. Finally, Jewish law would question whether one can legally bind oneself to a course of action involving physical danger. Since pregnancy does involve some risk, such a contract may violate Jewish ethical principles.

On the basis of these considerations, Jewish tradition would question the legal validity of a surrogate contract. Nevertheless, according to the Talmud, a woman who makes such a contract has a moral obligation to fulfill her word. In this spirit the sages ruled: "He who exacted punishment from the generation of the Flood and from the generation of the Tower of Babel will also exact punishment from one who does not abide by his word."[26]

Obviously, civil law, not Jewish law, is used when a contract is drawn up today between a surrogate mother and an infertile couple. In such a case, we follow Samuel's dictum in the Talmud: *dinah d'malkhutah dinah* ("the law of the land is the law").[27] If the law of the land permits it, a Jewish couple would be permitted to arrange a contract with a surrogate mother. Yet such a couple should be warned that the law is in a state of flux, with legislation pending in numerous states. There is a possibility that the legal validity of a surrogate arrangement will not be upheld by the courts, and the case will become a custody battle between the surrogate mother and the biological father.

After the Baby M case, legislators are turning to religious leaders for guidance on this difficult issue. From a Jewish perspective, it would be wrong to outlaw a procedure that has the potential of helping so many couples and works smoothly in the overwhelming majority of cases. Judaism would respect the rights of adults to consent to and be morally bound by such an arrangement. Yet Jewish tradition would recommend that such a contract not be absolutely legally binding. In my mind, the only sensible approach for state legislatures would be to permit such arrangements while allowing a waiting period after birth before the birth mother's rights are terminated. Surrogate motherhood would then be handled precisely like an adoption. Such an escape clause for the birth mother might be an anathema to an infertile couple, but it would avoid the heartache of the Baby M case and serve to make such contracts more socially acceptable. Such legislation can only help infertile couples in the long run.

To prevent a surrogate arrangement from degenerating into a custody battle, the surrogate mother must have a clear understanding of the consequences of her actions. She should have experienced pregnancy and already had children, be psychologically stable, and, if married, have the full support of her husband. She should also have psychological counseling both before insemination and throughout the course of her pregnancy.

Using a married woman as a surrogate mother can present another problem. In discussing AID, we mentioned that both Jewish law and civil law in many states presume that a woman's husband is the father of her biological child. These laws work in favor of AID but against surrogate motherhood. To overcome this presumption, the surrogate's husband would have to clearly agree to the insemination, avoid sexual relations with his wife during the insemination period, and unequivocally state that he is not the biological father. Obviously, his support and cooperation are vital.

Another difficulty that could arise in a surrogate mother arrangement is that every state in the union outlaws baby buying. Paying a woman a fee to place her baby for adoption, even if the biological father is paying the fee, can easily be construed as baby buying. Occasionally a woman is willing to carry a pregnancy for an unknown couple for altruistic reasons, with no compensation. Even in this rare case, there are fees such as medical, counseling, and living expenses that the couple should pay. The legal problems are serious and should be studied carefully by any couple contemplating surrogate parenting.

Advocates of surrogate mothering deny that it is baby buying. In her book *New Conceptions,* Lori Andrews writes:

The use of a surrogate mother differs in some important ways from paying a pregnant woman for her child. First, the contract is made before the woman is pregnant, and thus it is less likely that she will be taken advantage of. Moreover, since the adopting father is the natural father, the child is more likely to be given a good home.[28]

Unfortunately, the courts may not necessarily interpret it this way.

A final argument has been raised particularly by feminists who are opposed to surrogate mothering. They have claimed that it will set up a class of poor "breeder women" producing babies for the rich. I find this to be a specious argument. First, it assumes that all surrogate mothers are poor, an argument shown false by my first example in this section. Second, it does not respect the carefully considered choice of those women, both rich and poor, who have decided to become surrogates out of a desire to help an infertile couple. Finally, it plays into the vicious stereotype that infertility is a rich person's disease and a solution can be bought for money.

With all these legal and ethical questions, why would a couple prefer a surrogate mother over adoption? There are a number of reasons. Many couples believe adoption is too difficult. Adoption is difficult but not impossible (see Chapter 8) and is generally far less costly than hiring a surrogate mother. Some couples fear that with an adopted child, there is no control over genetic background. This is true, but a good agency or intermediary can screen the biological parents of a child being placed for adoption. Besides, people who work with adoptive families have discovered that environment is as important as genetics in defining the character, personality, and even the intelligence of a child.

The main reason couples prefer a surrogate mother is to ensure a biological connection from the husband to the child. From my counseling experience, men seem to need this biological connection even more than women. From a halakhic perspective, this may even make some sense. A husband can fulfill the technical halakhic requirement of "be fruitful and multiply" with a surrogate; he cannot do so when he adopts. However, most men who seek a surrogate are motivated not by halakhic considerations but by an emotional need for biological continuity. Nevertheless, men ought to seriously consider adoption.

An important thesis of this book is that biology is secondary in Judaism. The man and woman who nurture and raise a child take priority over the man and woman who provide the genetic material. Jewish tradition teaches that whoever raise an orphan in their home, Scripture considers them as if they gave birth to that child. Given a choice between adoption and surrogate motherhood, Judaism would opt for adoption.

The question remains: If, after careful consideration of the emotional and legal ramifications of surrogate motherhood, a couple choose to go ahead, what is the status of the child? Here we follow the laws of adoption (see Chapter 7). The baby follows the religion of the surrogate mother. If she is not Jewish, the baby is not Jewish and must be formally converted, including ritual circumcision for a boy and immersion in a *mikvah* for both a boy and a girl. Also, a converted child cannot be a Kohen or Levi.

If the surrogate mother is Jewish, the baby is Jewish. If she is married, both she and her husband must clearly indicate that he is not the biological father. We would then treat the case as if she was unmarried and depend on her word as to the identity of the father. This follows the ruling of Rabban Gamliel in the Mishnah: "If she [a single woman] is pregnant, and they say to her, 'what is the status of this embryo?' and she answers, 'It is by so-and-so and he is a priest,' Rabban Gamliel and Rabbi Eliezer say, she is believed."[29] Therefore, if the husband who donated the sperm is a Kohen or Levi, so is the child.

Obviously, this is a complicated question. Any couple contemplating a surrogate mother arrangement should see not only a competent attorney but also a sensitive rabbi.

To summarize the Jewish view on surrogate motherhood:

1 Surrogate motherhood raises numerous legal and ethical questions, including the validity of a contract for purposes of conceiving a baby, the possibility of baby buying, and the ethics of developing a poor class of "breeder women." Of these objections, the first is the most serious in terms of Jewish law.

2 Jewish tradition would question whether a surrogate contract could be legally binding but would consider it morally binding. However, we follow civil law in these matters with the warning that the law is currently

in a state of flux, with huge legal and emotional risks if something goes wrong.

3 States ought to enact legislation permitting such contracts, with an escape clause for the mother if she changes her mind within a certain waiting period.

4 Adoption would be preferable to surrogate motherhood because it raises fewer legal and emotional problems. Judaism teaches that a man does not need a biological connection with a child in order to be the true father.

5 If a surrogate mother is used, the status of the child follows that of the surrogate. If she is gentile, the child must be converted. If she is married, her husband must clearly approve and sign a document waiving any claim to paternity. The surrogate is then believed as to the identity of the biological father.

6 For a Jewish woman to become a surrogate mother and help an infertile couple have a baby is a great *mitzvah*. However, such a woman must be stable enough to understand the seriousness of her decision and the potential for heartbreak should she change her mind.

Embryo Transplants

One other method of conception is becoming available through modern medical technology. Doctors have successfully implanted an embryo in a woman who has a normal uterus but is unable to produce eggs. In fact, doctors have successfully performed a complete ovary transplant. These techniques resemble surrogate mothering, without the legal complications. These methods are certainly permissible by Jewish law and should be encouraged if they can help an infertile couple have a child. The only question is the status of the baby. Or, to put it more simply, who is the mother?

The matter of an ovarian transplant is simple. Jewish legal scholars have determined that a transplanted organ becomes part of the living body of a recipient. For example, by Jewish law when a person dies, his kidneys, even if removed, must be buried with him. However, if the kidney is donated to a recipient, it becomes a living part of his body and will eventually be buried with him. Similarly, when a woman receives an ovarian transplant, that ovary becomes part of her body and she should be considered the mother of a baby produced by the new ovary.

A more difficult halakhic problem is raised when a fertilized ovum is transplanted into another woman's uterus. This procedure is sometimes done by flushing a fertilized ovum from a donor and transplanting it into the host mother. Also, it is done as a result of in vitro fertilization, whereby extra fertilized eggs are transplanted into another woman.

Several questions are related to the problem of who the mother is. If the donor is gentile and the host mother Jewish, is the baby Jewish? Do we need a *pidyon ha-ben* if it is the donor's second child but the host mother's first child? Who is the mother according to Jewish law regarding various questions of incest?

Several sources indicate that the mother, for purposes of Jewish law, is the birth mother, not the donor. One such source is the aggadic story regarding the birth of Dinah to Leah. According to the legend, Dinah was originally a boy. However, Leah, in a moment of prophecy, saw that there were twelve tribes destined to be born from Jacob. She had six sons, the maidservants had two sons each, leaving two sons yet to be born. Leah saw that she was carrying a son in her womb and realized that only one son would then be born to her sister Rachel. Saddened for Rachel, she prayed and her fetus was changed in utero to a female.[30] The story is told slightly differently in Targum Yonatan (Gen. 30:21). According to this Aramaic version of the Bible, there was an actual embryo exchange. The embryo of Dinah moved from Rachel to Leah; the embryo of Joseph from Leah to Rachel. According to this legend, Dinah was conceived in Rachel, was born in Leah, and is called the daughter of Leah. This would indicate that the birth mother gives a child its status.

There is a principle that we cannot learn Jewish law from an aggadic story. Yet there also is a halakhic precedent brought by Rabbi Solomon Freehof that the birth mother is the mother by Jewish law.[31] A pregnant woman who converts to Judaism also converts her fetus. At conception, the mother is gentile; at birth she is Jewish. The baby is Jewish, indicating that the mother's status at the moment of birth determines the baby's status. These sources indicate that, for purposes of Jewish law, the donor is irrelevant. This would parallel the case of artificial insemination, in which the status of the donor did not affect the status of the child.

There is an opinion that disagrees, teaching that a child receives its status on the fortieth day after conception. Dr. Fred Rosner writes:

> Based on several Jewish sources, [Rabbi Azriel] Rosenfeld concludes that if fetal transplantation is performed after forty days post conception, the child is considered to be the legal offspring of its biological parents since the child became "completed" while still in the biological mother's body, and therefore, she is regarded as having given birth to it.[32]

At this point, there have been no cases of a fetus being transplanted later than a few days after conception. Therefore, it seems reasonable to conclude that, by Jewish law, the mother is the woman who gives birth, not the woman who donates the egg. We follow her status in determining such factors as the Jewishness of the child and the need for a *pidyon ha-ben*.

Conclusions

Many readers of this chapter will be surprised at some of its conclusions, since religion is usually perceived as conservative, teaching people to accept their fate as God's will. Yet this chapter advocates aggressive action to heal infertility. It quotes Jewish sources in order to support the use of radical and sometimes controversial medical techniques to help an infertile couple conceive.

Jewish tradition has never accepted passivity in the face of human suffering. Neither Sarah nor Rachel nor Hannah was passive when she failed to conceive. Judaism teaches that doctors are commanded to heal, and the acquisition of medical skills and knowledge is a gift from God. Whether the treatment be drugs or surgery, artificial insemination or in vitro fertilization, Jewish tradition would permit its use. The overriding concern is to fulfill the commandment "Be fruitful and multiply."

Does this mean that anything is permitted? The answer is no. We must look at the overall purpose of any procedure. Judaism would frown on artificial insemination of a single woman who simply wants to avoid the encumbrances of marriage. It would not permit the transfer of a fertilized ovum to another woman because the mother wants to avoid the discomfort of pregnancy. It would certainly outlaw the use of in vitro fertilization to clone an identical replica of a human being or to create a super race. Any technology can be misused; that is the lesson of the Tower of Babel. However, using technology to help a childless couple conceive is certainly permissible. We might even say that it is obligatory.

A couple facing infertility should seek the best medical help they can find. They should aggressively pursue pregnancy to the maximum that their emotions and financial resources will allow. Jewish tradition advocates nothing less. And the couple should feel the moral support of the entire Jewish community in their quest.

When men fight, and one of them pushes a pregnant woman and a miscarriage results, but no other damage ensues, the one responsible shall be fined according as the woman's husband may exact from him, the payment to be based on reckoning.

(Exod. 21:22)

⊠ 6

Pregnancy Loss

Let us begin by considering three couples with fertility problems. Their experiences are different, yet they share something. All three are Jewish, all three were childless and desperately wanted a child, and all three wives managed to become pregnant.

The first couple achieved pregnancy three times. Each time the pregnancy ended in miscarriage. They have sought medical treatment, but doctors have been unsuccessful in finding the cause of the recurring miscarriages. Meanwhile, they have become more depressed and anxious, unsure whether they can face another pregnancy. The woman poured out her frustrations in a letter to me: "First of all, with each miscarriage it became clear that no one in the community knows how to respond. . . . While the Jewish community has prescribed mourning routines for the death of an individual, it seems that a miscarriage is treated as a minor occurrence that is barely acknowledged. Still, we bear the emotional scars of having experienced the deaths of three potential children."

The second couple also achieved pregnancy. Everything went fine for the first six months, and then the wife began to suspect that something was wrong; the baby was not responding normally. She expressed her fears to her doctor, who was unusually reticent. Later she realized that her doctor did not believe in abortion and so was reluctant to share with her the full truth. A second doctor told her that her baby was badly deformed; in the seventh month of pregnancy she had an abortion.

The third couple successfully carried their baby to term. However, their son was born prematurely, with serious circulatory and respiratory problems. After lying in an incubator in the hospital's neonatal unit for six days, the baby died. This young couple had prepared for the joy of bringing a new baby home; instead, they faced their first encounter with a funeral home and a cemetery.

This couple came to me a year after the death of their child. They told me of their discussion with the rabbi and funeral director. Their son's body would be circumcised in the funeral home. There would be no funeral, no mourning, no *shiva*, no *Kaddish*. The baby would be buried in a corner of the cemetery, and they would be expected to go about their lives as if nothing had happened. Now, a year was almost past, and they were plaintive: "Rabbi, can't we light a *yahrzeit* candle and say *Kaddish*? We need to mourn for our son."

Infertility is not only the inability to become pregnant; it is also the inability to carry pregnancy to term and give birth to a viable baby. Many couples become pregnant, only to lose the baby along the way. Sometimes they miscarry, or the baby is stillborn. Sometimes they must face the painful decision whether to abort a fetus that is diseased or deformed. And sometimes an unhealthy baby is born, only to linger for days or weeks in a hospital nursery before succumbing.

In many ways, pregnancy loss is even more painful than infertility. An infertile couple mourn the loss of a dream, the dream of a child they cannot conceive. With pregnancy loss, a child has been conceived. A real baby, who can usually be identified as a boy or girl, has been lost. Whether the loss is from a miscarriage, a stillbirth, the abortion of a deformed fetus, or the death of a newborn, the pain and loss are profound. There is a need to mourn.

Marc Silver wrote a sensitive newspaper column after he and his wife chose to abort a fetus afflicted with Tay-Sachs disease. The column was entitled "After Our Abortion, No One Said 'I'm Sorry.' " His words capture the feelings of a couple who have suffered a pregnancy loss:

> We lost this child, the chance to hold her, love her and raise her; we lost the joy of anticipation about her future; we lost the many little questions we had. Would she be a good sleeper? Would she inherit the musical talent on both sides of our families? Who would she look like? What would she become when she grows up? I think the worst part of our loss was the awareness that we would never know this child. My image of her will always be frozen in time: delicate and tiny, she was like a flower just beginning to bloom.
>
> All we wanted to hear from people were the words "I'm sorry." We wanted to know that we weren't alone, that others felt for us and understood our sorrow. We were grateful that modern medicine prevented us from the tragedy of having a Tay-Sachs child, but our gratitude did not mitigate the sense of loss.[1]

Jewish law has no mourning rituals for this type of death. This absence gives a clear message to the bereaved couple; their loss was not a real loss, their baby was not a real person. A couple who miscarry are usually told, "There was probably something wrong with the fetus. You can always have another." This is beside the point. Another will be beloved, but it cannot replace the one that was just lost. That fetus may have been only a few months old, or it may have been deformed. The couple may even have chosen to abort it, yet that loss is real.

Susan Borg and Judith Lasker have written a sensitive book on this issue called *When Pregnancy Fails.* In their chapter on religion, they describe the pain associated with the lack of religious ritual at times of pregnancy loss:

At birth and at death especially, the community joins with a family in religious rites either of celebration or of mourning. Even without formal religious ceremonies, such significant events as a birth or a death are still announced and marked in some public fashion.

Yet when these two events occur together, there is rarely any ritual. Even if an infant lives for several days or weeks, the ceremonies are brief or non-existent. There is seldom the coming together of family and community in a way that offers hope and comfort. All the psychological and social benefits of birth and death rituals are withheld from the family; once more they are given the message, in yet another way, that their loss isn't very important, that their baby wasn't a real person.[2]

Judaism, like many other religions, does not fully recognize the loss of a fetus or a premature baby. Only when a baby survives thirty days is it considered fully viable by Jewish law. Only then are there the full mourning practices, including *shiva* and *Kaddish.* Most of Jewish law was crystallized in an age when many babies were born and a high percentage did not survive. If families were to fully mourn every infant, they would have been in a constant state of mourning.

Yet the absence of mourning rituals should not make the parents feel that their baby was not a real person or that its death was not a real loss. Judaism does recognize the existence and loss of a fetus forty days and over. A full-term baby is a living human being, and after the head comes forth the baby cannot be killed even if the birth process threatens the mother's life. In truth, there are different stages of existence and viability for a baby from conception through birth until thirty days. By exploring these stages, we can better understand how Judaism views pregnancy loss.

Pregnancy Loss from a Jewish Perspective

From the perspective of Jewish law, there are four stages in the development of a baby, with discrete criteria for each stage: (1) the first forty days after conception; (2) the forty-first day until birth; (3) the first thirty days of life; and (4) after thirty days. Let us explore each stage.

The first forty days after conception. Judaism does not teach that life begins at conception; on the contrary, for the first forty days an embryo is considered mere water. The decision arises in an interesting context. The daughter of a Kohen can eat *terumah* (special offerings that a priest and his family can eat). If she marries a Yisrael, she can no longer eat *terumah*. If she is subsequently widowed and has no children, she can once again eat *terumah*. The question is, what if she is pregnant? The Gemarah answers the question: "Rav Hisda taught, let her immerse [in a *mikvah*] and eat (*terumah*) for forty days. If she is not pregnant, she is not pregnant. If she is pregnant, the fetus is merely water."[3]

This decision, arising in the context of the laws of priesthood, was applied by the rabbis to other cases. Thus, Judaism is more permissive toward abortion during the first forty days (although it never condones abortion without good reason). If a woman miscarries within forty days, a subsequent pregnancy would be considered the firstborn. If it is a boy, that baby would require a *pidyon ha-ben*.

For halakhic purposes, Jewish law treats a miscarriage in the first forty days as a nonevent. It is the same ruling that allowed us to permit in vitro fertilization (see Chapter 5). Whereas right-to-life advocates, who claim that life begins at conception, have denounced in vitro fertilization, Judaism, which considers such an embryo "mere water," permits in vitro fertilization.

Most miscarriages within forty days of conception pass unnoticed. There is not the sense of loss and grieving that a woman who miscarries later in pregnancy would feel. In truth, it makes sense not to give an embryo of forty days the same consideration as a more developed fetus. Such an embryo has not begun cell differentiation or the development of nerve cells. If death is considered the cessation of brain activity, then we would be hard put to call a ball of cells with no brain activity a life. It is at best a potential life. Therefore, its loss has no halakhic consequences.

The forty-first day until birth. After forty days a fetus is still not considered a full life, but it does have a status in Jewish law. The quote at the beginning of this chapter speaks of a pregnant woman who loses her fruit as the result of a man's carelessness. Although the man must pay a fine to the husband, he is not charged with murder, as he would be if the fetus had the status of a human being. To kill the fetus is a crime and a monetary payment must be made, but it is not murder.

On the basis of this verse, Judaism has never equated abortion with murder. In fact, Judaism has permitted abortion, and even required it under certain circumstances. The Mishnah teaches:

If a woman is having difficult labor, we can cut up the fetus in her womb and remove it limb by limb, since her life takes precedence over its life. When the majority [of the fetus] has come out, we do not touch it, for we do not put aside one life for another.[4]

Commentators have understood "the majority of the fetus" to be the head; only when the head comes out does the fetus have a full claim on life. Before that, it is considered by Maimonides to be a pursuer (*rodef*) who can be killed to save a life.[5]

These prooftexts show that a fetus in the womb does not have a full claim on life in Jewish law. It is not yet considered a *nefesh* (living thing). Judaism would allow abortion under certain circumstances. (The question of fetal abnormalities will be discussed later in the chapter.) However, that does not mean that the fetus is "mere water," with no status in Jewish law. In a number of areas, that fetus does have halakhic status. When a woman miscarries after forty days, there are halakhic consequences.

Jewish law teaches that when a fetus begins to take on a human form (at about three months), it becomes the firstborn for purposes of a *pidyon ha-ben*. If the woman miscarries at that point, a future boy will not require a *pidyon ha-ben*. To quote the exact law in Rabbi Hayim Halevy Donin's *To Be a Jew:*

> A first-born male child who is born following a previous miscarriage by the mother does not require a Pidyon HaBen, if the miscarriage took place after the third month of pregnancy. If the miscarriage took place during the first forty days of pregnancy, a Pidyon HaBen for a son born afterwards is required. After forty days and until such time as the fetus develops definite characteristics, a Pidyon HaBen is still required, but the blessing recited by the father is omitted. In all such questions, the guidance of a rabbi should be sought.[6]

Jewish law recognizes the status of a baby who is miscarried in another area, the laws of *mikvah*. The Torah teaches that a woman who gives birth counts seven days after the birth of a male, fourteen after the birth of a female (see Lev. 12:1–5). She then counts seven clean days and immerses herself in a *mikvah*. A woman who miscarries after forty-one days must keep the same laws. The Mishnah teaches, "If a woman miscarries on the fortieth day, we do not worry that it is a child. However, on the forty-first day she sits the count for a male, a female and a *niddah* [menstruating woman]."[7] She must wait the maximum number of days, that is, fourteen days plus an additional clean seven, before going to the *mikvah,* as if she gave birth to a full-term female child.

The laws of both a *pidyon ha-ben* and *mikvah* reflect the view that an actual child was lost, although there is no formal mourning. There is one other law that recognizes the reality of a miscarriage. The Mishnah teaches that if a couple live together ten years without a child, they cannot put off fulfilling the *mitzvah* of procreation any longer (see Chapter 2). The original principle (not practiced since the Middle Ages) is that after ten years a man must find a new wife. But the Mishnah also states that "if she miscarries, they count from the time of the miscarriage." In other words, when a miscarriage occurs, the count starts over; the couple has ten more years to try to conceive.

Miscarriage is a sad event, but it is also a hopeful sign, since it is evidence that pregnancy can occur. A couple can take encouragement that they are fertile and that the next pregnancy may produce the child they want.

The first thirty days of life. From the moment a child's head emerges from the womb, it is a full human being with all the rights thereof. By Jewish law it can own property and inherit, and to kill the child would be an act of murder.[8] Even if the completion of the birth threatens the mother's life, the baby cannot be killed, for one life is not set aside for another. This child is clearly a "life."

Yet the child still is not considered a fully viable human being. In the Book of Numbers, Moses is commanded by God to take a census of the tribe of Levi. "Record the Levites by ancestral house and by clan; record every male among them from the age of one month up" (Num. 3:15). On the basis of this verse, the Midrash teaches, "Because an infant of one day old is not definitely viable, but one of a month old is definitely known to be viable."[9] Only after thirty days is an infant presumed to be a *bar kyama* (viable).

This law has many practical consequences. First, a *pidyon ha-ben* takes place on the thirty-first day, when the child has been established as a *bar kyama.* In the sad event that the baby dies before thirty days, the usual laws of mourning do not apply. There is no rending of clothing.[10] The Talmud teaches, "Before thirty days an infant [who dies] is taken out in arms and buried by one woman and two men. We do not stand in the rows and do not say the blessing for mourners or the traditional consolations. After thirty days it is buried in a casket."[11]

After thirty days. After thirty days, a baby is a *bar kyama*. Its viability has been proved, and it is considered fully human. If the baby should die, it receives all the rites of mourning, including *Kaddish* and *shiva*. Only now is it fully recognized as a "life" by Jewish law.

Dealing with Miscarriage

My wife recently received an invitation to a baby shower. She was quite surprised, because her European parents had taught her not to buy baby gifts until the baby is born. To do so would be to tempt the "evil eye"; Jews therefore do not have baby showers. This is one of Judaism's oldest superstitions. Yet like many superstitions, it contains a grain of wisdom. One never knows how a pregnancy will turn out. The proper time for celebration seems to be after the birth.

In fact, a miscarriage occurs in 15 to 20 percent of all conceptions. Usually it happens so early in pregnancy that it passes unnoticed, at the point when the embryo is "mere water," to use Rav Hisda's term. The problem comes for the couple dealing with a miscarriage later in pregnancy, when they have begun to anticipate the arrival of a baby.

A miscarriage can occur for a number of reasons. Most occur in the first twelve weeks, usually because of an abnormality in the embryo. If a woman habitually miscarries early in pregnancy, she and her husband should see a genetic counselor to try to find a cause. A miscarriage that occurs later (thirteenth to twentieth week) usually involves a normal fetus that did not attach properly to the uterus or the placenta. Sometimes the cervix is overly weak or dilates early (called an incompetent cervix). A woman should check to see if a congenital problem with the uterus or cervix caused the miscarriage. Such problems can sometimes be corrected surgically. Hormonal deficiency or various diseases may also cause miscarriage.

Guilt is often associated with miscarriage. A woman may feel that she is the cause; if she had been less active, rested more, or gone to the hospital earlier, she might have prevented the miscarriage from occurring. Actually, there is no medical evidence that a woman's activity increases the likelihood of miscarriage. In his book *Pregnancy, Birth and Family Planning,* Dr. Alan Guttmacher writes, "You cannot shake a good human egg loose any more than you can shake a good unripe apple from the apple tree."[12] It is rare that a woman could have done anything to prevent the miscarriage. There are usually valid medical reasons why the pregnancy failed.

Still, a couple will react to miscarriage with shock, anger, and grief, all the normal emotions associated with loss. They need a chance to mourn. It is insensitive to treat a miscarriage as a nonevent or to tell a couple, "A miscarriage is nature's way of sparing you from having an imperfect baby." There may be truth to that statement, but it does not relieve the sense of loss. The couple must mourn the loss of this baby before going on to try for another.

Here Judaism does give us insight. There is no formal mourning, but, as pointed out earlier, Jewish law does recognize a miscarriage as a real event and the baby as a real person. The laws of *pidyon ha-ben, mikvah,* and infertility are all affected. The miscarriage cannot be ignored. It must be acknowledged and discussed, particularly by the husband and wife. By openly discussing the baby they lost, a couple can help the healing process begin.

Judaism recognizes the reality of miscarriage in another way. Usually Orthodox authorities forbid birth control for a couple with no children. However, an exception has been made by many authorities for a couple who suffer from habitual miscarriages. Rabbi David Feldman, a Conservative rabbi, writes, "In the matter . . . of chronic miscarriages, where contraception was requested in order to be spared this futile pain, many authorities reason that since no viable child would in any case be born, one might permit an otherwise forbidden contraceptive."[13] The pain is real, and Jewish authorities recognize it.

Habitual miscarriage can be viewed as any other form of infertility. The best medical treatment should be sought to see if a congenital or a genetic problem is the cause. Ultimately, no couple should have to suffer the pain of repeated unsuccessful pregnancies. Judaism puts the greater emphasis on raising a child, not on giving birth. Such a couple should seriously consider adoption.

Amniocentesis and Jewish Law

Modern medical techniques have raised serious dilemmas for halakhic authorities. One of the most difficult is the question of amniocentesis. The primary purpose of this procedure is to test if a fetus is normal or abnormal, with the option of aborting an abnormal fetus. Obviously, right-to-life groups strongly oppose this procedure. Judaism has always been more liberal on questions of abortion, but it has never been permissive. The question is, does Judaism permit the deliberate abortion of a fetus because it is diseased or deformed? If the answer is no, there can be no room to permit amniocentesis.

Amniocentesis is usually performed between the fifteenth and sixteenth weeks of pregnancy. A hollow needle is inserted through the abdominal wall and uterus to obtain amniotic fluid. Usually ultrasound is used so that the position of the fetus can be shown, ensuring that the doctor will not pierce it with the needle. Still there are risks. Infections can occur, and about 1 percent of the time amniocentesis can cause miscarriage. For this reason, doctors recommend the procedure only for women over thirty-five or women with a history of fetal abnormality.

Amniocentesis can identify a number of abnormalities, as well as other information, such as the sex of a child. It can be used to tell if the baby has Down's syndrome, a chromosomal abnormality resulting in mental retardation and other medical problems. It can also recognize such developmental abnormalities as spina bifida (open or malformed spine), which often leads to paralysis and possibly brain damage. For Jewish couples, amniocentesis can be particularly valuable in that it can identify Tay-Sachs disease and other Jewish genetic diseases. Tay-Sachs is a devastating disease in which a vital enzyme called hexosaminidase A is missing. A baby with Tay-Sachs disease develops normally for five or six months, then begins to deteriorate. The baby loses the ability to sit and hold up his or her head and eventually becomes blind, suffers convulsions, and cannot swallow food. Death occurs in the third or fourth year of life.[14]

As mentioned, amniocentesis cannot be performed until the fourth or fifth month of pregnancy, and it takes about three weeks to find out the test results. Therefore, if a couple is contemplating terminating the pregnancy, abortion would not take place until the end of the second trimester. How does Jewish law view an abortion that is undertaken because of fetal abnormality?

Judaism does not equate abortion with murder. Abortion is permissible and sometimes mandatory if there is a threat to the mother's life or health. The question is, does giving birth to an abnormal baby constitute such a threat? Judaism does not permit abortion simply out of pity for the baby, just as it does not permit infanticide of a deformed baby. Even a sick baby has a full claim on life. The only criterion whereby Judaism can countenance abortion is a threat to the mother's health.

There are precedents for permitting an abortion when the mother's mental health is threatened. A very extreme case is found in the Talmud.[15] It involved a pregnant woman condemned to be executed. (Capital punishment was discussed in the Talmud theoretically but rarely applied in practice.) The Talmud permits an abortion in such a case rather than delaying the execution, for such a delay would cause pain and anguish to the mother. The legal precedent established is that the mother's pain comes first.

This is the basic principle of halakhah. An abortion

would be permitted when birth would cause either harm or degradation to the mother. It is not permitted simply out of pity. This principle is summarized by Rabbi David Feldman:

> The principle that a mother's pain "comes first," however, is the most pervasive of all factors in the consideration of the abortion question. It produces the following generalization: if a possibility or probability exists that a child may be born defective and the mother would seek an abortion on grounds of pity for the child whose life will be less than normal, the Rabbi would decline permission. Since we don't know for sure that he will be born defective, and since we don't know how bad that defective life will be (in view of the availability of prosthetic devices, etc.), and since no permission exists in Jewish law to kill born defectives, permission on those grounds would be denied. If, however, an abortion for that same potentially deformed child were sought on the grounds that the possibility is causing severe anguish to the mother, permission would be granted. The foetus is unknown, future, potential, part of "the secrets of God"; the mother is known, present, alive and asking for compassion.[16]

Thus, Jewish law seems to sanction abortion of a defective fetus when there is good cause to believe that the mother's well-being will be threatened. It should be noted, however, that many Orthodox authorities have not permitted abortion on the grounds of fetal abnormalities. Rabbi J. David Bleich writes, "Until very recently virtually all rabbinic authorities who have addressed themselves to the question of the permissibility of destroying a defective fetus have ruled that the presence of physical or mental abnormality does not, in itself, constitute halachic grounds for sanctioning termination of pregnancy."[17]

However, Bleich continues by analyzing the more liberal opinion of Rabbi Eliezer Waldenberg, an eminent Orthodox authority on medical ethics, who permits the abortion of a fetus known to have Tay-Sachs disease. He allows such an abortion through the seventh month but not beyond that since by then a fetus may be viable. Rabbi Waldenberg based his opinion on many earlier authorities, particularly Rabbi Jacob Emden, who permitted abortion in cases of "grave necessity."[18]

Thus, Jewish law would sanction amniocentesis when there is substantial fear that a baby would be born with a serious abnormality. Every Jewish couple who marry should be tested to see if they carry Tay-Sachs disease. If both the husband and the wife are carriers, the odds are one in four that a child will have the disease. Certainly they should have amniocentesis and have the opportunity to consider abortion rather than face the certainty of giving birth to a child who will suffer and die from this deadly disease.

For other diseases, the deciding factor is the mother's well-being. How painful will it be for her to raise a child with a particular birth defect? No abortion should ever be considered for light or superficial reasons such as the "wrong" sex. Parents who learn that a fetus has Down's syndrome should think twice before considering abortion. Most babies with this chromosomal condition turn out to be loving, beautiful children and adults. More and more synagogues are recognizing the importance of educational programs for mentally retarded children. And almost any rabbi, myself included, can speak with tears in his eyes of the bar or bat mitzvah of a child with Down's syndrome. These children, like any other, deserve a chance at life.

In the last few years, a new test has been developed called chorion villus sampling (CVS). The test involves a biopsy of the placenta, and it can indicate the same fetal problems as amniocentesis. The advantage of CVS is that it can be performed during the ninth week of pregnancy and results can be obtained within a day or so. If an abortion is chosen, the simpler dilation and curettage (D and C) method can be used. On the other hand, abortion following amniocentesis would take place near the end of the second trimester and require a saline abortion, a more complicated procedure. Also, aborting a second-trimester pregnancy is far more wrenching for a couple than is an earlier abortion. The disadvantage of CVS is that currently there is a higher rate of miscarriage than with amniocentesis. However, this may be lessened as doctors become more proficient with the procedure.

Ultimately, the decision whether to have CVS or amniocentesis is a very personal one. I know a Jewish woman, pregnant with her fourth child and almost forty, who went in for amniocentesis at her physician's recommendation. The doctor asked her whether she would abort an abnormal fetus. She answered absolutely no. The physician then told her that he saw no need for the test, and she had to agree. She was willing to take a chance and willing to share her love even with an imperfect child.

When a Baby Is Lost

Few events are as sad as the death of a newborn baby. Whether the baby is stillborn or lingers in a hospital incubator for several weeks or more, the loss is an overwhelming tragedy. A family who have made plans to bring home a newborn suddenly are forced to deal with funeral homes and cemeteries. Often they are young people, inexperienced with death. They are easy targets for shrewd undertakers who see the family as a source of good income. Some funeral directors will push a family to purchase a fancy casket and have a large funeral to pay proper last respects to their baby.

Any family who suffer this kind of loss should contact their rabbi immediately for help in handling the baby's burial in a respectful and traditional way. The rabbi will know which funeral home to recommend. (In my own community, there is a Jewish funeral home that will handle the death of an infant without charge.)

Jewish tradition teaches that there are no *kriyah* (the rending of garments), no funeral, and no formal mourning for an infant thirty days old or less. Such an infant is called a *nefel*, literally "one who fell." The Hevra Kaddisha (Jewish burial society) should prepare the body by washing it and wrapping it in a blanket. A simple box or casket should be used.

There is a well-established custom that the Hevra Kaddisha circumcises a baby boy who has not yet had a *brit milah*. They may insist on this procedure. Although it is a custom and is recognized as such by most religious authorities, it is not a law. Maimonides, in his code of law, never mentions it. One medieval commentator discourages the custom: "The Torah says [that a boy is circumcised] at eight days, and this one is not eight days old. When God gave the commandments, he gave them to the living and not the dead, for when a man dies he is free from the commandments."[19] He does admit that it is a custom in all communities. Yet it is a custom that may add to a family's pain, and the family should feel free to dispense with it.

The funeral should be a simple graveside service. Once again, there is no rending of garments and no *Tziduk Ha-Din* (a traditional graveside prayer). However, the baby should be given a Hebrew name and the *El Malei Rahamim* prayer said. This reiterates the fact that although there is no formal mourning, a real human being has died.

The question of reciting *Kaddish* is a difficult one. There certainly is no obligation to say *Kaddish*, just as there is no obligation to sit *shiva*. Yet one can always assume an obligation to say *Kaddish*, even if not obligated by Jewish law. The truth is that *Kaddish* is not a prayer for the dead but a reaffirmation of life and of faith in God. Therefore, it seems worthy that parents who suffer the tragic loss of a newborn be encouraged to reaffirm their faith by saying *Kaddish*. Since there is no formal *shiva*, it is not necessary to gather a *minyan* at the home; *Kaddish* can be said at the synagogue. If the family choose to say *Kaddish*, it should be said for thirty days and on the *yahrzeit*. On the *yahrzeit* it is also appropriate to light a memorial lamp.

Although Judaism may not recognize a child less than thirty days old as a viable life, to the parents that child is real and needs to be mourned. The mourning rituals may not be the same as those for an adult, yet by giving the

baby a name, holding a simple graveside service, and reciting *Kaddish,* a couple receive the support of Jewish tradition and the Jewish community in facing their loss. That
alone is a great comfort.

Genetic Engineering

One last issue remains to be addressed. We spoke about
the question of amniocentesis and whether or not it is permissible to abort a baby who has severe genetic defects.
Modern science has begun to understand the inner workings of the nucleus of the cell and is on the threshold of
cracking the genetic code. Using the techniques of recom-
binant DNA and gene splicing, scientists can manipulate
the very building blocks of life. Thus far, these techniques
have been used on bacteria and lower forms of life. It is
conceivable that genetic engineering will soon be applicable
to human beings. Using the techniques of in vitro fertilization, an egg can be fertilized outside the womb and
then can be genetically manipulated before it is implanted
in a woman's uterus.

There are obvious advantages to genetic engineering.
Someday it may be possible to cure such genetically based
diseases as hemophilia, diabetes, sickle cell anemia, and
Tay-Sachs. Yet these techniques can easily be abused. They
can be used for eugenic purposes, the attempt to create a
perfect species. Jews, of all people, should be most sensitive
to the use of genetic experimentation to create a better
species; we were victims of such experiments in Nazi Germany. Genetic engineering can be misused in other ways.
Wealthy people may use these techniques to make genetic
duplicates of themselves (cloning). Or scientists may be
tempted to grow a human being totally outside the womb
(ectogenesis).

Ultimately, by manipulating genes, humans have been
accused of playing God. Unlike ordinary medicine, the

genetic engineer is playing with the fundamental materials of life. Humans' ability to unlock the secrets of the atom has led to the threat of nuclear holocaust. There is great fear that unlocking the secret of the genetic code will lead to great dangers for humankind.

Judaism has always warned against playing God. The Talmud mentions that Rava created a man. Rabbi Zeira greeted the man but received no answer. He therefore said, "You are not human, return to the dust."[20] Out of this story grew the many legends of the golem, a man created through mystical techniques and the use of God's name. According to legend, Rabbi Loew, a leading rabbi in sixteenth-century Prague, created a golem from a handful of dust. It protected the Jews from those who would harm them. Eventually, Rabbi Lowe realized that the monster he created was out of control, and he was forced to take away its power. These stories point to the limits of humans playing God.

The question thus arises, Does Judaism permit genetic engineering? Or do these techniques raise such serious ethical problems that Judaism would outlaw them?

There are few sources to turn to for an answer. From the beginning, Judaism has recognized the importance of genetic considerations when choosing a mate. The Talmud teaches, "A man should not marry a woman from a diseased family or a leprous family."[21] This statement is mentioned in the context of a discussion on hemophilia, a disease known to be genetically linked even in talmudic times.

On the other hand, Judaism allows parents to take action to ensure not only that their offspring be healthy but also that they have other desirable qualities. There are traditions regarding the selection of a baby's sex through certain behavior during sexual intercourse. The Talmud teaches:

Rabbi Isaac, citing Rabbi Ammi, stated, "If the woman emits her semen first [that is, has an orgasm first], she bears a male child; if the man emits his semen first, she bears a female child, for it says in the Torah, 'a woman emits semen and bears a man-child' (Leviticus 12:2)."[22]

This was probably an ethical admonition to men to allow their wives to climax first. Yet it does indicate that a couple can act to select a sex for their child.

Similarly, there were ways to have a child who was more beautiful or learned. "Rabbi Yohanan used to go and sit at the gates of the place of immersion, saying, 'When the daughters of Israel come out from their required immersion, they look at me and may have sons who are as handsome as I, and as accomplished in Torah as I.' "[23]

These sources would indicate a Jewish view toward genetic engineering. A technique that would help Jewish babies be healthier, better human beings would be justified. Certainly, if a cure could be found for such dreadful diseases as Tay-Sachs or hemophilia, it should be used. Research into genetic engineering, which may lead to an eventual cure for these genetic diseases, should be encouraged and properly funded.

Yet, like any technological advance, genetic engineering has a dangerous potential for misuse. To clone a human being or grow a person in a laboratory would be contrary to Jewish ethics. Both involve the manipulation of the building blocks of life for self-gratification without serving any higher ethical purpose. It would be utterly abhorrent to Jewish ethics if these techniques were used to make a person taller so that he will be a better basketball player, smarter so that she will be a brilliant mathematician, or below intelligence to work as a slave. Hitler showed us the dangers of eugenics. Whenever genetic engineering is used, there must be a committee of ethical experts to ensure that these techniques are used to cure disease and improve human life, not to create a super species.

Like any other technology, genetic engineering is morally neutral. It can be used or abused. The lesson of the Tower of Babel is not that building skyscrapers is wrong but rather that humans should not challenge God. If humans use their God-given knowledge of genetics to cure diseases, they are to be praised. The fear of abuse should not prevent us from perfecting our knowledge of and ability to maneuver the genetic code. By finding a cure to genetic diseases, we would help many couples who are infertile not because they cannot conceive, but because they fear bringing a child with a genetic disease into the world.

A certain man of the house of Levi went and married a Levite woman. The woman conceived and bore a son; and when she saw how beautiful he was, she hid him for three months. When she could hide him no longer, she got a wicker basket for him and caulked it with bitumen and pitch. She put the child into it and placed it among the reeds by the bank of the Nile. And his sister stationed herself at a distance, to learn what would befall him.

The daughter of Pharaoh came down to bathe in the Nile, while her maidens walked along the Nile. She spied the basket among the reeds and sent her slave girl to fetch it. When she opened it, she saw that it was a child, a boy crying. She took pity on it and said, "This must be a Hebrew child." Then his sister said to Pharaoh's daughter, "Shall I go and get you a Hebrew nurse to suckle the child for you?" And Pharaoh's daughter answered, "Yes." So the girl went and called the child's mother. And Pharaoh's daughter said to her, "Take this child and nurse it for me, and I will pay your wages." So the woman took the child and nursed it. When the child grew up, she brought him to Pharaoh's daughter, who made him her son. She named him Moses, explaining, "I drew him out of the water."

(Exod. 2:1–10)

☯ 7

Adoption as a Jewish Option

My wife and I had just begun long-term treatment for infertility when we received an exciting phone call. There was a baby available for adoption. Were we interested? This opportunity required an immediate decision; there was no time to think it over or discuss it with our families. We were only beginning to consider adoption and still had strong hopes of achieving pregnancy with medical help. Yet such opportunities are rare. We chose to adopt.

Our initial reaction was that adoption meant giving up on pregnancy. It crossed my mind, "If we adopt, we are throwing in the towel, so to speak." I realize now that this is not true. Adoption and pregnancy are two different ways of achieving the same goal, creating a family. To succeed at one is not to give up on the other. I know many couples who adopted and then went on to have biological children. One particular couple comes to mind. They placed their name with an adoption agency and were warned that the waiting list was long. Through private sources they managed to adopt three children. Then the wife learned that she was pregnant. They were the parents of four children when the agency finally contacted them. The agency asked them three questions: Have you given birth to a child? Have you adopted? Are you still interested in adoption? They answered yes to all three questions.

To adopt is not to give up on pregnancy. On the contrary, adoption relieves most of the pressure of childlessness. It is an alternative way to raise a family, a way that is looked upon with favor in Jewish tradition. For any infertile couple it is worth considering.

I am often asked, "Can you love an adopted child as much as a child of your own?" The answer is simple. "This *is* a child of my own." Any adoptive parent will tell you the same thing. "Once you hold that child in your arms, that child is yours." That child is a natural part of your household, whether that child enters the household through pregnancy or adoption.

Adoption does raise certain problems. Civil law has stated that an adoptive relationship totally replaces a biological relationship. The adoptive child enters the family with all the legal rights of a biological child. Jewish law does not recognize adoption per se. It is true that the Talmud does say, "Whoever raises an orphan in his home, scripture considers him as if he gave birth to the child."[1] Yet the child's biological identity can never be replaced. If a non-Jewish child is adopted into a Jewish family, the child does not automatically become Jewish. He or she must be formally converted. If the father is a Kohen or Levi, the adopted child is not a Kohen or Levi. Some rabbis insist that the child can never be called by the adoptive father's Hebrew name, but must be called "_____ ben [or bat]

Avraham Avinu," the son or daughter of Abraham our Father. All of these issues will be discussed in this chapter.

The next chapter will discuss in detail the most difficult part of adoption, finding a child. This difficulty is true of all adoptions but particularly true for a family seeking a healthy, white newborn. To find a baby takes a huge amount of energy and can often be quite expensive. The organized Jewish community will do little to help. Jewish couples who wish to adopt will often meet anti-Semitism on the part of social workers, agencies, judges, and the biological mothers themselves.

Few procedures are as intrusive to one's personal life as adoption. A couple must share with social workers every detail about their marriage, finances, physical health, lifestyle, child-rearing philosophy, and fertility problems. Some agencies will insist that a couple exhaust all medical procedures and that they sign a paper agreeing to seek no infertility treatment while on the agency list. I personally find such a demand unethical.

I raise these issues to show that adoption is difficult. It takes energy, persistence, and money. Yet, as an adoptive parent, I will say that every moment of difficulty is worth it. There is no feeling like bringing that child home, and there is boundless satisfaction in providing a loving home for a child who otherwise might be homeless or neglected. Some couples are reticent about adopting a child; they worry about heredity. My own experience indicates that environment has far greater influence on a child than heredity. Providing a loving, nurturing environment for a child born to someone else can be a wonderful solution to infertility.

The Jewish View Toward Adoption

Adoption presents a strange irony from a Jewish perspective. On the one hand, adoption is as old as the Bible. The opening quotation in this chapter tells of the adoption of Moses by Batya, the daughter of Pharaoh; one of the earliest examples of adoption in the Bible. Throughout the Bible we find cases of a child being born to one set of parents and raised by another, a de facto adoption. Yet adoption de jure, adoption as a legal institution, is unknown to Jewish law. Only in modern Israel have rabbinic authorities been forced to establish procedures for the adoption of children. Israel had to coin a new term, *ametz*, to describe adoption because there was no word in classical Hebrew. Adoption in civil law means the total severing of a child's relationship to his or her biological parents and the establishment of an equivalent relationship with adoptive parents. Such a procedure is unknown in Judaism for reasons we will discuss later.

Still, de facto adoption was common in biblical times. The earliest example was an adult adoption. Abraham, childless in spite of God's promise, told God, ". . . 'Lord God, what can you give me, seeing that I shall die childless, and the one in charge of my household is Dammesek Eliezer!' Abram* said further, 'Since you have granted me no offspring, my steward will be my heir' " (Gen. 15:2–3). Abraham adopted his servant Eliezer to be his heir. This type of adoption was common in the ancient Near East, as we have learned from documents discovered by modern archaeologists.[2] It is interesting to note that when adoption as a legal institution was first developed in ancient Rome, its purpose was to provide an heir for a childless couple.

Examples of adoption can be seen in the stories of Sarah and Rachel. In both cases, children born of their handmaidens were brought into their homes and raised as their own children. (See Chapter 2 for a discussion of these stories.) Similarly, Jacob adopted his two grandsons. Jacob said to Joseph, " 'Now, your two sons, who were born to you in the land of Egypt before I came to you in Egypt,

---

*Abraham's original name in the Torah was Abram. God later changed it.

shall be mine; Ephraim and Manasseh shall be mine no less than Reuben and Simeon' " (Gen. 48:5). Because Ephraim and Manasseh were adopted by Jacob, they became proper names for two of the tribes.

Another famous example of adoption is the story of Esther that we read on Purim. "He [Mordecai] was foster father to Hadassah—that is, Esther—his uncle's daughter, for she had neither father nor mother. The maiden was shapely and beautiful; and when her father and mother died, Mordecai adopted her as his own daughter" (Esther 2:7). In all these cases, the adoption seems to be an informal arrangement. When Esther was orphaned, her cousin Mordecai brought her into his home and raised her. The Bible does not mention any legal documents or formal judicial decrees. Mordecai, acting on his own initiative, assumed responsibility for raising his orphaned cousin.

This type of informal adoption is discussed at length in the Talmud. It opens with the case of Michal, the wife of King David and daughter of King Saul. Michal was childless her entire life (see 2 Sam. 6:23), yet she is described as being the mother of five sons (see 2 Sam. 21:8). Actually, the five sons were born to Michal's sister Merab. In attempting to resolve this contradiction, the Talmud gives the classical justification for adoption:

> It is written, "the five sons of Michal the daughter of Saul." Rabbi Joshua answers you, Was it Michal who bore them? Surely Merab bore them. Merab gave birth to them and Michal raised them, therefore they are called by her name. This teaches that anyone who raises an orphan in his home, scripture considers him as if he gave birth to him.
>
> Rabbi Haninah learned it from here, "And the women her neighbors gave it a name saying, there is a son born to Naomi" [Ruth 4:17]. Was it Naomi who bore him? Surely Ruth bore him. Rather Ruth bore him and Naomi raised him, therefore he is called by her [Naomi's] name.
>
> Rabbi Yohanan learned it from here. "And his wife Yehudiah [another name for Batya, the daughter of Pharaoh, mentioned at the end of the verse] gave birth to Yered the father of

Gedor, Heber the father of Soco, and Yekutial the father of Zanoah" [various names for Moses; see Rashi's comment: 1 Chron. 4:18]. Was it Batya who bore him? Surely Yocheved bore him. Rather Yocheved bore him and Batya raised him, therefore he is called by her name.

Rabbi Elazar learned it from here, "You have with Your arm redeemed Your people, the children of Jacob and Joseph, Selah" [Pss. 77:16]. Was it Joseph who bore them? Surely Jacob bore them. Rather Jacob bore them and Joseph sustained them, therefore they are called by his name.

Rabbi Samuel ben Nahmani said in the name of Rabbi Yohanan, Anyone who teaches the son of his companion Torah, scripture considers him as if he gave birth to him. One verse says, "These are the generations of Aaron and Moses" [Num. 3:1] and then it says "These are the sons of Aaron" [Num. 3:2]. Aaron bore them and Moses taught them [Torah], therefore they are called by his [Mose's] name.[3]

The Jewish attitude toward adoption is clear from this passage. The child's spiritual parents, not the biological parents, give the child his or her name and identity. An orphan is called by the name of the parent that raises him or her, not the parent that gives birth. The real parents are the ones who physically sustain the child by providing for his or her needs and who spiritually sustain the child by teaching the Torah. We return to a theme mentioned frequently in this book. In Judaism, being the biological parent is secondary. The real parents are those who provide a home for, take care of, and teach a child.

Another midrashic passage makes this point explicitly:

"But now, O Lord, Thou art our father" [Isa. 64:7]. The Holy One, blessed be He, said, "You have ignored your own fathers, Abraham, Isaac and Jacob, and me you call father?" To which they replied, "You do we recognize as our father."

It can be compared to an orphan who was brought up with a guardian that was a good and trustworthy man, and brought her up and looked after her most carefully. Later he wished to marry her, and when the scribe came to write the marriage document he asked her, "What is your name?" to which she replied, "So-and-so," but when he asked her, "What is the name of your father?" she was silent. Whereupon her guardian said to her, "Why are you silent?" and she replied, "Because I know of no other father save you, for he that brings up a child is called a father, and not he that gives birth."

Similarly, the orphan is Israel, as it says "We are become orphans and fatherless" [Lam. 5:3]. The good and faithful guardian is the Holy One, blessed be He, whom Israel began to call "our father" as it says, "But now, O Lord, Thou art our father" [Isa. 54:7]. God said, "You have ignored your own father and now call me your father" . . . Lord of the Universe! He who brings up children is called the father, not he who gives birth.[4]

In Jewish tradition, the ones who raise a child are called mother and father, not the ones who give birth. Judaism has a long history of adoption de facto. Since biblical times, Jewish couples have taken an orphan into their homes, raised and sustained that child, and called that child by their name. Judaism sees such an adoption as a great *mitzvah*. Yet adoption as a judicial act does not exist. Jewish law does not recognize it as a legal institution. Only in modern times has the rabbinate in the state of Israel established legal procedures for adoption.

There is a reason for the absence of adoption as a legal procedure in Jewish law. Halakhah places great importance on a child's biological identity and status. Such identity is permanent and cannot be changed by a legal procedure such as adoption. It is birth that gives a child identity as a Jew or gentile and as a Kohen, Levi, or Yisrael. This identity does not change because of a judicial decree. Even after adoption, the child would maintain his or her relationship with the biological parents. Technically, the child would inherit from the biological parents. Similarly, biological siblings would be forbidden from marrying one another by the laws of incest. For these reasons, Judaism has never established adoption as a judicial procedure.

We can understand this lack of a procedure for adoption in Jewish law if we compare Judaism with other legal systems. Adoption as a legal procedure has its roots in ancient Rome. One of the major purposes of the law was to provide an heir for a childless couple. Ancient Rome placed great emphasis on proper inheritance but little emphasis on blood lines.

In contrast, our legal system in the United States grew out of British common law. In common law, adoption was unknown. England did not pass an adoption law until 1926. To quote one authority regarding adoption in the United States:

Our laws and social workers treat adoption as though it were something extraordinary. Our legal system has a surprising amount of trouble with it, and traditional adoption agencies have never done much to dispel the impression that they are helping people out of an unnatural and peculiar difficulty. The roots of this attitude grew out of British common law, which did not recognize adoption.

The English nobility placed greater stress on the role of blood ties than did practically any other group in history. Property and titles passed directly to the oldest son. If there was no oldest son, the nearest male relation was awarded the land and title. If there were no male kin, the line ended and the title fell out of use. Under this system, adoption was forbidden. It is because of this special emphasis on blood that British literature is full of wards, guardians, foundlings, and illegitimate sons. Informal adoptions were common enough, but adoptions protected by law were unknown and adoptive children were left in a legal limbo.[5]

Jewish law is closer to British common law than Roman law. In Judaism, there is great emphasis on bloodlines and *yichus*, one's family background. Whole sections of the Talmud discuss the question of determining the parentage of a child. Those legal systems that place an emphasis on bloodlines, like common law and Jewish law, will not have statutes regarding adoption.[6]

The lack of a legal process for adoption in Jewish law was problematic for the modern state of Israel, where all questions of personal status are handled by Jewish religious law. The Israeli rabbinate had to pass a *takanah*, or enact-

ment, regarding the adoption of children, and Israeli lexi-
cographers had to coin a new word. They chose the term
ametz, based on a root meaning "to make strong." This term
was chosen because of a verse in Psalms: "O God of hosts,
turn again, down from heaven and see; take note of that
vine, the stock planted by Your right hand, the stem you
have taken as Your own" (Pss. 80:15–16). The last line can
also be translated, "for the son that You adopted for Yourself." An adopted child is like a stem transplanted.

Even these enactments only partially established the
parent-child relationship within adoptive families. To quote
Menahem Elon, the leading authority on Jewish civil law:

> These enactments, and the rulings which followed them, gave
> permission for a legal relationship to be created between adoptive
> parents and adoptees similar to the relationship between parents
> and children. They did not permit, through adoption, the sev-
> ering of the natural relationship between an adoptive child and
> his biological parents. Such a severance would violate a basic
> principle of Jewish law, that a child's relationship to his parents,
> created naturally, cannot be changed or broken.[7]

Elon goes on to describe the Israeli law regarding
adoption as a compromise between Jewish law and the legal
systems of other nations. On the one hand, any claim by
the biological parents for the child to be returned to them
is not permitted, and the adoptive parents take on all responsibility for the welfare and maintenance of the child.
On the other hand, the child maintains his or her biological
status and is forbidden to marry into his or her biological
family.

The Israeli Adoption of Children act was passed in
1960.[8] This law permits the adoption of a child up to the
age of eighteen. (There is no adult adoption in Israel.) The
adopting parents must be at least eighteen years older than
the child. The adoption order severs all legal ties between
the biological parents and the child and gives the adopting
parents all legal responsibility for the child. However, in
keeping with Jewish law, the adoption order does not change
the child's biological status. Technically, an adopted boy

would still be forbidden to marry his biological sister, even if he never knew her. However, he would be permitted to marry his adopted sister.

The fact that a child's biological status can never be changed has another consequence. In Israel adoptions are relatively open. Upon reaching the age of eighteen, a child can apply to see the adoption records and learn about his or her biological family.[9] Israeli law and Jewish tradition have never sanctioned the secrecy that used to surround adoption in the United States.

Although adoption is unknown to the Jewish legal tradition, there is precedent for the establishment of a relationship between parents and children that is almost the equivalent of adoption. The Talmud speaks of parents being appointed as legal guardians for a child. Such a guardian is called an *apotropos* in Jewish legal sources. The court can appoint an *apotropos* by virtue of its authority as the father of orphans. The court even has the authority to remove a minor from his or her parent's home and appoint a guardian over that minor, if such a move is in the child's best interest.

The *apotropos* has legal authority over the property of the minor but is subject to the supervision of the court. He is also responsible for the physical care of the minor. The legal guardian is responsible for training the child in the commandments and providing whatever is necessary for a proper Jewish education.[10] Most authorities include in this requirement the responsibility for a boy's *brit milah* and *pidyon ha-ben*.

The *apotropos* shares many responsibilities of an adopted parent, but there is an essential difference: The child maintains his or her biological identity. The child would still inherit from the biological parents, not the *apotropos*. Again a child's biological status can never be broken, nor can artificial ties of parenthood be created by an act of the court.

This principle has serious consequences for couples adopting today. In planning the adoption, they must consider the child's biological status. The laws regarding a child will vary, depending on whether the child was born of a Jewish or gentile mother.

When the Biological Mother Is Jewish

Although the adoption of a child whose biological mother is Jewish is relatively rare, occasionally such adoptions do occur. Usually they take place within a family by a step-parent, a grandparent, or another relative. However, sometimes a Jewish woman will place a baby for adoption with a Jewish couple she does not know, working through an agency or an intermediary. I have been involved in several such adoptions.

The adoption of a Jewish child raises several questions of Jewish law involving the child's identity as a Jew. These questions are sufficiently serious that many Orthodox couples prefer to adopt a gentile child and have the child converted.

The most serious problem is that a child may be a *mamzer*. Unfortunately, the term *mamzer* has become a derogatory term in common usage. In this section, I will be using the word as a technical term within Jewish law, with no derogatory intent. First, it must be clarified that *mamzer* does not mean illegitimate in the usual sense of the word; a child born out of wedlock is fully legitimate in Jewish law. A child is a *mamzer* only if he or she is born as a result of adultery or incest. A *mamzer* is the offspring of relations between a married woman and a man who is not her husband or of relations between relatives forbidden to be married to each other, such as father and daughter or brother and sister.

The Torah teaches, "No one misbegotten shall be admitted into the congregation of the Lord; none of his descendants, even in the tenth generation, shall be admitted into the congregation of the Lord" (Deut. 23:3). A *mamzer*, although a Jew for all other purposes, may not marry a Jew of legitimate birth. A *mamzer* is considered tainted by

Jewish law, and his or her children will also be considered *mamzerim*. There is no problem with adopting a *mamzer* per se. The problem, at least in the Orthodox community, is raising a *mamzer* as a legitimate Jew and allowing that child to eventually marry a Jew of legitimate birth. In general, the question of *mamzerut* does not arise in the Conservative or Reform communities.

There are two cases in adoption that could raise the issue of a child being a *mamzer*. One case is the *asufi* (foundling), a baby whose parents are unknown. The second case is the *shetuki* (undisclosed), in which the mother is known but the father unknown or in which the mother refuses to disclose the father.[11] In both these cases, the rabbis have ruled the child may be a *safek mamzer* (doubtful *mamzer*). There is a principle in Jewish law that in cases of doubt regarding laws of the Torah we follow the stricter opinion. On this basis, a *safek mamzer* would not be permitted to marry a Jew of legitimate birth. This would raise serious questions of whether a traditional Jewish family could adopt an *asufi* or a *shetuki*; since most Jewish children placed for adoption fall into these categories, some Orthodox families may avoid adopting a Jewish child altogether.

To clarify, let us study each case individually.

Asufi. An *asufi* is a foundling whose parents are unknown. It would be extremely rare to find a Jewish foundling in America. We go by the majority of cases, and in America we would presume that any foundling is gentile. (The opposite is true in Israel; an abandoned baby found on the streets of Tel Aviv would be considered Jewish.)

Let us suppose that a baby of unknown parentage is found, and there are clear indications that the baby is Jewish. Perhaps a note is left with the baby's family history. The Talmud puts severe limitations on the definition of an *asufi*. Only if it is clear that the baby was totally unwanted and abandoned to die does it have a taint of illegitimacy. If there is the slightest indication that the baby was loved or cared for, it is considered fully legitimate. The Talmud provides several examples: a baby is not an *asufi* and is therefore legitimate if the baby is circumcised; if the baby was massaged with oil or wears an amulet; or if the baby is found near a synagogue or public thoroughfare where people congregate.[12] Almost anything that shows the baby has been properly cared for indicates that the baby is not an *asufi*, even if the baby is wrapped in a blanket.

According to Jewish law, only a Jewish baby clearly abandoned to die would be an *asufi* and therefore illegitimate. Such a case would be so rare as to be unheard of. For all practical purposes, the rabbis of the Talmud removed the category of *asufi*. Therefore, traditional Jews should have no qualms about adopting such an abandoned Jewish child.

Shetuki. The question of a baby whose biological mother is Jewish and whose father is unknown is more complicated. If the mother is married, there is a presumption that the husband is the father and the child is legitimate. If the mother is single, a problem could arise. The biological father could be a blood relation, making the child a result of incest and therefore illegitimate. It is true that the majority of men are not blood relations. Yet we cannot always use the rule of majority; if the biological mother went into the man's residence, there is a rule called *kavua*, which negates the law of majority.[13] Therefore, some Orthodox authorities forbid the adoption of a Jewish child whose biological father is unknown.[14]

In truth, it is not necessary to take that strict a view. There is a rule that the biological mother is believed regarding the legitimacy of her child. Even if she refuses to identify the father, her word as to the child's legitimacy is sufficient. Yet, even if she does not know who the father is, there is room for a more liberal ruling. Just such a case came before the eighteenth-century halakhic authority Rabbi Ezekiel Landau.[15] A child had been born to an unmarried mother by an unknown father. The mother had since died and the question arose: Was the child a *shetuki* and therefore illegitimate? Rabbi Landau gave a long analysis of the relevant sources and ruled that the child was fully legitimate.

Based on this source, there is no barrier to a traditional Jewish couple's adopting a baby born of a Jewish mother. In fact, a couple should be thrilled at the opportunity to provide a traditional home for a Jewish child. Only in the rare and sad case in which a child is definitely known to be the result of incest should a traditional couple consider passing up such an adoption. There are many Jewish couples less concerned with questions of *mamzerut* who would jump at a chance to adopt such a baby.

When the Biological Mother Is Gentile

According to Jewish law, a child born of a gentile mother is gentile. Adoption by a Jewish couple does not change that fact. The child will remain a gentile until he or she is formally converted to Judaism. To quote Rabbi Hayim Halevy Donin, a prominent Orthodox authority:

For a non-Jewish adopted child to be regarded as Jewish in the view of the religion, he or she must go through a formal conversion. Even if the child is raised as a Jew, and grows up to be an ultra-devout, ultra-orthodox person whose Jewish faith is unquestioned, whose religious commitments are without reservations, and whose devotion and loyalty to the Jewish people are beyond question, his legal status as a Jew is denied him unless he has also gone through the rite of conversion.[16]

The conversion process is simple and should not be neglected. (See Appendix 1 for a detailed description of the conversion ceremony and its blessings.) A boy is circumcised normally, with a special blessing indicating that the circumcision is for purposes of *gerut* (conversion). If the boy has already been circumcised, a symbolic circumcision is done. This is called a *hatafat dam brit* (literally "drop of blood of the covenant") and involves taking a symbolic drop of blood. Then, when a boy or girl is slightly older, there must be a ritual immersion (*tevilah* in Hebrew). The immersion is usually performed in a *mikvah*, although it can be done in a lake, ocean, or any other natural body of water. A swimming pool is not considered a kosher *mikvah*.[17]

The immersion can be performed any time. Some rabbis prefer to wait until the child is old enough to understand, but others recommend that it be done as early as possible. Delaying the ritual might cause it to be neglected altogether. Both of my children were ritually converted before they were six months old. Three rabbis constitute themselves as a *beit din* (court of law) and witness the immersion. They then give the child a Hebrew name and officially welcome him or her into the Jewish community. If it is handled appropriately, the entire conversion procedure can be beautiful and meaningful for parents. Many families follow it up with a meal or refreshments to celebrate the event.

For various reasons, some families are resistant to the conversion procedure. Many do not see the necessity for it. One family claimed that it sounded too much like baptism. I answered that we Jews invented the ritual first, and the Christians borrowed it from us. In Jewish tradition, immersion in a *mikvah* symbolizes rebirth; it is the symbolic birth of the adopted child into the Jewish community.

Immersion in a *mikvah* is required by all Orthodox and Conservative rabbis. Many Reform and some Reconstructionist rabbis dispense with the ritual, claiming that it is sufficient to give the child a Hebrew name and enroll him or her in a religious school. To quote the Reform Responsa Committee regarding the status of an adopted child:

> The naming of such a child should occur in the same manner as with any other child. In most Reform congregations this would be considered sufficient ritual conversion for girls and also for a large number of boys. This act, along with Jewish education, would bring the child into the covenant of Judaism in the same manner as any natural child.[18]

Parents should carefully consider before following such

advice. An adopted child might grow up in a Reform or Reconstructionist temple and later choose to affiliate with, or marry someone from, a more traditional synagogue. If the child has not been properly converted, numerous problems could ensue. For this reason and because of the intrinsic beauty of the ritual itself, many Reform rabbis do require, or at least strongly recommend, immersion.

One basic ethical question remains regarding the conversion of a child. What gives Jewish parents the right to adopt a gentile child, convert the child without his or her knowledge, and raise him or her as a Jew?

The Talmud asks this question. The rabbis answer that a court is permitted to act for a person's benefit without his permission. Conversion to Judaism is considered to be a benefit for the child. To quote the talmudic text:

Rav Huna taught, "A minor proselyte can be immersed by permission of a beit din [court of three rabbis]." What does this teach us? That it is to his benefit, and we can act to a person's benefit without his permission. It has been taught, "We can act for a person's benefit without his permission, but we cannot act to a person's detriment without his permission." Rabbi Joseph said, "When he reaches the age of majority, he can protest... if he reaches the age of majority plus one hour, if he has not protested he can no longer do so."[19]

This section of Talmud gives the basic law of a child proselyte, which is recorded in the later codes.[20] A minor can be converted by permission of the *beit din*. At the age of majority—twelve for a girl, thirteen for a boy—the child can protest the conversion. If he or she protests, the conversion is annulled. However, if he or she continues to live as a Jew for even a short time beyond the age of bar or bat mitzvah, the conversion is considered permanent.

There is some disagreement among legal authorities about the form of this protest. Some say that the child must reconvene a *beit din* and formally renounce the conversion. Others say that it is sufficient simply to stop living as a Jew. In my opinion, the child ought to do some public act to reaffirm his or her Jewish identity upon reaching the age of majority. The bar or bat mitzvah of an adopted child would be such a reaffirmation.

Certain truths are evident from this law. First, Judaism would never permit keeping an adoption a secret from the child. A child cannot reaffirm a conversion if he or she never knew the conversion took place. Second, it is particularly important to give an adopted child a strong Jewish education and a positive feeling about being Jewish. If the child feels good about being Jewish, he or she will reaffirm it upon reaching the age of majority. Finally, the bar or bat mitzvah takes on a special significance for an adopted child. It is the completion of a conversion begun years before. Jewish law has three requirements for conversion: circumcision, immersion, and acceptance of the commandments. The first two are done in infancy. With the bar or bat mitzvah come the acceptance of the commandments and the public commitment to living as a Jew.

Practical Questions of Jewish Law

In the beginning of this chapter, we laid down the theoretical foundations for adoption in Jewish law. We turn now to a number of practical questions asked by adoptive parents.

What Hebrew Name Is Used by an Adopted Child?

In Judaism, a child is called by a Hebrew name, the son or daughter of the father's name (e.g., Yosef ben Yaakov). All Reform Jews and many traditional Jews also use the mother's name (e.g., Yosef ben Yaakov v'Rachel). This Hebrew name will be used at the *brit milah* or naming, upon receiving an *aliyah* to the Torah, for wedding and divorce documents, and after death on the tombstone.

The question is, which parents' names are used, the biological parents or the adoptive parents? If an adopted child is converted, do we call him [or her] ben [or bat]

Avraham Avinu (son [or daughter] of Abraham our Father), as we do for adult converts, or _____ ben [or bat] [adoptive father]?

Authorities in all three movements have ruled that a child can be called by the name of his or her adoptive parents. This is based on the statement quoted earlier, "Anyone who raises an orphan in his home, Scripture considers him as if he gave birth to him." Rabbi Moshe Feinstein, a leading Orthodox halakhic scholar, writes:

His name can be called in Israel so-and-so the son of so-and-so, using the name of the adoptive father. Although technically he should be called the son of Abraham our father, but since the one who raises him wants to use his name, it is permissible to do so.[21]

Other Orthodox authorities have disagreed.[22] They insist that using the adoptive parents' names could create confusion and possibly invalidate a future marriage or divorce document. They insist that a child be called _____ ben [or bat] Avraham Avinu. Or if the adoptive parents' names are used, there should be an indication that the child is adopted. Some rabbis put *hager* (the convert) before the child's name, others say *ha-migadlo* (the one who raised him) after the father's name.

Most authorities see no need for this stringency. We no longer live in an age where adoptions are kept secret, so that a reminder must be tacked onto a Hebrew name. It seems unnecessary to remind a boy that he is adopted every time he is called to the Torah or when the *ketubbah* is read at his wedding—especially when so many Jewish sources state clearly that the true parents are not the biological parents but the adoptive parents. The child should be called by their name.

Have Adoptive Parents Fulfilled the Mitzvah to "Be Fruitful and Multiply"?

In a certain technical sense, parents who adopt have not fulfilled the *mitzvah* of procreation. This does have some halakhic consequences. For example, a woman with one or more adopted children who gives birth to a son may be obligated to have a *pidyon ha-ben*. A *pidyon ha-ben* is required for the son who opens the womb; it is irrelevant if there are older adopted children in the family.

Similarly, if a man dies leaving adopted children but not biological children, most Orthodox rabbis would consider him to be technically childless. His widow may be required to go through the ceremony of *halitzah* before she can remarry.

These laws serve as a reminder that Judaism sees giving birth as a basic *mitzvah*. Adoption should not be pursued simply to avoid pregnancy or because one fears overpopulation. Adoption is a wonderful option, but only when pregnancy is not possible or not recommended for medical reasons.

Technically, the requirements of the *mitzvah* may not have been fulfilled. Yet life is lived on more than a technical level. By taking children into one's home and raising them as Jews, a couple are certainly fulfilling the purposes of the *mitzvah*. In fact, Rav Joseph Soloveitchik has said that raising adopted children does constitute a partial fulfillment of the commandment "Be fruitful and multiply."[23]

Earlier in this book I spoke of Ben Azzai, a Torah scholar who chose to remain a bachelor and dedicate his life to Torah study. The rabbis ruled that he was no sinner; his disciples would be considered his offspring. If students are considered the offspring of their teacher, how much more so are children considered the offspring of the parents who bring them into their home and raise them? Infertile couples should view adoption as an alternative way to fulfill the first commandment in Judaism.

What Ceremonies Are Used to Welcome a Newly Adopted Child into the Jewish Community?

There are a number of Jewish rituals to welcome a new baby into the Jewish community. These include a *brit milah* for a baby boy, a synagogue naming for a baby girl, and a *pidyon ha-ben* to redeem a firstborn son. Many couples also include a home ceremony for a baby girl, called a *simhat bat*.

As mentioned, Jewish law teaches that an *apotropos* (legal guardian) has the full responsibility for all *mitzvot* traditionally carried out by the father for his child. In a parallel manner, the adoptive parents would be responsible for the various ceremonies to welcome a newborn into the community.

If a baby boy is born of a Jewish mother, the *brit milah* should take place on the eighth day after birth. If the couple does not receive the baby until after eight days, the *brit milah* should take place as soon as possible. The adoptive father recites the blessing traditionally said by the father. The rabbi may wish to delete the words, *Yismach ha-av b' yotzei ha-latzav v'tagel imo b'free vitnah* ("May the father be happy with the offspring of his loins and the mother rejoice with the fruit of her womb").

If a baby boy is born to a gentile mother, it is not a requirement for the *brit milah* to take place on the eighth day. (If the eighth day is a Sabbath or festival, the *brit milah* must not take place.) However, many couples will try to have it on the eighth day if possible, to conform to traditional Jewish practice. The *mohel* says the blessings used at the *brit milah* of a convert. In this case there is traditionally no blessing said by the father. (However, the father may choose to add a blessing. See the appendix on the conversion ceremony for details.) If the baby is already circumcised, a symbolic circumcision is performed with no blessing.

A baby daughter is traditionally named in synagogue shortly after birth, with the father (and, where permitted, the mother) receiving an *aliyah* to the Torah. Many couples have also developed a new home ceremony called a *simhat bat* (literally, the joy of a daughter). This ceremony may include a prayer for the baby, the *sheheheyanu* blessing (said upon reaching an important occasion), the blessing over the wine, and other selected readings. Whatever ceremony parents would hold for their biological daughter should be held for an adopted daughter. However, if the baby's biological mother is gentile, some rabbis recommend that these ceremonies be delayed until after *mikvah*.

A *pidyon ha-ben* may be required for an adopted son only in certain limited circumstances. The child must be the firstborn of the biological mother, and it must be a natural birth, not a cesarean section. The biological mother must be Jewish; the ceremony is not required for a child born to a gentile woman. The biological father can be Jewish or gentile. The biological mother cannot be the daughter of a Kohen or Levi; similarly, the biological father, if known, cannot be a Kohen or Levi. If he is unknown, we assume that he was a Yisrael. Obviously, a great deal of information must be ascertained regarding the biological parents. Because of the complications, a rabbi should be consulted.

If it is required, the adoptive parents should arrange a *pidyon ha-ben*. The adoptive father should say the blessings and other statements traditionally required of the father. He should arrange a *pidyon ha-ben* for his adopted son even if he is a Kohen, or if he has older children. It is the child's status at birth and not the status of the adoptive parents that establishes the requirement for a *pidyon ha-ben*.

In Appendix 1, I have included a special prayer to name an adopted child. This can be recited by the rabbi at the *brit milah*, at the baby-naming, at the *simhat bat*, or after the *mikvah*.

What Is the Status of an Adopted Child as a Kohen or Levi?

Once again it is the status at birth, not the status of the adoptive parents, that establishes the category of Kohen, Levi, or Yisrael. If the biological mother is a Jew and the biological father is a Kohen or Levi, the child is a Kohen or Levi. If the biological mother is a Jew and the biological father is a Yisrael, a gentile, or unknown, the child is a Yisrael. If the biological mother is gentile, the child must be converted, and all converts take on the status of Yisrael.

This status does not change as the result of adoption. A man may have a long, distinguished family history as a Kohen, but adopting a son does not make that son a Kohen. Biology, not adoption, establishes a child's status.

My own experience has taught me that this law is the most difficult for adoptive parents to accept. Most people are proud of their family history as a Kohen or Levi. They want their adopted child to continue that tradition. One adoptive father who was a Kohen told me, "I have always gotten the first *aliyah*, as did my father. Why will that be denied to my son? I have always gone up on the holidays to pronounce the priestly blessing. Why can't my son do it?"

While I sympathize with these feelings, the law is unequivocal. Perhaps as adoption becomes more open and acceptable, this will be less of a problem. The Jewish community is becoming used to adopted children in its midst. We have more Jewish children who do not match their parents biologically, children with significantly darker or lighter skin than their parents, even children with Oriental or black features. We are learning to accept this fact. Perhaps we should accept the fact that a Kohen will be called for the first *aliyah*, whereas his adopted son will receive the third *aliyah* as a Yisrael. After all, Kohen, Levi, and Yisrael are facts of biology. As adoption becomes more common, biology should become less and less important to the Jewish community. The same principles apply in determining if a daughter is a "bat Kohen" or "bat Levi."

What Are the Laws When an Adoptive Parent Dies?

The loss of a parent is always painful regardless of whether that parent is related by biology or adoption. Judaism has developed traditions for mourning the death of a parent, which can give an individual a feeling of community and of spiritual solace. These include *kriyah* (the tearing of clothing or a symbolic ribbon), sitting *shiva*, and reciting the mourners' *Kaddish* for eleven months.

One does not need to be a blood relative to mourn. Tradition is full of examples of students saying *Kaddish* for teachers or other relatives taking on the obligation to say *Kaddish* for a man with no children. Some people even hire a stranger to say *Kaddish*. In view of this, there is no barrier to an adopted child taking on the full obligations of mourning for his or her parents. These include *kriyah*, *shiva*, and *Kaddish*. There are no differences in the laws of mourning for an adoptive and a biological parent, just as there is no difference in the depth of the loss a child feels for a parent.

Similarly, in the sad case of the loss of an adoptive child, the full laws of mourning apply to the parents. The only exception would be an adoptive father who is a Kohen and who is strict about the laws of not visiting a cemetery. He may avoid going to the cemetery, but he should certainly keep the other laws of mourning.

What Are the Laws Regarding Forbidden Marriages?

The Book of Leviticus lists a number of relations forbidden for marriage by the laws of incest. The fact of adoption does not change the prohibition of marriage to biological relatives. A biological brother and sister, separated at birth and raised in two separate families, would be forbidden to marry if they meet as adults.

On the other hand, adoptive brothers and sisters technically are permitted to marry. Rav, one of the leading rabbis of the Talmud, was the offspring of a marriage between a stepbrother and a stepsister.[24] However, such a marriage between adoptive siblings, although technically permissible, would be considered by most rabbis to be unseemly and improper.

An important issue has been raised by many religious authorities. Since, in most cases, the biological family of an adopted child is unknown, would it not be possible that the child could accidentally marry a blood relative? In fact, such a possibility is remote. We go by the majority of cases and do not concern ourselves with the remote possibility of accidental incest.

One final issue may arise in the Orthodox community. A Kohen is not permitted to marry a woman convert, even if she was converted as an infant.[25] This would seem to preclude the marriage of a Kohen to an adopted girl converted as an infant. However, there are opinions that disagree. Shimon bar Yohai ruled in the Talmud that if the girl was converted at less than three years of age, she can marry a Kohen.[26] With a rise in adoptions, perhaps it is worthwhile for the Orthodox community to accept Shimon bar Yohai's ruling. Most Conservative and Reform rabbis do not place these restrictions on the marriage of a Kohen.

Does Judaism Permit the Adoption of a Nonwhite Baby?

With the difficulties of finding a white baby to adopt, many Jewish couples are adopting across racial boundaries. Some have adopted black or biracial babies from the United States. Others have adopted from abroad, particularly from Korea, Vietnam, and South America. Many South American babies have Indian blood and are quite dark skinned. Some Jewish couples have adopted babies from India. The question arises, Can a baby who is nonwhite be raised as a Jew?

To begin with, Judaism is not a race. There are black Jews, brown Jews, and Oriental Jews. Many are converts, but some are born of families who have been Jewish for generations. One merely has to walk the streets of Israel to appreciate the racial diversity of the Jewish people.

There is no halakhic problem in adopting a child of another race and raising that child as a Jew. The child must obviously be converted, as would any other child born of a gentile mother. Such a child would also have the right to protest the conversion upon reaching the age of bar or bat mitzvah. Still, I have seen black and Korean Jewish children become bar or bat mitzvah and make a serious commitment to the Jewish people and the Jewish religion.

There is no halakhic barrier to an interracial adoption,

but there are still social consequences to such adoptions. We will discuss these in the next chapter.

What Does Judaism Teach About Open Adoption?

There is a tendency today toward more openness in adoption. The biological and the adoptive parents have a greater opportunity to learn about one another. Sometimes they can meet, using first names to ensure confidentiality. Sometimes a biological mother can meet several prospective couples before deciding who will receive her baby. Occasionally, a biological mother and the adoptive parents have an ongoing relationship even after the baby is placed. This sometimes includes the exchange of letters, or even visits, throughout the childhood of the adopted youngster.

Judaism has never accepted the secrecy or sense of stigma previously associated with adoption. In the Jewish view, placement of a baby by a birth mother and adoption of that baby by a couple are both acts of love. These can be approached with greater openness. In addition, some kind of meeting or exchange of information is often best for the psychological well-being of the biological mother. Placing a baby for adoption is a tremendous loss; knowing where the baby is going will alleviate part of that sense of loss. For these reasons, many lawyers, social workers, and counselors have recommended greater openness in adoption.

However, there is a limit to openness. The limit is anything that threatens the integrity of the adoption. The best interest of the child dictates that all ties be broken with the biological parents. The adoptive parents must know that several years down the road the biological parents will not show up and demand the child back. Maintaining the integrity of the adoption usually means that there must be some anonymity. In my opinion, a meeting arranged by an intermediary between the biological mother and the adoptive parents is a good idea. First names only should be used and general information exchanged. An exchange

of more specific information, including last names and telephone numbers, might make it more difficult for the biological mother to let go and for the adopting parents to
find peace of mind. Such an exchange should be avoided.

How Is Adoption Viewed by the Jewish Community?

I have been exploring how adoption is treated in Jewish
law, yet many couples seeking to adopt have a more practical question. How will their adoption be viewed by the
Jewish community? Will their child be fully accepted as a
Jew?

We must remember that adoption as a formal, judicial
act is relatively new to the Jewish community. Adoption as
we know it today was unheard of in the shtetls. A family
may have taken in an orphaned Jewish child to raise as
their own, but it was an informal arrangement with no
legal procedure tied to the act. To bring the child of a
Christian woman into one's home to raise as a Jew would
have been unthinkable.

Therefore, the Jewish community is only beginning
to become accustomed to adoption. Among the more in-
sular Orthodox communities, including the Hasidic community, adoption is not practiced. In fact, the Lubavitch
movement has stated its opposition to formal legal adoption. It has ruled that adoptive parents lavish physical af-
fection on children, and it is forbidden to have such physical contact with one who is not a blood relative.[27]

This has not been a concern of more modern Orthodox Jews. However, adoption is still relatively new in Orthodox circles. In researching this book, I spoke with numerous Orthodox couples. Some were told by their rabbis
that it was forbidden to adopt a baby born of a Jewish
mother because of a fear of illegitimacy. Others were told
that it was forbidden to adopt a baby born of a gentile
mother because such a child could not become truly Jewish.
It is clear that a consistent attitude toward adoption has
not emerged from Orthodox leadership. As more infertile
Orthodox couples build families through adoption, it is

hoped that the community will become more sensitive to their needs.

In a similar way, many Jews who are first-generation immigrants have difficulty with adoption. They may have trouble accepting an adopted grandchild, or they may favor biological grandchildren over adopted grandchildren. Couples should be patient. Time and love should win them over. If family members are unable to accept the adoption to the point where it becomes destructive to the family, the rabbi should be consulted on the best action to take.[28]

For most liberal Jews, adoption presents less of a problem. Religious schools of the Conservative and Reform movements are filled with adopted children, and adoption is often discussed openly. The Jewish community accepts these children. However, problems do sometimes arise when the adopted Jewish child is of another race, particularly black or Oriental. (This question will be discussed in the next chapter.)

As recently as a generation ago, most adoptions were kept secret, not only in the Jewish community but also in the community at large. There was still a stigma attached to adoption, and parents felt a need to protect their child from the pain associated with it. Often the children themselves were not told, a practice that is counter to Jewish law. Today some Jews still are uncomfortable with adoption. Couples often hear many unthinking and insensitive comments. When my wife and I adopted our son, most people wished us a *mazel tov*. However, one rabbi gave us an odd, pitying look that seemed to ask, "What is the matter with you that you had to turn to adoption?"

Adoption is a joyous occasion. As it becomes more common and more open, it will be more accepted by all groups within the Jewish community.

[Abbaye's] father died when his mother conceived him, and his mother died when she bore him. . . . But that is not so, for Abbaye frequently said, "my mother told me." That was his foster mother.

(Kiddushin 31b)

8

Finding Children for Jewish Couples

Abbaye, a fourth-century scholar, was one of the great rabbis of the Babylonian Talmud. His name is mentioned on almost every page, particularly when he is involved in intricate arguments on points of Jewish law with his colleague Rava. Abbaye was also an adopted child.

Abbaye was orphaned as an infant and raised by his uncle, Rabi Bar Nahmani, and a foster mother. He constantly quoted pieces of wisdom in the name of his adoptive mother, who obviously had a great deal of influence on him. Abbaye was one of the earliest examples in literature of a successful adoption.

The case of Abbaye raises a basic question argued in adoption circles. Is the purpose of adoption to provide homes for orphaned and unwanted children? Or is its purpose to find children for childless couples? Abbaye is a classic example of adoption as viewed by most social workers today. For them, the purpose of adoption is to find homes for children who are orphaned, abandoned, or unwanted. Many social workers would object to the title of this chapter. They would claim that it should be called Finding Homes for Unwanted Children. One worker serving a Jewish agency wrote in reaction to an article on private adoption, "[A]n agency has a different perspective and obligation. The agency's responsibility is to find the best possible home for a particular child, regardless of the child's age."[1]

Most children handled by agencies today are older and often have physical and emotional problems. Some are parts of sibling groups seeking to be adopted together. Many are nonwhite. Agencies have assumed a huge responsibility in finding parents for these children. Handling the adoption of healthy infants is only a small percentage of their work.

On the other hand, most Jewish couples who wish to adopt are looking for healthy white infants. They are infertile couples, trying to experience the totality of parenthood by raising a child from infancy. Most agencies do not see their task as helping these couples. Many couples, including my wife and me, have called adoption agencies and been treated rudely because they inquire about adopting an infant. I have been made to feel guilty by agency social workers for not considering the adoption of a "special needs" child at this stage in my life. One social worker from a major agency said, "Rabbi, you should be lucky that you have experienced the joy of raising one child from infancy. There are so many children with special needs." I understood her concerns, but my own priorities were different at that time.

In adoption circles, a false dichotomy has been set up between two views of adoption. To quote one book on adoption:

Instead of talking about families, many adoptive parent organizations say the purpose of the adoptive process is to provide children for those who want them. This view raises protests from people working to find homes for waiting children, because they see adoption primarily as a way to help needy children. Both of these viewpoints focus on the here and now, and neither of them is broad enough to grasp the idea of serving families that won't even exist until the children and adults are brought together. Adoption is an attempt to share the future, so it is dangerous to base decisions on the needs of the moment.[2]

This assessment is correct. Adoption is an alternative way of creating families. Adoption workers have a responsibility to find homes for needy children, yet they also have a responsibility to find children for childless couples. No couple seeking to adopt should be made to feel guilty whether they are searching for an older child, a special needs child, or a healthy infant.

This chapter is written from a particular point of view. Its goal is to help infertile Jewish couples who seek to build a family through adoption. My own experience has taught me that any couple who wish to adopt can adopt. And they can adopt the kind of child they *want*. It takes a commitment of time, effort, and money. Yet adoption can be accomplished. Daily, Jewish couples are adopting older children, special needs children, infants from other countries and of other races, and healthy white infants, born in the United States. Any couple who set out to adopt can do so, often within a year.

Adoption Can Be Done

Stories circulating today about adoption can frighten many childless couples away. There are stories of a baby shortage, with a waiting time of five to seven years for a healthy white infant. There are stories of fantastic sums of money, as much as $50,000, being exchanged for a baby on the black market. There are stories of illegal adoption schemes and shady operators. Unfortunately, there is some truth to all these stories.

Yet each year thousands of couples do adopt. Their adoptions go smoothly, creating loving homes for children in need. Each year thousands of birth mothers choose to place their newborns for adoption. There are numerous reasons; usually the birth mother is single or divorced and too young or too poor to raise a child properly. Sometimes the birth mother is married but unable to keep the baby for a variety of reasons—from illness to poverty. In all these cases, the birth mother is not placing the baby because she wants to abandon him or her. On the contrary, placing a baby is an act of love. It takes a heroic kind of love to give up a baby so that the child will have a better chance in life.

Adoption can be completed successfully. Any couple who truly wish to adopt can find the kind of child they want. Admittedly, it is not always easy. Adoption means revealing a private part of one's life, a couple's infertility. An agency will want detailed information, including financial and medical reports. Independent adoption requires a couple to tell the world, letting friends, relatives, and professional acquaintances act as adoption advocates. To be successful, adoption cannot be private and secretive.

A couple seeking to adopt should first search their own souls, preferably with the guidance of a rabbi or professional counselor. Have they truly had a chance to mourn the loss they suffered as a result of infertility? Can they take a child into their home and love that child, although they do not share the child's biological heritage? Is their marriage strong enough to withstand the emotional roller coaster of adoption? Do both husband and wife want to adopt? Would they consider an older child, a child with special needs, or a child of another race?

Both partners in a marriage must be emotionally ready for adoption. I know a couple who recently celebrated the adoption of a baby girl, sending out beautiful announcements that their daughter had been "placed in our arms." Yet for years this couple had not considered adoption. The husband felt that he could not relate to a child that was not "his own." He needed to work through his own discomfort with adoption before they could begin their search.

It is also important that a couple share their quest to adopt with their parents, siblings, and other relatives. As much as parents need time to become used to the fact that their child will be adopted, grandparents need to prepare themselves for an adopted grandchild. One older couple in my synagogue received a call from their daughter and son-in-law. "Guess what? You have a new grandson. We just adopted a baby from Korea." The grandparents were in shock and called me. "Rabbi, we did not even know they had a problem. How can we be *bubba* and *zayda* to a Korean grandson?" "Give it time," I said. Several months later the grandparents brought me pictures of their new grandson at a Passover seder. They simply needed time to become used to the idea. Their children had been unfair not to share their quest to adopt with their parents.

Sometimes grandparents and other family members are reluctant to accept an adopted child into the family. This is particularly true of European-born grandparents, who are often more old fashioned about the proper way to build a family. Such grandparents need to be educated about the importance of adoption in Jewish history. Ideally, time and love will win them over.

Another issue should be raised by Jewish couples seeking to adopt. For better or worse, Jews tend to be achievement oriented, particularly when it comes to academics. They want intelligent children who will succeed in school and go to college. With adoption, there is not the control over a baby's genetic background that there is with pregnancy. Certainly the home environment plays a role in a child's academic achievement, but we cannot discount the genetic factor.

Any couple who adopt a child must accept that child

for what he or she is, without particular academic expectations. In preparing this book, I had a long conversation with a social worker who runs support groups for Jewish infertile couples. She told me that many of the couples said they would adopt only a child whose birth mother was college educated. Two couples preferred Oriental to white American-born babies because they thought the Oriental children would do better in school. The social worker commented, "If you are going to love this child for what this child produces for you, you should wonder why you want to adopt."

A final point must be made. No couple should ever look at adoption as second best or as settling for less. Adoption is an alternative way to build a family, with its own particular needs. Families may even have children through both birth and adoption. Just as it is not fair to consider an adoptive child as second best, the opposite is also true: a parent should not favor an adopted child. I once read an Orthodox manual that recommended particularly gentle treatment for adopted children because the Torah commands us not to vex the orphan. An adopted child is not an orphan and deserves to be treated like any other child. An adopted child, like a family's biological child, should be loved for what he or she is.

Parents seeking to adopt should carefully discuss these considerations. If they are ready to open their hearts and their home to a child born of someone else and to love and accept that child fully whatever his or her genetic background, they should pursue adoption. If they are persistent, they will succeed.

This chapter will not present all the details of how to find a child to adopt. There are numerous excellent how-to books for the general reader. Two such books are Lois Gilman, *The Adoption Resource Book* (Harper & Row, 1984), and Edmund Blair Bolles, *The Penguin Adoption Handbook* (The Viking Press and Penguin Books, 1984).

The remainder of this chapter will cover some particular issues faced by Jewish couples seeking to adopt. The most basic issue is religion.

The Religious Issue

In 1955 a controversial decision was handed down by a court in Massachusetts. It denied the adoption of twins to a Jewish couple because the twins had been born to a Catholic mother, even though she was not a practicing Catholic, had not baptized the twins, and had agreed to the adoption by the Jewish foster parents. The court strictly construed a Massachusetts statute saying that children should be given to adoptive parents of the same faith. The court "found the mother's Catholicism an inborn status dictating adoption by Catholics only."[3]

The decision was strongly criticized by jurists at the time and would probably not be upheld by any appeals court today. In fact, current legal trends seem to indicate that the request of the mother is the only legal basis for religious matching; insisting that adoptive parents be of the same religion when no such request is made by the birth mother may be unconstitutional.[4] Most states do not have rigid rules regarding the religion of the adoptive parents. When such statutes are on the books, they tend to be worded vaguely, allowing clear discretion to the courts. For example, the law might state: "Whenever possible, the child should be placed with parents of the same religion as the natural mother, always taking into consideration the best interests of the child." Words like "whenever possible" and "the best interests of the child" give agencies and judges some leeway in choosing a home for a child. If any judge today tries to obstruct an adoption on religious grounds, the adoptive parents should appeal. They will probably win.

Still, most adoption agencies and intermediaries will respect the religious preferences of the birth mother. One director of a prominent agency told me that he tries to get the birth mother to sign a religious waiver. He explains to the mother that this will allow the agency to find the best possible home and not be hampered by religious restrictions. Yet if the birth mother does make a religious request, the agency is bound to honor it.

Respecting the birth mother's religious request is the proper thing to do. Yet it works to the disadvantage of Jewish couples. Most babies available for adoption today come from birth mothers with religious traditions that forbid abortion, such as Catholicism and fundamentalist Protestantism. Such mothers would be the most likely to insist on adoptive parents who share their religion. Jewish babies are much more difficult, although not impossible, to find. Jews can understand the feelings of a Christian birth mother who wants her baby to go to a Christian home; we would want a baby born of a Jewish mother to go to a Jewish home.

Although the religious question does put Jewish couples at a disadvantage, Jewish couples are constantly adopting babies born of other religions. They are adopting through agencies, including sectarian Christian agencies. They are adopting from overseas, often from countries that are primarily Catholic. They are adopting independently and discussing the religious differences face to face with the birth mother. We will deal with these types of adoption and how the religious question can be handled.

Older Children and Foster Children

Any couple who seek to adopt should seriously consider taking an older child. Such a child usually has special needs, whether emotional or physical. Often such children have lived in a variety of foster homes. They are sometimes called "waiting children" because they grow up waiting to be adopted. These children need loving parents.

A couple who would consider the adoption of a child with special needs should contact their local county youth services. The county agency is usually searching for homes for these children and will know of other agencies that handle such adoptions. They may also have photo listings of children available for adoption from throughout the state and often from other states. Other sources of information are adoptive parent groups, organizations that have adopted children from similar backgrounds or with similar needs.

It is a great *mitzvah* to provide a home for children with special needs. Yet such adoptions are difficult. Many waiting children have been traumatized by the shuffling between homes and may be slow to open up and trust new adoptive parents. It is important that any couple who adopt a special needs child get proper counseling from the social worker at the agency.

For Jewish couples, there is another difficulty. Rarely are such waiting children Jewish. A parent feels ambivalent enough about raising a child born of a Christian mother as a Jew from birth. As one mother wrote me, "Each December, when the world is aglow with Christmas, I am keenly aware that I have taken something from my daughter. I look to Friday evenings and holidays as an opportunity to offer her something special in return." It is far more difficult to bring an older Christian child, with fresh memories of Christmas, into a Jewish household and change that child's religion. It may be worthwhile to ask a child to give up the celebration of Christmas for the stability of a loving household. Yet adopting an older child and converting that child to Judaism is a serious matter that should be discussed at length with the social worker.

An alternative for parents who want to provide a home for a child with special needs is foster care. Children are placed in foster homes when their biological parents are unable to care for them but they have not yet been released for adoption. Foster care can last from a few weeks to an entire childhood. Of late, there is a tendency to get children out of foster care and into adoptive homes as quickly as possible. New York law has recently mandated an eighteen-month to two-year limit to make children in foster care available for adoption. Foster parents often are given the first choice to adopt the child.

There are Jewish children in need of foster care. Often they are handicapped or retarded, with parents who are unable to cope. Many of these children are placed with Christian parents because Jewish parents are unavailable. While I was recently trying to find a foster home for a thirteen-year-old girl, a social worker told me, "Jews are so generous when it comes to giving money. But when it comes to opening their homes, they have much greater difficulty."

Hakhnasat orhim, the opening of one's home to guests, is an important *mitzvah*. Included in this *mitzvah* would be opening one's home to a child in need. Any couple who would consider opening their home for a Jewish child in need of foster care should call their local Jewish Family Service. If they live in the New York City area, they should contact:

Ohel Children's Home, Family Services
4423 16th Avenue
Brooklyn, NY 11204

Adopting an Infant

A young Jewish woman called a prominent adoption agency in New York to inquire about adopting a white infant. The social worker who took the call told her such adoptions were impossible; babies were not available. The social worker went on to lecture her. "Why don't you adopt a black baby? Or an older child with special needs? If you could not open your heart to accept a child other than a healthy white baby, I have to question your motives to adopt."

The young woman hung up feeling depressed and guilty, asking herself what was wrong with her that she wanted a white baby. She refused to call another agency. One year later, working through an independent agent, she and her husband adopted a baby from El Salvador. I recently participated in the conversion of that beautiful child, who is now a happy little Jewish girl.

One fact is clear, there is a baby shortage in America today. There are far more couples interested in adopting babies than there are babies available for adoption. The reason is not simply the easy availability of abortion. Even with abortion, hundreds of thousands of babies are born out of wedlock each year. The difficulty stems from the social acceptability of single mothers keeping their babies. It is estimated that more than 90 percent of the time a single mother will keep her infant. Even so, thousands of babies are adopted each year by those couples who most actively seek them out.

It is possible to adopt an infant. Every couple I have ever counseled who have earnestly tried to adopt an infant have succeeded. I tell couples not to limit their sights to Jewish babies; a baby born of a gentile mother can be converted to Judaism (see the previous chapter). There are two basic methods of adoption, agency and independent (nonagency). I will explore the implications of both types of adoption for Jewish couples.

Agency Adoption

Most couples who want to adopt first turn to agencies. Yet for Jewish couples who prefer an infant, the quest through an agency can be extremely disappointing. Most agencies, particularly those run through the state or county government, handle mostly special needs children. Their waiting lists for infant adoptions are likely to be closed. Most agencies that handle infant adoptions today are clearly sectarian, connected with various religious organizations. These are usually Catholic, Lutheran, or evangelical Christian groups.

One unfortunate fact will become clear: there are few Jewish agencies handling the placement of babies with Jewish couples. In preparation for this book, I conducted a survey of all the Jewish Family and Children's Services around the United States, including a number of questions about adoption practices. The results are enlightening.

Fifty-six agencies responded to my survey. Thirty-four were licensed adoption agencies. Many had given up their licenses in recent years because of a lack of available babies. Many of the agencies that maintained their licenses handled a minimum number of adoptions over the past ten years; several had done none. Many maintained their licenses to conduct home studies, particularly for couples adopting from other agencies or abroad. Most expressed a strong bias against independent adoption (discussed subsequently) and would not do a home study for such an adoption.

The survey of these Jewish social service agencies was generally discouraging. Many expressed strong reservations about the feasibility of adoption today. One social worker wrote, "I think we would be more helpful to people to help them accept not being able to be parents. The solutions available are terribly flawed. Adoption as a life experience, while helpful, is also seriously flawed. So we should dampen the zeal of people and help them to direct their energy to other fulfilling experiences." Another agency told me to warn readers of "the need to work only with a licensed agency rather than potentially unscrupulous individuals." However, although this social worker pushed agency adoption, his agency has not placed a baby in years.

The picture is not entirely gloomy. Several Jewish social service agencies are doing exciting work in adoption. Some, led by the Jewish Family Service in Boston, have developed "identified" adoption programs, which combine the advantages of agency and independent adoption. (I will discuss this type of adoption later in the chapter.) Some agencies sent beautiful brochures that describe their adoption programs to potential biological mothers. Two agencies, which asked to remain unidentified in this book because they serve only a small geographic area, have hired full-time adoption workers to do outreach and counseling for potential birth mothers. They have established relationships with abortion clinics, women's centers, government agencies, and other sources for women who might consider placing a baby. One of these agencies successfully completed twelve adoptions with Jewish couples in the past year.

It is obvious that the organized Jewish community should and could do more to help couples who seek to adopt. I will offer some suggestions in the next chapter. Meanwhile, in most communities, Jewish couples will have to look to other sources for babies.

I recommend the following steps for couples who would like to adopt through an agency:

1 Call the local Jewish Family Service. You may be lucky enough to live in a city with an active adoption program. Push the agency to do more to help Jewish couples.

2 Call all other local adoption agencies, including those affiliated with other religious organizations. They often receive funds from the United Way and are required to do at least some adoptions on a nonsectarian basis. Persistence is the key; keep calling back and do not be put off by surly telephone receptionists. If their waiting list is closed, ask when it will be reopened. Let them know you are serious.

3 Jewish babies sometimes become available to agencies that seldom deal with Jewish clients. One Catholic agency found a birth mother who was looking for a Jewish home, and the agency had a difficult time finding a couple to take the baby. One rabbi adopted a daughter when a local social worker called county agencies in out-of-the-way rural areas and found a Jewish baby available in an area with few Jews. The county agency was thrilled that a rabbi would take the baby.

4 There are several large, private agencies around the country that have been responsive to the needs of Jewish couples. These agencies often serve limited geographic areas. They are also quite expensive; at

this writing their fees were in the neighborhood of $10,000 or more. To mention a few: The Edna Gladney Home, Fort Worth, Texas; Golden Cradle Home, Bala Cynwyd, Pennsylvania; Chosen Children, Lake Worth, Florida; Chosen Children Adoption Services, Louisville, Kentucky.

5 Consider adoption from abroad. Jewish couples have successfully adopted from South America, Korea, India, and other countries. However, adopting a baby of another racial or ethnic background can cause certain social problems that will be discussed subsequently.

International adoptions are usually handled by agencies, although sometimes private intermediaries can do the work. Not all agencies in foreign countries are willing to place a child with a Jewish couple. However, many will make such placements, particularly if they know that the child will have a good religious upbringing. Most of the couples I have interviewed about adopting from abroad said they were required to provide a letter from a rabbi stating that they would raise the child with a belief in God.

Couples who are interested in international adoption should contact a parent group that can provide specific information. These groups include:

Latin American Parents Association (LAPA)
P.O. Box 72
Seaford, New York 11783

Organization for United Response (OURS)
20140 Pine Ridge Drive NW
Anoka, Minnesota 55303

Families Adopting Children Everywhere (FACE)
P.O. Box 102
Bel Air, Maryland 21024

International adoption can be complicated and expensive, and the best source of information is other couples who have succeeded.

6 A couple might request an agency to do a home study, even if there are no babies currently available. I recently received a call that a Jewish baby in another state was available for immediate adoption. Only couples with a completed home study would be considered. A home study is also usually required for an interstate independent adoption.

7 Many Jewish couples have asked me about adoption of a baby from Israel. I have heard of one couple who succeeded with such an adoption, but I imagine that they had connections most people do not have. As a general rule, such adoptions are impossible for couples who do not live in Israel. In fact, many Israeli couples are adopting babies from abroad, particularly South America, because of a baby shortage in Israel.

There are very strong feelings in Israel that every Jew belongs there, as anybody who has ever visited the Jewish homeland can confirm. It would run strongly against Israeli policy to allow an Israeli child to be adopted by parents outside the country. While it is true that many Israeli children are born into difficult social circumstances and severe poverty and that many children grow up in orphanages and children's homes, adoption by American Jews is not an option for these children.

8 After a couple have explored all the agency options, they should consider independent adoption.

Independent Adoption

Most Jewish couples who adopt infants today do so independently, not through any agency. They work through an intermediary, often a doctor, lawyer, or rabbi. Sometimes they make arrangements directly with a birth mother. Independent adoption is sometimes called private adoption, or gray market adoption. I find this last name offensive, because it implies that independent adoption is related to black market baby buying. At this time, independent adoption is perfectly legal with certain restrictions in every state except Massachusetts, Connecticut, Michigan, Delaware, Minnesota, and North Dakota.

Independent adoption is the quickest and often the least expensive way to find a baby. There are other advantages, such as the ability to have greater contact with the birth mother than an agency will allow and the ability to pick up the baby directly from the hospital. (Agencies usually put the baby in foster care until the parental rights are terminated, which can take several months.) There is one major disadvantage: independent adoption is risky. A biological mother has a certain amount of time, which varies by state, in which to change her mind. Some couples have kept a new baby in their home for several months, only to lose that baby when the birth mother changes her mind. Independent adoption is not for the faint of heart or for those who are ambivalent about adopting.

There are ways to minimize the risk. The first is to work only through a trusted intermediary. Try to insist that the biological mother have counseling; this is an advantage of agency adoption. Unfortunately, many lawyers and doctors who act as intermediaries ignore this important service. It is a traumatic experience to give up a child for adoption, and the pain and guilt can be overwhelming if the mother does not have adequate support and counseling. Meeting the birth mother can also minimize risk; a birth mother will be more comfortable and less likely to change her mind if she sees the kind of parents who will be raising her child. She may also be more reluctant to hurt a couple whom she has met and talked to.

In spite of the risk, most Jewish couples turn to independent adoption. One reason is that there is no other choice, since there are so few Jewish agencies. Also, Jews have an advantage in the area of independent adoption. The best sources of babies are doctors, lawyers, social workers, and other professionals, and Jewish professionals are often willing to help Jewish couples adopt, particularly when they know that these couples have nowhere else to turn.

In some states that do not permit independent adoption, an alternative called identified adoption is developing. This approach shares many of the advantages and risks of independent adoption. A couple find the birth mother on their own or through an intermediary. They refer her to an agency that handles the adoption. This type of adoption has become a standard practice at the Jewish Family Service in Boston, and in Hartford, Connecticut, a program was recently implemented. Detroit has a program in which any couple who refer a potential birth mother to the agency will receive first consideration for the next baby available.

Most Jewish couples who pursue independent adoption wonder if religion will be a factor. Will a birth mother who is non-Jewish be willing to place with a Jewish couple? Should a Jewish couple lie about their religion to the birth mother?

My advice is not to lie, but not to volunteer information if not asked. If a birth mother asks, "Are you Christian?" and a Jewish couple say yes, it can jeopardize the adoption later down the line if the truth becomes known. Besides, the birth mother does have a right to choose the religion in which her baby will be raised. It is possible that a birth mother will refuse to place her baby with a Jewish couple. If the couple are persistent, they will get the next baby that comes along.

Let me share the story of two couples. One couple advertised in a local paper to adopt and received several inquiries. One potential birth mother talked two hours with this couple and seemed impressed—until she asked their religion. When they said Jewish, she said, "Let me get back to you." They never heard from her again.

Shortly afterward, they received a second phone call. This birth mother also asked if they were Jewish. When the couple answered yes, the birth mother asked whether it bothered them to answer that question. The couple said, "No. We want to be honest with you as we hope you are with us. We believe in God, and we will raise the child in our religious tradition." The birth mother answered, "I want my child to have a religious upbringing. That is good enough for me." This Irish-Catholic mother gave her baby to a Jewish couple for adoption.

The second couple were Orthodox Jews. The birth mother insisted on a face-to-face meeting. After much soul searching, the husband felt that he had to be honest about his own religious convictions, so he wore his skullcap at the meeting. The couple discussed their religion with the birth mother. She told them that she was going to give up eating pork for the remainder of her pregnancy, and she gave them her son to adopt.

There are birth mothers who will refuse to give a baby to a Jewish couple. There are others who are delighted to give their baby a Jewish home because they believe that Jews make good parents. Most birth mothers simply want a good home for their baby, a home where religious and moral values will be stressed. Often the issue of religion does not even arise. If it is not mentioned, there is no reason for a couple to bring it up. Yet if it does arise, it should be treated honestly.

I recommend the following steps for couples seeking to adopt independently:

1 Talk to a good attorney, and find out the laws in your state. Questions to be asked include: Is independent adoption legal? Must there be an intermediary? Is it a requirement that the birth mother know the names of the adoptive parents? (California requires this.) How much time does the birth mother have to change her mind? When are her rights terminated? What rights does the birth father have? What expenses can the couple legally pay? Is it legal to advertise for a baby? What protocol should be followed if the couple come into contact with a birth mother?

2 Tell everybody that you are looking to adopt. Networking is the key to successful independent adoption. You never know who has contact with a potential birth mother. It is particularly valuable to tell rabbis and other clergy, doctors (particularly obstetrician-gynecologists), lawyers, teachers, social workers, and couples who have adopted. One couple found their son

by speaking with waitresses whenever they ate out. One waitress knew a pregnant college student and made the match.

3 Some couples print up hundreds of resumes and send them to doctors and lawyers. This method, once very popular, probably has been overused. Still, it cannot hurt. One Jewish couple sent such a resume with a cover letter to lawyers throughout their state, particularly those located in small communities. A Jewish attorney in a small community, recognizing that the couple were Jewish, found them a baby.

4 Put a separate telephone in your home with an unlisted number. Then do your own outreach for a birth mother. Put fliers up in such places as launderettes, supermarkets, trailer parks, and college campus bulletin boards. Advertise in newspapers (not legal in every state), particularly in small blue-collar communities. Also advertise in Jewish newspapers. If a birth mother calls, put her in touch with your attorney and, optimally, with a counselor.

5 If the birth mother desires it, agree to meet her face to face on a first-name basis. My experience has convinced me that adoption is more comfortable for both the birth parents and the adoptive parents if they see one another as human beings and not nameless abstractions. For some more thoughts on this subject, see the Afterword, "A Letter to My Child's Birth Mother."

6 Avoid any black market situations. Such situations are tempting, but your adoption will always be in jeopardy. If the birth mother asks for money, tell her that she and you can go to jail. If necessary, call the district attorney. Avoid any attorney who demands a large retainer up front without a baby immediately available. Avoid situations in which large amounts of cash are exchanged in paper bags or you are asked to commit perjury. You do not need to be involved in these situations; you can adopt legally.

7 Do not give up. Every couple I know who have sought to adopt independently and persisted have succeeded.

I am often asked how to handle the issue of a *brit milah* in an independent adoption when the birth mother is not Jewish. A couple links up with a pregnant woman and wants to know what to say to her regarding circumcision. My advice is that, ideally, they would want to take the baby home from the hospital uncircumcised and arrange for a *brit milah* on or close to the eighth day. However, if they feel that this might present a risk to the adoption, they may wish to have the birth mother arrange a hospital circumcision and later do a symbolic circumcision as part of the conversion process. The attorney can advise a couple on how to handle this situation.

Before leaving the subject of adoption, let me turn to two more important points. First is the question of adoption across racial lines, a practice becoming more prevalent in the Jewish community. The second is a major ethical issue that has become a scandal in adoption circles: baby buying.

Adopting Across Racial Lines

With the shortage of white babies, it is becoming popular to adopt across racial lines. Such children may range from South American babies who, because of Indian blood, look like dark Sephardic Jews, to Oriental babies from Korea and Vietnam and black babies from the United States. As mentioned in the previous chapter, there are no halakhic barriers to such adoptions. Judaism is not a race. Such a child must be properly converted to Judaism and would then become fully Jewish.

Interracial adoption is one area in which Jewish law is far more liberal than Jewish social values. The Jewish community, and particularly Jewish relatives, may not be as quick to accept the child as a Jew. A couple should carefully consider the consequences of an interracial adoption. That beautiful Korean baby boy will become a Korean Jewish teenager. Will he find Jewish girls to date, and will he be accepted by these girls' Jewish parents? It may be relatively easy to find a black baby girl to adopt. Yet when she becomes a teenager, will she find herself in a conflict between her religious identity as a Jew and her racial identity as a black? Any couple seeking to adopt should remember that they are not simply getting a baby. That baby will become a child in school, a teenager, and eventually an adult. What will the biracial adoption mean as the child grows older?

Some parents choose to adopt a child of another race or from another nation with the view that they are rescuing that child and providing that child with a better life. This is not a reason to adopt. To quote one rabbi who is an authority on adoption:

> The adoptive family . . . needs to have a realistic view of their act. Adoption is a way of building a family, and not a form of charity. The child needs not only to be loved and cared for, but to be treated like any other child in the family. If the adoption saves a child from starvation or illness, that is not at all relevant. The child should be no more grateful than a child who was born into the family.[5]

A family contemplating an interracial adoption must carefully analyze their own motivation. Are they adopting this child because they want him or her to be fully part of their family? Are they adopting out of guilt? Do they have a rescue fantasy? Do they live in the kind of community where an interracial adoption will be accepted? Have they given their parents and other family members an opportunity to get used to the idea? Are they prepared to give the child a pride in his or her own ethnic background as well as his or her Judaism?

The last question is a vital one. In her book *Mixed Families: Adopting Across Racial Boundaries*, Joyce Ladner describes the controversy over the adoption of black babies by white families. In 1972 the National Association of Black Social Workers passed a resolution condemning transracial adoption. To quote part of the resolution:

Black children belong physically, psychologically and culturally in Black families in order that they receive the total sense of themselves and develop a sound projection of their future. Human beings are products of their environment and develop their sense of values, attitudes and self-concept within their family structures. Black children in white homes are cut off from the healthy development of themselves as Black people.[6]

Ladner describes the sense of outrage at this resolution by many white parents who have adopted across racial lines. They feel their adoptions were done out of love and not with political implications. Still, Ladner writes that many such parents have a political agenda of their own, even if it is understood only on the unconscious level:

Many of these parents have a commitment to the goals of an integrated society whereby individuals are judged on their own merit instead of being evaluated on their racial group membership. Their commitment is also to justice, equality, understanding, and acceptance of all people, without regard for their racial, cultural, religious, or other background.[7]

Jews would certainly favor an integrated society where individuals are judged on their own merit. Yet Jews would see a limit to total integration. They also would understand the importance of ethnic identity. Go back and reread the resolution passed by the black social workers, substituting the word *Jewish* for *Black*. If as Jews we want our children to have a total sense of self, we can understand why blacks want the same thing for their children.

If a Jewish family adopt a child who is black, Oriental, Indian, or Hispanic, the child should be given a sense of ethnic identity not only as a Jew but also as a member of his or her particular racial or ethnic group. In Lois Gilman's *The Adoption Resource Book* is a section called "Helping Children Build Their Special Identities," which includes listings of a number of camps and other programs for children from Korean backgrounds. This sense of dual identity is no different from that of American Jews who can identify with their ethnic background as German, Lithuanian, or Polish Jews or of Israelis who can identify as Moroccan, Yemenite, or Georgian Jews. Social workers who counsel adopted children know that there is great curiosity about one's ancestral background. If this is true of white children, how much more is it when children of another race are adopted by white families?

Many Jews who adopt from overseas face another difficulty. They must often deal with agencies that have little knowledge or sympathy for Judaism. One couple I spoke with had great difficulty explaining to a Catholic agency in South America the wife's divorce and remarriage. The agency believed that a woman who was divorced could not possibly be religious, and it took more than one letter from their rabbi to clarify that Judaism permits divorce. Another couple had a conflict with a Korean agency over their son's *brit milah*. The agency refused to let a *mohel* perform the circumcision, nor would it let a rabbi in the hospital room when a doctor performed it. The couple told me that they would like to adopt again from Korea, but only a girl this time.

Interracial adoptions do present numerous difficulties. Yet here, as in many areas, the attitude of the Jewish community is changing. The recent airlift of Ethiopian Jews to Israel has brought a large black Jewish community to the attention of the world. As conversion to Judaism is becoming more frequent, Jews of all races are becoming more common. It is hoped that, in a generation, the Jewish community will become accustomed to Jews of all races and ethnic backgrounds in its midst. Meanwhile, parents should proceed with caution when pursuing an interracial adoption.

Black Market Babies

A young Jewish couple were seeking to adopt their second child. One day a phone call came in from an attorney. A young woman had just delivered a baby girl. She would place the baby with them for adoption if they would pay her hospital bill and give her $15,000. They turned down the offer, but within a day she had a customer.

I recently received a telephone call from a Jewish woman who was placing her six-month-old son for adoption. Two Christian couples had offered her $10,000, but she wanted the baby in a Jewish home. However, the Jewish parents had to match the offer. I told her that she and the adoptive parents would end up in jail, but she was insistent on getting the money. I contacted the district attorney, who had the child welfare agency remove the baby from her home.

Baby buying, or black market adoption, is illegal in every state. The practice also is counter to Jewish ethics. Judaism teaches that a price cannot be put on a human life. Human beings are created in God's image and have an infinite value in the eyes of God, not whatever price the black market will bear. Babies are not a commodity. Black market adoptions must be fought by all people who care about children and adoption. They should be scrupulously avoided. Not only are they illegal and immoral but also they are exceedingly risky. There is nothing to prevent a greedy birth mother or a shady intermediary from demanding more money and threatening to take the baby back if the demands are not met.

Yet the legal definition of a black market baby is confusing. The two cases of baby buying described previously are clear. Let us compare them with two cases that are more questionable.

1 An agency is willing to provide a baby to a couple within six months. The agency demands an up-front fee of $14,000.

2 A birth mother is prepared to place her baby with a couple she has met. She has nowhere to live for the final three months of her pregnancy. The couple provide her with an apartment and a food allowance, as well as payment for medical expenses.

In many states, the former is legal and the latter is illegal. Paying reasonable expenses such as housing and food has been construed as baby buying. These restrictive laws put a particular burden on Jewish couples, who often must use independent adoption because no other alternative is available. States that permit independent adoption should allow the adoptive parents to pay reasonable expenses for the birth mother.

Admittedly, there is a subjective line between reasonable and unreasonable expenses. Medical, legal, and counseling fees plus room and board for the last months of the pregnancy would be reasonable. Paying for college tuition or a trip to Europe for the birth mother would not be reasonable. Yet, what about paying for a major car repair so that the birth mother can drive to her doctor's appointments? What about buying airplane tickets so that she can live with relatives during pregnancy? These issues are not black and white; that is why independent adoption has been labeled "gray market."

Still, by making independent adoptions easier and allowing payment for reasonable expenses, states can discourage black market adoptions. Women sell their babies when they feel that there is no other choice. If a woman knows that her housing, medical, and legal expenses can be handled by the adoptive couple, she will be less tempted to demand a high price for her baby in desperation.

Raising an Adopted Child

There is an old Jewish saying, "It is easier to have children than to raise them." Raising Jewish children in our Christian society is difficult. Raising an adopted Jewish child presents additional challenges of its own.

Consider three cases. The first involves a family with a young adopted preschooler in our community. I called them with the hope that they would participate in a workshop for Jewish adoptive parents. They answered me in very strong language. "Rabbi, who told you that our son is adopted? We do not consider our son to be any different from any other child. We have no intention of telling him that he was adopted. And we would appreciate it if you would keep this adoption secret and not contact us again."

The second case is mentioned in an article by Deborah Silverstein that appeared in the *Journal of Jewish Communal Service*. She described a thirteen-year-old adopted girl who refused to celebrate a bat mitzvah because she didn't "feel Jewish." The girl was going through a difficult identity crisis, compounded by various family problems at home.

The girl's attempts at gathering information about her birth family had been so threatening to the adoptive parents that they refused to supply her with any information. The question had triggered the parents' grief and fear of rejection and loss. The parents' refusal only reinforced the adoptee's doubts about her own identity and origins.[8]

The third case involved an adult adoptee in my own community, a delightful young woman who is a professional dancer. When I invited her to join my congregation, she answered, "Rabbi, I am really not Jewish. I was adopted as an infant and raised in an Orthodox Jewish home by wonderful people, but I don't consider them my real parents. I am right now searching for my birth parents, and when I find them I will know who I really am."

All youngsters, particularly upon reaching adolescence, tend to go through an identity crisis. This crisis is compounded by the facts of an adoption, particularly if a child's birth parents are not Jewish. To quote Deborah Silverstein again:

Many of the issues inherent in the Jewish adoption experience converge when the child reaches adolescence. At this time, three factors intersect: 1) an acute awareness of the significance of being adopted; 2) the profound meaning of being a Jew in history; and 3) a biopsychosocial striving toward the development of a whole identity.[9]

It is true that the overwhelming majority of adopted youngsters weather this identity crisis and become healthy,

well-adjusted members of the Jewish community. Silverstein writes, "It is a tribute to human resourcefulness how
many adoptees negotiate the shoals successfully."[10] Yet
building a family through adoption is different from building a family through pregnancy, and adopted children have
certain special needs. This will become apparent to adoptive families the first time their child brings home a school
assignment on genetics and heredity.

First, a child has a right to a complete identity, and
part of that identity is his or her biological heritage from
another set of parents. That identity is not canceled by a
legal document, even if those parents are unknown. The
child has a right to as much information as possible about
those parents. On this subject, Judaism has wisdom to share,
for our tradition teaches that a child never loses his or her
biological identity, even after adoption.

With this in mind, it is important that parents tell their
child about his or her adoption openly and lovingly. In my
opinion, the first couple described here, who were so intent
on secrecy, are making a bad mistake. Their son is bound
to find out that he was adopted, possibly through a friend
or relative, and such information during adolescence or
adulthood can be devastating. Such information from a
stranger would probably place a permanent barrier in the
trust relationship between parents and child. It is far better
that a child be told and that this information be part of his
or her earliest memories.

In *The Adoption Resource Book*, Lois Gilman has an excellent chapter called Raising the Adopted Child. In it she
writes:

> There is general agreement, however, that children must be told
> about their adoption and must be helped to understand it in
> order to grow. Parents must be open and accepting of adoption.
> They must acknowledge that their family is built by adoption,
> and that the process of building a family by adoption is different
> from that of building families by birth.[11]

From the youngest age, a child should be told in the

most loving tone of voice, that he or she is adopted. The word *adopted* should be familiar long before its meaning is comprehended. The story of a child's adoption should become a favorite childhood story, reinforced by photographs and other memories.

As a child becomes older, questions should be answered honestly, openly, and according to a child's age level. For this reason, parents should try to acquire as much information as possible about the birth parents. Most adopted children fantasize about their birth parents. Such fantasies are normal and do not constitute a threat to the adoptive parents. On the contrary, sharing information can help a child develop a more complete identity and sense of self.

For Jewish children, there is another reason why adoption cannot be a secret. If the child is born to a gentile mother, as most adopted children are today, the child must be formally converted. Jewish law teaches that he or she has the right either to protest or to affirm the conversion upon reaching the age of majority. Obviously, such a reaffirmation can take place only if the child knows of his or her adoption. The bar or bat mitzvah of an adopted child is the time for reaffirming that conversion and publicly accepting one's Jewishness. In a sense, it is the completion of the conversion.

The notion of telling a child about his or her adoption and sharing information about the birth parents is relatively new. A generation ago it was often customary to keep adoptions a secret. Adoption was associated with illegitimacy and was considered shameful. Judaism has never placed the stigma of illegitimacy on a child born out of wedlock or insisted that the child's background be kept secret. On the contrary, Judaism has seen the adoption of a child as an act of love and a wonderful way to build a family. It has taught that adoption should be handled in an open and loving manner. Fortunately, the rest of the world is catching up with the openness of the Jewish position.

Another question is raised by the last two cases de-

scribed previously—the thirteen-year-old refusing to become bat mitzvah and the adult who denied her Jewishness.
By Jewish law, if an adopted child is formally converted
and does not protest that conversion at the age of bar or
bat mitzvah, that child is fully a Jew. However, because the
child has the right to protest the conversion, it is particularly vital that parents give the child a positive self-image
as a Jew.

Deborah Silverstein describes the consequences of a
negative self-image for Jewish adolescents:

> Many adolescent adoptees . . . become further confused by Jew-
> ish discontent, alienation, and self-hatred. They choose not to
> identify as Jews. Parents who have neither resolved their infer-
> tility conflicts nor been helped to deal with their own issues about
> being Jewish or about adopting non-Jewish children convey to
> the adolescent the desirability of not being Jewish. . . . The par-
> ents' metacommunication to the child is acted out by adolescent
> adoptees who deny being Jewish, lack a Jewish peer group, date
> only non-Jews, do not become Bar or Bat Mitzvah, refuse to
> participate in Confirmation, and hold the so-called "Jewish traits"
> in contempt. Clearly, part of the emancipation process and the
> search for a positive self-image for these youngsters involves
> distancing themselves from Jews—an "identity rejection"—and
> returning to the majority group of their birth. According to
> Halachic principles, of course, this is their right. On a personal
> level, however, it has disastrous consequences because it leaves
> the adolescent conflicted and without moorings during a crucial
> developmental stage, thereby creating more loss and rejection,
> leading to increased feelings of guilt and rage.[12]

By her own admission, Silverstein is describing a worst-
case scenario of certain families who have come for counseling. Most Jewish adoptees have as strong a sense of
Jewish identity as their nonadopted peers. Yet it is important that an adopted child be raised with positive self-identity, both as a Jew and as an adoptee. Parents, through
counseling if necessary, should work through their fertility
problems before turning to adoption. They should never

consider adoption as settling for second best. It is also important that parents feel good about themselves as Jews and strive to communicate that positive Jewish identity to their child. It is for this purpose that Silverstein recommends ongoing workshops on Jewish identity and Jewish rituals for adoptive families.

Let me bring one example of such a positive Jewish approach. A rabbi adopted a baby girl born of a gentile mother and converted the baby. The girl grew up in an observant Jewish household and attended a Jewish day school. As the girl's twelfth birthday approached, the rabbi felt that his daughter needed to reaffirm her Jewishness more strongly than a child born into a Jewish family. Arrangements were made to make the girl's bat mitzvah at the age of twelve particularly joyous and meaningful, including a family trip to Israel. The girl has become a delightful Jewish teenager, active in her youth group and committed to her people and her religion.

It is important for the adopted child to meet and socialize with other adopted children so that adoption seems the most natural thing in the world. In the last few years, an organization called Stars of David has been formed for Jewish families with adopted children. For information, contact:

Stars of David
24 Lisa Lane
Reading, MA 01867

I recently spoke at the first meeting of a new Stars of David chapter in our community. To quote part of my speech:

Let me share another reason why Stars of David has an important role for all of us. What is our most important role as parents? It is to give our children a strong self-esteem, to make them feel good about themselves. Now, I am a rabbi and my children are that tiny minority known as "Rabbi's kids." It can be difficult for them; they are constantly in the public eye. Therefore, my wife and I make a point of getting together on a regular basis with other rabbis and their families. We want our kids to know and feel comfortable with other rabbis' kids.

Each of our children here is part of two minorities, they are Jewish and they are adopted. Obviously, it would not be healthy only to mingle with adopted children any more than it would be healthy only to mingle with Jewish children. I want my children to meet all sorts of children from all sorts of backgrounds as they grow up. Yet, on a regular basis, I think it will be good for them to get to know and play with other Jewish adopted children. It will help them build up that vitally important sense of self-esteem, and let them know that there are other children with similar backgrounds.

As our children play together, we adults can share ideas on issues of adoption. Yet, we can also share ideas on issues of Judaism and on how to make our children better Jews. We can talk about exposing our children to the Sabbath, festivals, synagogue life, Israel, and the whole range of Jewish experiences.[13]

One final issue must be discussed. We read about adopted children searching for their biological parents. Although such searches are far less frequent than the media would lead one to believe, they are a source of concern for many adoptive parents. For Jewish parents there is a double concern, that the search may mean not only a rejection of them but also a rejection of Judaism.

Judaism has always taught that parents do not own their children; the job of parents is to raise them as responsible adults and hope for the best. As adults, the children have a right to make basic decisions, including whether to search. Adoptees have emphasized that such a search is not a rejection of the adoptive parents. Often it is necessary for the child's psychological well-being.

For all these reasons, adoptive parents should be as open and supportive as possible when a child undertakes a search for his or her biological parents. They should share whatever information they know. The parents will probably find that their help and support will strengthen their relationship with their adopted child.

Parenting is always difficult. The key to successful parenting is giving a child a positive self-image, a sense of belonging and of being loved. Parents have a responsibility to help a child feel good about all aspects of his or her self, as an adoptee, as a Jew, and as a human being.

It is not your obligation to finish the task, nor are you free to desist from it.
(Pirkei Avot 2:16)

⊙ *9*

An Agenda for the Jewish Community

When a Jewish couple are infertile, it is a problem not only for that particular couple but also for the entire Jewish community. The Jewish community today is faced with zero population growth, even negative population growth. We are living in an age when every Jew counts. Every time an infertile couple are able to conceive a child, or when that couple adopt a child, one more Jew is added to the Jewish community.

In researching this book, I have spoken to infertile couples from all over the United States. The one emotion they all shared was the loneliness of infertility. Childless couples felt that they had no place in synagogues, with their strong emphasis on families and children. Jewish tradition places a great emphasis on children, and it is often painful for infertile couples to participate in activities within the Jewish community. Many couples shared with me feelings of being totally alone, with no one else to share their pain. They certainly expressed a sense that they could not turn to the organized Jewish community for support. Some even have become totally alienated from the Jewish community.

If 20 percent of young Jewish couples have an infertility problem, the organized Jewish community cannot afford to ignore their needs. It has a responsibility to help these couples. Jewish tradition does contain wisdom that can guide a couple through the available options, whether it be childlessness, unconventional medical techniques, or adoption. This wisdom must be made available. The Jewish community can also address the emotional needs of infertile couples and help them deal with their sense of loss, guilt, and anger. It is important that Jewish social service agencies set up support groups for infertile couples.

The most important service the Jewish community can provide for infertile couples is in the area of adoption. Today there is a strange irony. There are few successful Jewish agencies that are providing babies for childless couples. Most Jews who seek to adopt children are forced to turn to lawyers, doctors, and other independent sources. Yet the very agencies that are doing nothing to help Jewish couples have been outspoken in condemning independent adoption.

It is possible to set an agenda for the Jewish community to help infertile couples. This agenda would include (1) sensitizing rabbis and social workers to the needs of infertile couples; (2) presenting positive alternatives to abortion within the Jewish community; and (3) having the Jewish community reenter the adoption business. Let us explore each of these items.

Sensitizing Rabbis and Social Workers to the Needs of Infertile Couples. I recently conducted a workshop entitled "The Infertile Jewish Couple" at a national rabbinic convention. I was pleased with the attendance and participation, but it struck me that most (but not all) of the participants were rabbis dealing with infertility in their own lives. Most rabbis, unless they have faced it themselves, are unaware of the depth of pain faced by a couple who are unable to conceive a child. Many are also unaware of the solutions that Jewish tradition can offer these couples. It is important that rabbis, as interpreters of Jewish tradition, be able to use the wisdom of Judaism in counseling infertile couples. The following facts, which are explored in greater depth in this book, may be useful to rabbis:

1 Judaism sees companionship, not procreation, as the ultimate purpose in marriage.

2 Divorce because of childlessness, although mentioned in the Mishnah, has not been accepted in Jewish ethics.

3 Jewish tradition has recognized from the beginning that infertility is a couple's problem and cannot be blamed on the wife or the husband alone.

4 Judaism encourages aggressive medical treatment to solve the problem of infertility. Passivity is not a Jewish value.

5 There are sources in Jewish tradition that permit artificial insemination, in vitro fertilization, surrogate motherhood, and other unconventional medical techniques. Judaism, unlike the Catholic Church and other religious traditions, does not consider such procedures "unnatural."

6 When a pregnancy is lost through miscarriage or stillbirth, the loss is a real one and parents have a right to mourn.

7 Adoption has a long, positive history in Judaism. Adoption is possible for any couple who have the will and persistence.

8 A baby born of a gentile mother must be properly converted, preferably in the first year of birth. All the ramifications of a conversion should be explained to a couple.

It is also important that social workers employed by Jewish social service agencies be aware of the needs of infertile Jewish couples. Workshops should be held for Jewish professionals on the emotional and religious implications of infertility. Jewish agencies can then set up support groups to help Jewish couples.

A number of communities, including my own, have set up conferences on infertility, adoption, and the Jewish couple. In my own community the conference was co-sponsored by our local Jewish Family Service agency and RESOLVE. It included two keynote addresses followed by workshops on such topics as a medical update on infertility treatment, the emotional impact of infertility, methods of adoption, and raising the adopted child. Our conference attracted many couples who were marginally involved with the Jewish community and who commented that this was the first time the Jewish community had reached out to them. As a direct result of the conference, a support group was established through the Jewish Family and Children's Service.

Synagogues also need to be more sensitive to infertile couples in their programming and publicity. To quote one rabbi's Rosh Hashanah sermon:

Ours is a community with a heavy emphasis on family. Just peruse the Temple bulletin and see what you come up with . . . family education unit, Shabbat family dinner, religious school family picnic. . . . We haven't meant to exclude or offend, we just haven't been sensitive enough to the fact that amongst our members are not only singles of all ages, but married couples who may have chosen not to have children, and those who desperately want to be counted as families, but are without children and feel incomplete.[1]

There is a need for infertility support groups to help Jews of all levels of religious conviction. This need is particularly strong in the Orthodox community. In an Orthodox synagogue, the pressure on a couple to have children shortly after marriage is considerable. A childless couple feel a huge sense of loneliness in a community where large families are the norm. Many Orthodox couples have been made to feel guilty by their peers; perhaps they have been using birth control, a practice frowned upon by Orthodoxy. In addition, such traditional observances as *mikvah* can directly contribute to infertility problems.

Finally, it is important for halakhic authorities in all the religious movements to study the issues of infertility and Jewish law. For example, artificial insemination by donor has been forbidden by authorities in all three movements of American Jewish life. The Orthodox in particular have labeled the practice an abomination. Even Reform authorities have questioned the propriety of AID. Much that has been written in English on the subject is extremely negative. Yet traditional Jewish sources do not bear out this negative stance.

The truth is that as new medical techniques are developed to help couples conceive, Jews will use them. Since the first commandment underlying all Judaism is "Be fruitful and multiply," Jewish couples should not feel as if they are breaking the tenets of their religion in order to have a baby.

Presenting Positive Alternatives to Abortion Within the Jewish Community. I recently heard a rabbi speak to a group of Christian clergy on the Jewish view of abortion. He began his speech with the words, "Judaism condones abortion." I felt compelled to disagree with him publicly.

Judaism does not condone abortion. It is true that, unlike the Catholic and certain Protestant churches, Judaism does not equate abortion with murder. There are times when Judaism permits and even requires an abortion. Judaism would require an abortion if continuing the pregnancy would be a threat to the mother's life or health. Most authorities would also permit abortion in cases of rape and incest or of a diseased or deformed fetus. Clearly, from a Jewish perspective, abortion is not murder.

Yet abortion is not permitted by Jewish tradition because a pregnancy is unwanted or inconvenient. There is an irony in Jewish life today. While thousands of Jewish couples are desperate to adopt babies, thousands of other Jewish women are choosing to abort unwanted pregnancies, with the approval of the Jewish community. I recently counseled a young Jewish woman about an accidental pregnancy. She had gone to a Jewish social service agency, where a counselor had pressured her to have an abortion. The counselor was totally insensitive to this woman's belief that she could not kill the growing life within her. After meeting with me, I referred her to a counselor who was more sympathetic. After she gave birth, her baby was placed for adoption with a childless Jewish couple.

Unfortunately, abortion has become too widespread within the Jewish community. It is the automatic response to an unwanted pregnancy. Often it is simply a form of birth control. I am saddened when I learn of Jewish professional couples who abort a pregnancy because the timing is bad. I am more sympathetic to yet still sorry to hear of Jewish college-age girls who choose abortion to solve the problem of an unwanted pregnancy before they consider the emotional consequences of the abortion or the alternatives open to them.

It is time to organize a movement within the American Jewish community to provide an alternative to abortion. Such a movement would counsel women facing unwanted pregnancies. It would present an accurate Jewish viewpoint on abortion. It would provide the support, housing, medical care, and counseling needed by these young women. Christians have far outdistanced the Jewish community in providing such a support network.

A support network could present all alternatives to a woman in this difficult situation. If she chooses abortion, she will know that she has done so after learning about and considering all the options. If she chooses to keep and raise her baby, the organization would help her acquire the material and emotional support she would need. This might even include free membership in a synagogue and provisions for the child to have a proper Jewish education.

It is my hope that adoption would be presented as a positive, loving option, something that our current society does not do. Today, if a couple adopt a baby, most of us react with joy for them. However, if a woman places a baby for adoption, we are shocked. I often hear, "How can she give up her baby?" Only when we present adoption as an act of courage and love, and often the wisest choice, will more Jewish babies become available for adoption.

I should clarify that in presenting alternatives to abortion, I am not advocating a repeal of *Roe v. Wade*, the Supreme Court decision that guaranteed a woman's right to an abortion during the first two trimesters of pregnancy. I advocate freedom of choice. However, freedom of choice means that all choices must be intelligently presented. This includes the choice to carry the baby to term and then either to raise it or to place it for adoption. This is the choice that Judaism advocates. We have a responsibility to intelligently present that choice to women facing unwanted pregnancies.

Having the Jewish Community Reenter the Adoption Business. There was a time not many years ago when every major city in the United States had a Jewish adoption agency. Often there were more babies available for adoption than couples willing to adopt. Agencies were forced to actively seek homes for these children.

Obviously, social attitudes have changed the situation today. The availability of abortion and the acceptability of unmarried mothers who keep their babies have created a baby shortage. Agencies saw the number of infants drop precipitously. Some gave up their licenses to handle adoptions. Others kept their licenses but became inactive, handling only an occasional adoption every few years.

Today only a few scattered cities have active adoption programs under Jewish community auspices. Most Jewish couples who seek to adopt turn to nonsectarian agencies or independent sources. Meanwhile, Catholic and various Protestant agencies have maintained active adoption programs.

The time has come for the Jewish community to reenter the adoption business. It must develop the same kind of activist program to find babies for Jewish couples as it had years ago to find couples for Jewish babies. Such programs have already been successfully implemented by the Jewish Family Service in a number of cities.

The key to a successful program is an activist attempt to find pregnant women who are willing to work with the agency. A full-time social worker should be hired for just that purpose. This cannot be a 9 to 5 job; the social worker would have to be on call 24 hours and be prepared to visit a maternity ward in the middle of the night if an adoptive situation arises. He or she would have to develop relationships with abortion clinics, women's health centers, and other community and government agencies that might refer clients. This is one area where the more liberal Jewish attitude toward abortion can work to our advantage. If a woman is wavering about having an abortion, an abortion clinic may be more willing to refer her to a Jewish agency than to a Catholic agency because the latter will be so staunchly against abortion.

A Jewish adoption agency can also advertise in the newspaper and other media. Today, abortion clinics advertise in most cities. An agency that offers an alternative to abortion and provides support services for a pregnant woman should feel as free to advertise.

For the program to succeed, there must be active outreach to pregnant women. When programs like this have been established in other cities, they have appealed to gentile as well as Jewish women. A good program would provide excellent medical care, ongoing counseling, and other services for women, possibly including housing.

Another way agencies can help Jewish couples is to set up an identified adoption program. Such a program is described in the previous chapter. In identified adoption, a couple on their own finds a woman who is willing to place her baby with them. They refer her to the agency, which provides the counseling and other services she may need. Identified adoptions combine the advantages of independent and agency adoption. In the past, agencies have reacted quite negatively to independent adoptions. This is a way for agencies to become involved with couples who locate a birth mother through independent sources, providing emotional support for both the couple and the birth mother.

Ideally, a Jewish Family Service can set up a small support group of three or four Jewish couples. They would provide regular workshops on all aspects of adoption, including how to find babies. The group would commit themselves to work together until all had adopted. The agency would handle the adoptions. Afterward, the agency would provide ongoing workshops and support groups on raising adopted children. As mentioned in the preface, I participated in a support group like this with great success. Of the four couples in our group, all adopted within a year.

The activist adoption program described previously does not have to be expensive, particularly in comparison with other programs run through the Jewish community. Much of the cost will be covered by agency fees charged to the adoptive parents. Such a program can be established in all cities with a large Jewish population. All that is needed is the will to act.

An activist adoption program run through the Jewish community can do more than find adoptable children. For many marginal Jews, it is their link to the Jewish community. One couple found a baby through an excellent identified adoption program in the Boston area. They told me, "Until our baby arrived, we had no ties to the Jewish community. Thank God the agency was there for us. They not only taught us how to adopt and convert our baby. They taught us how to be Jews."

Part of the strength of the Jewish community is the willingness to help Jews in need. Jews have mustered their resources to help their fellow Jews fight discrimination, poverty, and a host of personal and family problems ranging from alcoholism to unemployment. A Jew in crisis knows that he or she can turn to the Jewish community for help. Infertility may rank low on the list of problems facing the Jewish community today, but for thousands of couples it is at the center of their consciousness. Their self-identity as Jews is linked to their ability to have children and pass their heritage on to them.

A Letter to My Child's Birth Mother

I never had direct contact with the birth mothers of my children. If I had, I probably would have written a letter like this:

Dear Birth Mother:

I think about you all the time. I often wish we had met; it would have made the adoption process more humane for both of us. After all, in a way we are partners. We shared in the creation of this child.

You gave our child the most valuable gift: life. You provided half the genes and a nurturing womb for the first nine months of existence. And you decided to give the child a chance at the kind of life you were unable to provide. So you placed your child with us for adoption.

We are providing the necessities for a happy, successful life. We will give this child a name, a family, a sense of belonging, a religion, an education, the material possessions it needs. Most of all, we will provide the child with love.

I realize that it took great courage to go through with this adoption. I am sure people asked you, "What kind of mother are you? How can you give up your baby?" I therefore make you this promise: I will never use the words "give up" when referring to you or to any other birth mother who places her baby for adoption.

In today's world, placing a baby for adoption is an act of love. This was not always so. There was a time when adoption was linked to illegitimacy and shame. A woman with an unwanted pregnancy had little choice; abortion was unavailable, and single parenthood was socially unacceptable. So a woman would disappear, only to resurface some nine months later without her baby and forever scarred by the experience. The whole procedure was shrouded with secrecy.

This is not so today. You had a choice. Abortion is easily available; I imagine some people put pressure on you to have an abortion. Yet, you felt this potential life growing in your womb, and you could not bring yourself to destroy it. You could have kept the baby. It is common today for a single mother to raise a child; among celebrities, it is the thing to do. Yet, you believed that your baby deserved more than you were in a position to provide.

So you chose to place your baby. It was an act of love and courage. You deserve credit, and better treatment than you probably received by those who arranged the adoption. For one, the veil of secrecy should have been lifted, at least somewhat. You should have been permitted some knowledge of where your baby was going. You should have been allowed to meet us.

We could have met you in a neutral place on a first-name basis; that way our anonymity and yours would have been protected. You could have learned something about us, our family, our values, our hopes for this child we plan to raise. We could have learned something about you and the birth father; information we could someday share with our child.

There are other things that a birth mother deserves: the best medical treatment available during the pregnancy and birth, the best legal advice to see that your interests are protected, adequate counseling to support you through this difficult decision. We would have been willing to do anything to help you except pay for the baby, because I think we both agree that a child is not a commodity to be bought and sold on the open market.

Let me tell you a little about us. We always dreamed of being parents; I can never describe the pain we felt as the years went by and we were unable to have a baby. The closest I can come is to repeat the words of Rachel in the Bible, "Give me children, or I shall die" (Gen. 30:1). We went to doctors, tried surgery, drugs, whatever it took; we came to realize how imprecise a science medicine is. Besides, our real goal was not pregnancy, but parenthood. So we chose adoption.

It is strange that despite the prevalence of adoption in our society, it still causes such difficulty for so many people. They feel that to be a parent, you must have a genetic link to your child. People often ask us, "Can you really love a child who is not yours?" Our answer is, "The moment that we held that child in our arms, that child became 'ours.' " Families are built through love as well as through biology.

Others have asked us whether we feel that we are settling for second best. Our answer is an unequivocal "no." Adoption may not have been our first choice, but it was a wonderful answer to our fertility problem. At one point we were angry at God for our infertility; today we thank God. Were it not for our inability to conceive, we never would have brought this beautiful child into our home.

We were not ashamed of the fact that we wanted to adopt. We told our friends and our family; we wanted them to be prepared when we brought our child home. We want the world to know that we approached adoption with great joy. It is not second best, but simply an alternative way to build a family.

You should also know that we will tell our child about the adoption. We will do so in as loving a manner as possible, starting at the youngest age. Adoption is a beautiful thing and should not be shrouded in secrecy. Besides, a child has a right to know. Biology and genetics are part of a child's makeup, just as family and religion are. Our goal as parents is to give our child a strong sense of self-esteem. A child must be comfortable with all aspects of its heritage, including biology.

We will share with our child as much information as we can about you and the birth father. Don't worry, we will not compromise your anonymity or your right to privacy. On the other hand, we feel that the natural curiosity about one's biological ancestors does not compromise our role as the child's parents.

Adoption procedures in this country leave much to be desired. They are too secretive, too costly, with too much room for fraud. There is still a stigma attached to adoption, and the courts still approach it as something unnatural. We must tell society that every adoption placement begins with two acts of love. It is an act of love when a birth mother places a baby and an act of love when strangers accept that baby into their home and hearts.

Thank you for your act of love.

Sincerely,
An adoptive father

Notes

Notes to Chapter 1

    1. Berakhot 31b.
    2. Ibid.
    3. Lori B. Andrews, *New Conceptions* (St. Martin's Press, New York, 1984), p. 3.
    4. Ibid., p. 2.
    5. Sherman J. Silber, *How to Get Pregnant* (Charles Scribner's Sons, New York, 1980), pp. 59–60.
    6. Ibid., p. 11.
    7. Kiddushin 29b.
    8. See "Marriage," *Encyclopedia Judaica,* Vol. 11 (Keter Publishing House, Jerusalem, 1971), pp. 1050–1051.
    9. Sanhedrin 36b.
    10. Avot 2:4.
    11. Song of Songs Rabbah 1:4.

Notes to Chapter 2

1. Sherman J. Silber, *How to Get Pregnant* (Charles Scribner's Sons, New York, 1980), p. 26.

2. Makkot 23b. There are many attempts at listing these commandments, the most influential being Maimonides's *Sefer Ha-Mitzvot*.

3. David M. Feldman, *Marital Relations, Birth Control and Abortion in Jewish Law* (Schocken Books, New York, 1974), p. 22.

4. Yevamot 6:6.

5. Yevamot 65b.

6. Kiddushin 2b.

7. Immanuel Jakobovitz, *Journal of a Rabbi*, p. 216, quoted by David M. Feldman in *Marital Relations, Birth Control and Abortion in Jewish Law* (Schocken Books, New York, 1974).

8. Meshekh Hokhmah to Genesis 9:7, quoted by David S. Shapiro in *Jewish Bioethics*, F. Rosner and J. D. Bleich, eds. (Sanhedrin Press, New York, 1979), p. 65.

9. Yevamot 65b.

10. Avot 5:25.

11. Kiddushin 29b.

12. Sotah 44a, based on Deuteronomy 20:5–7.

13. Yevamot 62b.

14. Yevamot 62a–b.

15. Yevamot 62b.

16. Maurice Lamm, *The Jewish Way in Love and Marriage* (Harper & Row, San Francisco, 1980), p. 132.

17. Robert Gordis, *Love and Sex* (Women's League for Conservative Judaism, 1978), p. 135.

18. Eugene Borowitz, *Liberal Judaism* (Union of American Hebrew Congregations, New York, 1984), p. 135.

19. Genesis Rabbah 8:9.

20. Hayim Halevy Donin, *To Be a Jew* (Basic Books, New York, 1972), p. 123.

21. David Abudarham, *Birkat Erusin 98a,* quoted by Maurice Lamm in *The Jewish Way in Love and Marriage* (Harper & Row, San Francisco, 1980, p.122.

22. Bava Kamma 92a.

23. Sanhedrin 19b.

24. Yevamot 64a.

25. Yevamot 64a.

26. Nahum M. Sarna, *Understanding Genesis* (Schocken Books, New York, 1970), p. 128.

27. Yevamot 64a.

28. Ibid.

29. Nedarim 64b. The exact quote is: "Rabbi Joshua ben Levi taught: A man without children is considered like a dead man as it is written, 'give me children and if not I shall die.' And it is taught, four are considered like they are dead, a poor man, a leper, a blind man, and a man without children."

30. Elisabeth Kübler-Ross, *On Death and Dying* (Macmillan Publishing Co., New York, 1969).

31. Genesis Rabbah 71:10.

32. Nehama Lebowitz, *Studies in Genesis* (World Zionist Organization, Department for Torah Education and Culture, Jerusalem, 1974), pp. 331–336. Also, see Ramban and Radak on this passage.

33. *Akedat Yitzhak* on Genesis 3:20.

34. Rashi on Genesis 6:9.

35. Taanit 2a.

36. Berakhot 10a.

37. Berakhot 40a.

38. Ketubbot 1:1.

39. Sotah 11b.

40. Bava Kamma 82a.

41. Gittin 70a.

42. Yevamot 64b.

43. Ketubbot 62b.

44. Yevamot 6:6.

45. David M. Feldman, *Marital Relations, Birth Control and Abortion in Jewish Law* (Schocken Books, New York, 1974), p. 36.

46. Eliezer ben Joel Halevi, quoted in David M. Feldman, *Marital Relations, Birth Control and Abortion in Jewish Law* (Schocken Books, New York, 1974), p. 39.

47. Song of Songs Rabbah 1:4. This translation is from Francine Klagsbrun, *Voices of Wisdom* (Pantheon Books, New York, 1980), pp. 152–153.

48. Gittin 90b.

49. Yevamot 65b.

50. Yevamot 65a.

51. Ibid., Tosefot d.h. *sh'beno.*

52. Rama on Eben Ha-Ezer 1:3.

53. Yevamot 61b.

54. Yevamot 8:2.

55. Yevamot 75b.

56. Eben Ha-Ezer 5:11.

57. Yevamot 63b.

58. "Aleinu" from the daily prayer book.

59. Berakhot 5b.

60. Bava Batra 116a.

61. Sanhedrin 19b.

Notes to Chapter 3

1. See note 4 in Chapter 1.

2. Nedarim 64b. See Chapter 2, note 29.

3. For a detailed discussion, see Elisabeth Kübler-Ross, *On Death and Dying* (Macmillan Publishing Co., New York, 1969).

4. Bava Mezia 2:11.

5. Berakhot 31b.

6. Linda P. Salzar, *Infertility: How Couples Can Cope* (G. K. Hall Co., Boston, 1986), p. 114.

7. Melvin Taymor and Ellen Bresnick, *Infertility,* quoted by Lori B. Andrews in *New Conceptions* (St. Martin's Press, New York, 1984), p. 111.

8. Linda P. Salzar, *Infertility: How Couples Can Cope* (G. K. Hall Co., Boston, 1986), pp. 5–6.

9. Pesahim 64b.

10. Sotah 37a.

11. Sukkah 26a.

12. For the story of Ben Azzai, see Chapter 2.

Notes to Chapter 4

1. Much of the information in this section was taken from Sherman J. Silber, *How to Get Pregnant* (Charles Scribner's Sons, New York, 1980). Dr. Stephen Winters read this chapter and added numerous valuable comments.

2. Niddah 31a.

3. Ramban on Leviticus 26:11.

4. See Berakhot 60a; Baba Kamma 85a–b.

5. Midrash Samuel 4:1.

6. Seymour Siegel. An unpublished responsa, prepared for the Committee of Law and Standards of the Rabbinical Assembly (1978).

7. Editorial, *Journal of the American Medical Association,* Vol. 220, No. 5, May 1, 1972.

8. Niddah 13b.

9. Zohar, Vayeshev 188a, quoted by David M. Feldman, in *Marital Relations, Birth Control and Abortion in Jewish Law* (Schocken Books, New York, 1974), p. 115.

10. See Yevamot 34b.

11. Eliezer Waldenberg, in Abraham Steinberg (ed.), *Hilchot Rofaim v'Refuah* (Mossad Ha-Rav Kook, Jerusalem, 1978), p. 154.

12. Yevamot 76a.

13. Eliezer Waldenberg, in Abraham Steinberg (ed.), *Hilchot Rofaim v'Refuah* (Mossad Ha-Rev Kook, Jerusalem, 1978), pp. 154–155.

14. Moses Tendler (ed.), *Medical Ethics* (Committee on Religious Affairs, Federation of Jewish Philanthropies, New York, 1975), p. 36.

15. Orah Hayim 618:1.

16. Teshuvot Zekan Aharon, II Eben HaEzer #97.

17. Quoted by David M. Feldman, in *Marital Relations, Birth Control and Abortion* (Schocken Books, New York, 1974), pp. 152–153.

18. Niddah 61a.

19. A number of books have appeared in English on the laws of *mikvah.* Among the best is Norman Lamm, *A Hedge of Roses* (Philipp Feldheim, New York, 1966).

20. Marsha Sheinfeld, "Infertility in Orthodox Judaism." *RESOLVE Newsletter,* June 1982, pp. 5–6.

21. Moses Tendler (ed.), *Medical Ethics* (Committee on Religious Affairs, Federation of Jewish Philanthropies, New York, 1975), p. 37.

22. Igrot Moshe, Yoreh Deah Vol. 2, No. 84.

23. Rachel Adler, "Tumah and Taharah-Mikveh," in R. Siegel, M. Strassfeld, and S. Strassfeld (eds.), *The Jewish Catalog* (Jewish Publication Society, Philadelphia, 1973), p 168.

24. Yoma 85b.

Notes to Chapter 5

1. Lori B. Andrews, "Yours, Mine and Theirs," *Psychology Today*, Vol. 18, No. 12, December 1984, p. 20.

2. Gerald Kelly, "Moral Aspects of Sterility Tests and Artificial Insemination," *Linacre Quarterly*, Vol. 15, No. 1–2, 1949, quoted by Immanuel Jakobovits, in *Jewish Medical Ethics* (Bloch Publishing, New York, 1959), p. 245.

3. "Instruction on Respect for Human Life in Its Origin and on the Dignity of Procreation," *Origins*, Vol. 16, No. 40, March 19, 1987, p. 700.

4. Ibid., p. 708.

5. Seymour Siegel. An unpublished responsum, prepared for the Committee of Law and Standards of the Rabbinical Assembly (1978).

6. See the previous chapter.

7. Lori B. Andrews, *New Conceptions* (St. Martin's Press, New York, 1984), p. 160.

8. Immanuel Jakobovits, *Jewish Medical Ethics* (Bloch Publishing, New York, 1959), pp. 248–249.

9. Moses Tendler (ed.), *Medical Ethics* (Committee on Religious Affairs, Federation of Jewish Philanthropies, New York, 1975), p. 36.

10. Hagigah 14b–15a.

11. Tur Zehav on Yoreh Deah 195:7.

12. Lori B. Andrews, *New Conceptions* (St. Martin's Press, New York, 1984), p. 174.

13. Moshe Feinstein, *Igrot Moshe*, Eben Ha-Ezer, No. 10.

14. Solomon Freehof, *New Reform Responsa* (Hebrew Union College Press, New York, 1980), p. 204.

15. Hullin 11b.

16. Eben Ha-Ezer 4:14.

17. Eben Ha-Ezer 4:15.

18. See Yevamot 65b.

19. J. David Bleich, "Test-Tube Babies," in *Jewish Bioethics*, F. Rosner and J. D. Bleich, eds. (Sanhedrin Press, New York, 1979), p. 84.

20. Carl Wood and Ann Westmore, *Test-Tube Conception* (Prentice-Hall, Englewood Cliffs, N. J., 1984), p. 98.

21. Yevamot 69b.

22. See J. David Bleich, "Test-Tube Babies," in *Jewish Bioethics*, F. Rosner and J. D. Bleich, eds. (Sanhedrin Press, New York, 1979) and Solomon Freehof, *New Reform Responsa* (Hebrew Union College Press, New York, 1980), p. 206.

23. See Lori B. Andrews, *New Conceptions* (St. Martin's Press, New York, 1984), p. 134.

24. See Tosefta Nedarim 6:7.

25. Bava Batra 168a.

26. Bava Mezia 4:2.

27. Nedarim 28a and other places in the Talmud.

28. Lori B. Andrews, *New Conceptions* (St. Martin's Press, New York, 1984), p. 226.

29. Ketubbot 1:4.

30. Berakhot 60a, JT Berakhot 9:3.

31. Solomon Freehof, *New Reform Responsa* (Hebrew Union College Press, New York, 1980), pp. 217–218.

32. Fred Rosner, "Genetic Engineering and Judaism," in *Jewish Bioethics*, F. Rosner and J. D. Bleich, eds. (Sanhedrin Press, New York, 1979), p. 416. For further discussion, see Azriel Rosenfeld, "Generation, Gestation and Judaism," *Tradition*, Vol. 12, Spring 1971, pp. 78–87.

Notes to Chapter 6

1. Marc Silver, "After Our Abortion, No One Said 'I'm Sorry,' " *Washington Post Health* Magazine, June 4, 1986, p. 6.

2. Susan Borg and Judith Lasker, *When Pregnancy Fails* (Beacon Press, Boston, 1981), p. 139.

3. Yevamot 69b.

4. Oholot 7:6, see also Rashi on Sanhedrin 72b, d.h. *lav nefesh hu.*

5. Rambam, Hilkhot Rotzeah u'Shmirat Ha-Nefesh 1:9.

6. Hayim Halevy Donin, *To Be a Jew* (Basic Books, New York, 1972), p. 277.

7. Niddah 3:7.

8. See Niddah 44b.

9. Numbers Rabbah 3:8.

10. See Yoreh Deah 340:30.

11. Moed Katan 24a–b.

12. Quoted by Susan Borg and Judith Lasker, in *When Pregnancy Fails* (Beacon Press, Boston, 1981), p. 33.

13. David M. Feldman, *Marital Relations, Birth Control and Abortion in Jewish Law* (Schocken Books, New York, 1974), p. 120.

14. For an excellent article on Tay-Sachs disease, the reality of bearing a Tay-Sachs baby, and the pain of choosing an abortion, see Marc Silver, "Life after Tay-Sachs," *International Jewish Monthly*, June–July 1985, pp. 14–41.

15. Arakhin 7a.

16. David M. Feldman, *Marital Relations, Birth Control and Abortion in Jewish Law* (Schocken Books, New York, 1974), pp. 291–292.

17. J. David Bleich, *Contemporary Halachic Problems* (Ktav, New York, 1977), p. 112.

18. See She'elat Ya'avez no. 43, *Assia*, Adar 5736.

19. Or Zarua, quoted by Yekeztial Yehuda Greenwald, *Kol Bo al Avilut* (Philipp Feldheim, New York, 1973), p. 201.

20. Sanhedrin 65b.
21. Yevamot 64b.
22. Niddah 31a.
23. Berakhot 20a.

Notes to Chapter 7

1. Sanhedrin 19b.
2. Nahum M. Sarna, *Understanding Genesis* (Schocken Books, New York, 1970), pp. 122–123.
3. Sanhedrin 19b.
4. Exodus Rabbah 46:5.
5. Edmund Blair Bolles, *The Penguin Adoption Handbook* (The Viking Press and Penguin Books, New York, 1984), p. 23.
6. For a further discussion of the issue of bloodlines and Judaism, see my essay "Adoption: A New Problem for Jewish Law," *Judaism*, vol. 36, Number 4, Fall 1987.
7. Menahem Elon, *Mishpat Ha-Ivri* (Magnes Press, Jerusalem, 1973), p. 670, n. 78.
8. "Adoption," *Encyclopedia Judaica*, Vol. 2 (Keter Publishing House, Jerusalem, 1971), p. 302.
9. Eliezer Jaffe, "Child Welfare in Israel: An Overview on Institutional Care, Foster Care, and Adoption," *Journal of Jewish Communal Service*, Vol. 55, Winter 1978, p. 179.
10. Rambam, Hilchot Nahalot 11:10.
11. Kiddushin 4:2.
12. Kiddushin 73a.
13. There is a principle that someone who separates himself to have relations with a woman does so from the majority of the community. However, if the man remained fixed (*kavua*) and the woman went into him, this majority principle cannot be used. See Ketubbot 15a, Sanhedrin 79a.
14. For example, see Melech Schachter, "Various Aspects of Adoption," *Journal of Halacha and Contemporary Society*, Vol. 4, Fall 1982, pp. 97–98.
15. Noda Biyehudah, Eben Ha-Ezer #7.
16. Hayim Halevy Donin, *To Be a Jew* (Basic Books, New York, 1972), p. 282.
17. The Conservative movement has permitted the use of a swimming pool if no *mikvah* is available. See Benjamin Kreitman, "May a Swimming Pool Be Used as a Mikvah?" (Hebrew), *Proceedings of the Rabbinical Assembly*, Vol. 33, 1969. According to Rabbi Isaac Klein, "Whenever possible, however, a regular *miqweh* should be used, not only because it is acceptable to all but also for psychological reasons. The atmosphere and associations should provide an experience of ritual purification." (Isaac Klein, *A Guide to Jewish Religious Practice* [Jewish Theological Seminary, New York, 1979], p. 222.)
18. Walter Jacob, ed., *American Reform Responsa* (Central Conference of American Rabbis, New York, 1983), p. 206.

19. Ketubbot 11a.

20. Rambam, Hilchot Isurei Biah 13:7; Shulkhan Arukh, Yoreh Deah 268:7.

21. Igrot Moshe, Yoreh Deah #161.

22. See Melech Schachter, "Various Aspects of Adoption," *Journal of Halacha and Contemporary Society*, Vol. 4, Fall 1982, p. 107.

23. Ibid., p. 94.

24. Sanhedrin 5a.

25. Shulkhan Arukh, Eben Ha-Ezer 6:8.

26. Yevamot 60b.

27. Louis Jacobs, "The Lubavich Movement," *Encyclopedia Judaica Yearbook, 1975–6* (Keter Publishing House, Jerusalem, 1976), p. 163.

28. Michael Gold, *Adoption and the Jewish Couple* (United Synagogue of America, Commission on Jewish Education, New York, 1987), p. 18.

Notes to Chapter 8

1. Eleanor Keys, "Adoption: What a Good Agency Provides," *Shma*, 12/230, March 19, 1982, pp. 76–78.

2. Edmund Blair Bolles, *The Penguin Adoption Handbook* (The Viking Press and Penguin Books, New York, 1984), p. 18.

3. Bernard J. Meislin, *Jewish Law in American Tribunals* (Ktav, New York, 1976), pp. 45–46.

4. For a complete discussion of this issue, see Barbara J. Dickey, "Religious Matching and Parental Preference," *Utah Law Review* Volume 1986, No. 3, pp. 559–575.

5. Michael M. Remson, *A Rabbi's Guide to Adoption* (CCAR, New York, 1981), p. 6.

6. Joyce A. Ladner, *Mixed Families: Adopting across Racial Boundaries* (Anchor Press/Doubleday, Garden City, N.Y., 1977), p. 75.

7. Ibid., p. 92.

8. Deborah Silverstein, "Identity Issues in the Jewish Adopted Adolescent," *Journal of Jewish Communal Service*, Vol. 61, no. 4, Summer 1985, p. 322.

9. Ibid., p. 321.

10. Ibid., p. 322.

11. Lois Gilman, *The Adoption Resource Book* (Harper & Row, New York, 1984), pp. 222–223.

12. Deborah Silverstein, "Identity Issues in the Jewish Adopted Adolescent," *Journal of Jewish Communal Service*, Vol. 61, no. 4, Summer 1985, p. 327.

13. This entire talk, entitled "Why Stars of David," is printed in *Startracks*, the Stars of David newsletter, Hanukkah 1986.

Note to Chapter 9

1. Rabbi Scott Glass, "To Find a Response," delivered to his congregation, Rosh Hashanah, 1986.

The Conversion Ceremony

A child born of a gentile mother and adopted by Jewish parents must be formally converted. The conversion ceremony consists of two parts, *milah* (circumcision) for boys and *tevilah* (immersion) for both boys and girls.

Milah. A *brit milah* should be performed as early as possible. It is preferable to do the circumcision on the eighth day after birth, but that is not a requirement, as it would be for a baby born Jewish. *Milah* for the purpose of conversion cannot take place on Shabbat or festivals.

The blessings are slightly different from those for an ordinary *brit milah*.

Mohel:

בָּרוּךְ אַתָּה יְיָ אֱלֹהֵינוּ מֶלֶךְ הָעוֹלָם, אֲשֶׁר קִדְּשָׁנוּ בְּמִצְוֹתָיו וְצִוָּנוּ לָמוּל אֶת־הַגֵּרִים.

"Praised art Thou, Lord our God, King of the Universe, who has sanctified us with His commandments and commanded us to circumcise proselytes."
[This portion is optional:

Father:

בָּרוּךְ אַתָּה יְיָ אֱלֹהֵינוּ מֶלֶךְ הָעוֹלָם, אֲשֶׁר קִדְּשָׁנוּ בְּמִצְוֹתָיו וְצִוָּנוּ לְהַכְנִיסוֹ בִּבְרִיתוֹ שֶׁל אַבְרָהָם אָבִינוּ.

"Praised art Thou, Lord our God, King of the Universe, Who has sanctified us with His commandments and commanded us to bring our son into the covenant of Abraham our father."

All present:

כְּשֵׁם שֶׁנִּכְנַס לַבְּרִית כֵּן יִכָּנֵס לְתוֹרָה וּלְחֻפָּה וּלְמַעֲשִׂים טוֹבִים.

"As he has entered the covenant, so may he attain the blessings of Torah, marriage, and good deeds."]

Rabbi (over wine):

בָּרוּךְ אַתָּה יְיָ אֱלֹהֵינוּ מֶלֶךְ הָעוֹלָם, בּוֹרֵא פְּרִי הַגָּפֶן.

בָּרוּךְ אַתָּה יְיָ אֱלֹהֵינוּ מֶלֶךְ הָעוֹלָם, אֲשֶׁר קִדְּשָׁנוּ בְּמִצְוֹתָיו וְצִוָּנוּ לָמוּל אֶת־הַגֵּרִים וּלְהַטִּיף מֵהֶם דַּם בְּרִית שֶׁאִלְמָלֵא דַּם בְּרִית לֹא נִתְקַיְּמוּ שָׁמַיִם וָאָרֶץ, שֶׁנֶּאֱמַר: אִם־לֹא בְרִיתִי יוֹמָם וָלָיְלָה חֻקּוֹת שָׁמַיִם וָאָרֶץ לֹא־שַׂמְתִּי. בָּרוּךְ אַתָּה יְיָ כּוֹרֵת הַבְּרִית.

"Praised art thou, Lord our God, King of the Universe, Who creates the fruit of the vine.

Praised art thou, Lord our God, King of the Universe, Who has sanctified us with His commandments and commanded us to circumcise proselytes, to take a drop of blood of the covenant. If it were not for the blood of the covenant, the heavens and earth could not exist, as it is written: 'If not for my covenant day and night, I would not create the laws of heaven and earth.' Praised art Thou, Who created the covenant."

If the baby is already circumcised, a symbolic drop of blood is taken from the penis. This is called *hatafat dam brit*. It is a simple, painless procedure and an absolute requirement of Jewish law. (After watching this procedure dozens of times on children of all ages, including my own son, I am convinced that it is less traumatic than having a drop of blood taken from the finger for a blood test.) There are no blessings said at a *hatafat dam brit*. Many parents prefer to wait and do the *hatafat dam brit* at the *mikvah*.

After the *brit milah* or the *hatafat dam brit*, the baby is given a Hebrew name. (See subsequent section for naming formula.) Some parents may prefer to wait until after *tevilah*.

Tevilah. The immersion in a *mikvah* can be done any time until bar or bat mitzvah age. I prefer to do it as young as possible, preferably between six months and a year. In my experience, a baby at this age will find the water less traumatic than a two- or three-year-old. In any case, it should not be done until the adoption is finalized or soon to be finalized. It would be wrong to convert a baby to Judaism if there is any possibility that the adoption will not go through.

Tevilah takes place at a *mikvah* (ritual bath). A *beit din* of three rabbis is convened. All clothing should be removed from the child; the water must touch every part of the body. One parent will want to bring a swimsuit so that he or she can bring the child into the water.

The child is quickly immersed so that water covers his or her head. The following two blessings are then recited, by the child, if he or she is old enough, or by the rabbi:

בָּרוּךְ אַתָּה יְיָ אֱלֹהֵינוּ מֶלֶךְ הָעוֹלָם, אֲשֶׁר קִדְּשָׁנוּ בְּמִצְוֹתָיו וְצִוָּנוּ עַל הַטְּבִילָה.

בָּרוּךְ אַתָּה יְיָ אֱלֹהֵינוּ מֶלֶךְ הָעוֹלָם, שֶׁהֶחֱיָנוּ וְקִיְּמָנוּ וְהִגִּיעָנוּ לַזְּמַן הַזֶּה.

"Praised art Thou, Lord our God, King of the Universe, Who has sanctified us with His commandments and commanded us regarding immersion.

Praised art Thou, Lord our God, King of the Universe, Who has kept us alive and sustained us and allowed us to reach this season."

The child is then immersed once more. (Some rabbis do it twice.) After the child is dressed, he or she receives a Hebrew name.

אֱלֹהֵינוּ וֵאלֹהֵי אֲבוֹתֵינוּ קַיֵּם אֶת הַיֶּלֶד הַזֶּה/הַיַּלְדָּה הַזֹּאת לְאָבִיו וּלְאִמּוֹ/
לְאָבִיהָ וּלְאִמָּהּ וְיִקָּרֵא שְׁמוֹ/שְׁמָהּ בְּיִשְׂרָאֵל _____ בֶּן/בַּת _____ .
יְהִי רָצוֹן שֶׁיִּזְכּוּ הוֹרָיו/הוֹרֶיהָ לְגַדְּלוֹ/לְגַדְּלָהּ לְתוֹרָה וּלְחוּפָּה וּלְמַעֲשִׂים טוֹבִים
וְנֹאמַר אָמֵן.

"Our God and God of our fathers, sustain this child for his/her father and mother and call his/her name in Israel _____ the son/daughter of _____ . May it be Thy will that his/her parents be privileged to raise him/her to a life of Torah, the marriage canopy, and good deeds and let us say, 'Amen.'"

Glossary of Hebrew Terms

Aggadah Folklore and other nonlegal material in the Talmud.

Aliyah (Lit. "going up") Going up to recite the blessing over the Torah.

Ametz Modern Hebrew term for an adopted child.

Apotropos Guardian.

Ashkenazim Jews whose ancestors are from Germany and Eastern Europe.

Asufi (Lit. "foundling") An abandoned child whose parents are unknown.

Bar Mitzvah (Lit. "son of the commandments") A boy when he turns thirteen and becomes responsible for the commandments.

Bat Mitzvah (Lit. "daughter of the commandments") A girl when she turns twelve and becomes responsible for the commandments.

Bris/Brit (Lit. "covenant") The ceremony of circumcision in which a Jewish boy is welcomed into the covenant.

El Malei Rahamim (Lit. "God who is full of mercy") Traditional memorial prayer for someone who has died.

Etrog Citron, fruit used during Sukkot festival.

Gemarah Discussions on the Mishnah that took place in Babylonian academies. The Mishnah and the Gemarah together make up the Talmud.

Ger Proselyte.

Haftarah Portion from Prophets recited in synagogue on Shabbat and festival mornings.

Halakhah (Lit. "the way") Jewish law.

Halitzah Ceremony of release, whereby a childless widow is released by her brother-in-law from the obligation to marry him.

Hanukkah Eight-day festival of lights, celebrating the Maccabees' victory over the Syrian-Greeks.

Hasidic (Lit. "pious") Group within Orthodoxy that emphasizes extreme piety and God's accessibility to the common Jew.

Hatafat Dam Brit Drop of blood taken to symbolize circumcision when a convert has already been circumcised.

Hevra Kaddisha (Lit. "sacred society") Jews who do the traditional preparations of a body for burial.

Huppah   Marriage canopy.

Kaddish   Doxology praising God. Mourners' *Kaddish* is said by mourners in memory of dead.

Kasher   Fit or proper.

Ketubbah   Marriage settlement a husband pays the wife in the event of divorce or the husband's death.

Kiddush   Blessing over wine sanctifying Shabbat and festivals. Also, refreshments served at a *simha*.

Kohen   Priest, descendant of Aaron.

Kriyah   Tearing of garment or ribbon at funeral.

Levi   Assistant to priests, descendant from the tribe of Levi.

Lubavitch   Largest and most outgoing of the various Hasidic groups.

Lulav   Palm branch attached to myrtle and willow, used in the celebration of Sukkot.

Mamzer   Child born as the result of incest or adultery.

Mezuzzah   Scroll of biblical verses, placed on doorposts of house.

Midrash   Rabbinic interpretations of biblical verses.

Mikvah   Ritual bath.

Milah   Ritual circumcision.

Mishnah   Collection of oral traditions compiled around the year 200 C.E. The Mishnah later served as the basis for the Talmud.

Mitzvah   Commandment (plural: *mitzvot*).

Mohel   Professional who performs ritual circumcisions.

Niddah   State of ritual impurity of woman during menstruation.

Pidyon Ha-Ben   Redemption of firstborn son.

Rashi   Foremost commentator on Torah and Talmud who lived in eleventh-century France.

Responsa   (Hebrew: *Teshuva*) Written answer to a query of Jewish law.

Rosh Hashanah   Jewish new year.

Sanhedrin   Body of seventy-one rabbis who were the ultimate religious authorities in Judea during the Second Temple period.

Seder   Ritual meal celebrated at Passover to recall the Exodus from Egypt.

Shabbat   Weekly day of rest beginning Friday at sundown.

Shema   Torah verses recited each morning and evening, containing the basic principles of the Jewish faith.

Shetuki   (Lit. "silent one") Child whose mother refuses to identify the father or whose father is unknown.

Shiva   Traditional week of mourning.

Siddur   Daily prayer book.

Simha   Joyous occasion.

Sukkah   Ritual booth in which a family eats during the festival of Sukkot.

Talmud   Great corpus of Jewish law and lore compiled around the year 500 C.E. Consists of Mishnah and Gemarah.

Tevilah   Ritual immersion in a *mikvah*.

Torah   Five books of Moses: Genesis, Exodus, Leviticus, Numbers, Deuteronomy.

Tosafot   Technical commentaries on the Talmud by Rashi's grandsons and others.

Tziduk Ha-Din   Prayer recited at burial that speaks of God's righteousness.

Yahrzeit   Anniversary of death, commemorated by lighting candle and reciting *Kaddish*.

Yisrael   Ordinary Jew, as opposed to Kohen or Levi.

Yom Kippur   Day of Atonement.

Index